Worlds at War,
Nations in Song

Worlds at War, Nations in Song

Dialogic Imagination and Moral Vision
in the Hymns of the Book of Revelation

KENDRA HALOVIAK VALENTINE

WIPF & STOCK · Eugene, Oregon

WORLDS AT WAR, NATIONS IN SONG
Dialogic Imagination and Moral Vision in the Hymns of the Book of Revelation

Copyright © 2015 Kendra Haloviak Valentine. All rights reserved. Except for brief quotations in critical publications or reviews, no part of this book may be reproduced in any manner without prior written permission from the publisher. Write: Permissions, Wipf and Stock Publishers, 199 W. 8th Ave., Suite 3, Eugene, OR 97401.

Wipf & Stock
An Imprint of Wipf and Stock Publishers
199 W. 8th Ave., Suite 3
Eugene, OR 97401

www.wipfandstock.com

ISBN 13: 978-1-4982-0488-0

Manufactured in the U.S.A.

New Revised Standard Version Bible, copyright 1989, Division of Christian Education of the National Council of the Churches of Christ in the United States of America. Used by permission. All rights reserved.

Nestle-Aland, Novum Testamentum Graece, 27th Revised Edition, edited by Barbara Aland, Kurt Aland, Johannes Karavidopoulos, Carlo M. Martini, and Bruce M. Metzger in cooperation with the Institute for New Testament Textual Research, Münster/Westphalia, © 1993 Deutsche Bibelgesellschaft, Stuttgart. Used by permission.

To Gil
Thank you for believing this should be a book.

Before the message there must be the vision, before the sermon the hymn, before the prose the poem.

Amos Wilder, Theopoetic

Contents

Acknowledgments | ix

1 Introduction: | 1
Reading the Book of Revelation after Waco

2 Hymns to an Immanent Creator and a Transcendent Lamb: | 15
Genre and the Book of Revelation

3 Hymns Celebrating the Presence of the Future: | 77
Chronotope and the Book of Revelation

4 Hymns Responding in Worship and Witness: | 138
Answerability and the Book of Revelation

5 The New Testament Psalter: | 180
The Book of Revelation as Moral Vision

Bibliography | 189

Acknowledgments

I AM GRATEFUL TO many for the privilege of graduate education. Columbia Union College, in Takoma Park, Maryland, under the presidency of Dr. Charles Scriven, granted me the study leave necessary to relish life and learning at the Graduate Theological Union in Berkeley. My initial advisor, Dr. James Bretzke, welcomed me into the GTU adventure, and the chair of my comprehensive exams, Dr. Joel Green, gave me many opportunities to learn through teaching and research assistantships. When I returned to full-time teaching at Columbia Union College, I enjoyed the enthusiasm of students in many different classes. I am especially grateful for the students who signed up for the "Book of Revelation" course each spring semester.

La Sierra University, in Riverside, California, under the presidency of Dr. Lawrence Geraty, and the dean of the School of Religion, Dr. John Jones, gave me the study leave necessary to complete my dissertation. I am grateful to Dr. Barbara Green, coordinator of my dissertation committee, for introducing me to Mikhail Bakhtin, for her care as a scholar, and for her commitment to engaged readings of Scripture. I am grateful to Dr. Martha Ellen (Marty) Stortz, committee member, for her amazing ability in the classroom to clarify and inspire ideas, and for her insights into moral vision. I am grateful to Dr. David L. Barr, committee member, for his many contributions to studies on the book of Revelation. Long before I asked him to participate on my committee, I appreciated his involvement with the Society of Biblical Literature, his articles and presentations, and the interdisciplinary nature of his work.

I am extremely fortunate to be part of many supportive circles of friends. During my years at Berkeley, Dr. John and Shirley Christian gave me the gift of a home on the weekends. Cheerie Lou Capman provided amazing technical support. Wil McLean spent hours double-checking quotes. Dr. Fritz Guy sent encouraging notes. Dr. Roy Benton, Dr. Doug Morgan, Dr. Zack Plantak, Bob Visser, Dr. Cynthia Westerbeck, and Bryan Zervos kept believing that I would finish. Dr. Roy Branson spent hours helping me clarify my project, and sharing his enthusiasm for the book of Revelation's contribution to the moral enterprise. The Sligo Seventh-day Adventist Church, especially the Branson/Ortner Sabbath School class, provided a place of conversation, faith and fellowship. The class also sparked a grass roots movement that concluded with the ordination of three women pastors, a first in this community.

I am grateful for the support of my brother, Brent, and sister-in-law, Kari. My husband, Gil Valentine, believed this manuscript should be a book. He encouraged me to contact potential publishers. I have appreciated the expertise of Chris Spinks, Karl Coppock and Matthew Wimer at Wipf and Stock.

My debt to my parents, Bert and Mary Haloviak, cannot be adequately expressed. The completion of this project would not have been possible without the countless conversations we shared, their insights into Scripture, the diversions from the project they provided, and their never-ending prayers and encouragement. They introduced me to the stories of the Bible long before I could read them for myself. I am especially grateful for dad's library, his assistance in many research endeavors, and his inspiring thirst for biblical studies. I am especially grateful for mom's calm and expertise during computer crashes, her many phone calls during my Berkeley years, and her personal commitment to daily worship which embodies the best of the book of Revelation.

1

Introduction
Reading the Book of Revelation after Waco

WORLDS AT WAR

DURING THE SPRING OF 1993 as I was gathering the necessary materials for applying to graduate schools, a tragedy took place in the United States which deepened my desire to do interdisciplinary work in New Testament studies and ethics. The tragedy took place on April 19, 1993, in Waco, Texas. After the flames engulfing the Branch Davidian compound, Mount Carmel, ceased, seventy-four people, including twenty-one children, were dead. Along with hundreds of thousands of television viewers, I watched the inferno as I had watched the preceding standoff between government agents and the Branch Davidians.[1] After fifty-one days the war between two very different worlds was over.

Relatives of people living in the compound, members who left prior to the standoff and survivors of the fire have provided information about life inside Mount Carmel.[2] The world has gradually learned about the convictions of the people living there and about the community's leader,

---

1. The standoff began on February 28, 1993, when ATF agents entering the compound were met with gunfire. Tabor and Gallagher, *Why Waco?*, 3.

2. Samples et al., *Prophets of the Apocalypse*, 173–216, includes documented interviews by the Christian Research Institute (CRI) with former members of the Mount Carmel community.

Vernon Howell, who had changed his name to David Koresh. A thirty-three-year-old former member of the Seventh-day Adventist (SDA) Church, Koresh aggressively recruited people (mostly from SDA churches in the United States, Great Britain, and Australia) to join Mount Carmel, which Koresh referred to as "Ranch Apocalypse." Life in the compound meant delegated jobs for the group's daily living, Bible study, and worship experiences. During the final years of Mount Carmel, Koresh's role included that of community leader and "husband" of all women (some as young as twelve years of age) on the compound, worship and rock band leader, spiritual guide, and interpreter of Scripture. Koresh took it upon himself to provide the community with a single and final interpretation of prophetic portions of the Old and New Testaments. Conversations that questioned Koresh's biblical interpretations or leadership decisions were rarely tolerated.[3] For members of the community, Koresh's voice was the only authoritative voice. No matter how complex the biblical text to be studied, Koresh explicated his one and only interpretation. After sharing such finalized meanings with the community, Koresh expected his word on God's Word to end all questions.

MOUNT CARMEL, SEVENTH-DAY ADVENTISM, AND THE SEARCH FOR MONOLOGIC TRUTH

For the Seventh-day Adventist denomination, my own faith community, the standoff in Waco, Texas, between government agencies and the people of Mount Carmel was a public relations nightmare. The first news reports identified Koresh's community as an offshoot of the Seventh-day Adventist Church, a protestant denomination with almost eight million members worldwide.[4] The denomination's world headquarters (located in Silver Spring, Maryland, just outside of Washington, DC) immediately sent representatives to Waco to inform reporters that the denomination was in no way connected with, or sympathetic to, the behavior of Koresh and his followers. The stockpiling of weapons on the compound was

---

3. Ibid., 186, includes a quote from a former Branch Davidian, Diana Ishikawa (pseudonym), who said to her interviewer, Richard Abanes, that "his [Koresh's] word was law." Later, 187, Ishikawa said that "he [Koresh] didn't like people complaining openly."

4. In 1993 Seventh-day Adventist membership was 7,962,210. By 2013, membership reached 18,143,745. Statistical information from "2014 Annual Statistical Report: 150th Report of the General Conference of Seventh-day Adventists for 2012 and 2013."

foreign to the traditional stance by Seventh-day Adventists as noncombatants in United States military actions.⁵ Like the rest of the country, Seventh-day Adventists were appalled at the allegations of child abuse and the reported sexual practices at Mount Carmel. Koresh certainly could not be an Adventist, for he did not act like one.

Ignoring, for the most part, Koresh's way of reading Scripture, SDA leaders and laity renounced his ethics, proclaiming Seventh-day Adventism's location within mainstream Christianity. Although some would later argue that Koresh held much in common with traditional SDA approaches to apocalyptic texts,⁶ by then the whole embarrassment would be over. Tragically, by then, the lives of seventy-four people would also be over. Few Seventh-day Adventist publications analyzed or even acknowledged the high percentage of former SDAs among Koresh's recruits.⁷ By emphasizing the stark differences in social ethics between Mount Carmel and Seventh-day Adventism, SDAs were able to maintain theological distance from the people of Waco. This distance would have been significantly reduced had Adventists known (or, in some cases, acknowledged) the religious backgrounds of Koresh's followers.

Although Koresh's moral behavior was clearly out of harmony with SDA practices, his approach to Scripture, especially to the book of Revelation, was familiar to the people who joined Mount Carmel, the vast majority of whom were former SDAs.⁸ As one Seventh-day Adventist

   5. Morgan, *Adventism and the American Republic*, 81–123.

   6. Newport, *Apocalypse and Millennium*, 172–236.

   7. Exceptions included Branson, "We Didn't Start the Fire," 2; Bursey, "In a Wild Moment," 50–52; Cooper, "Did David Die for Our Sins?," 47–48; Scriven, "Fundamentalism Is a Disease," 45–46; Teel, "Kissing Cousins or Kindred Spirits?," 48–49; and Warren, "Our Brothers and Our Sisters," 50.

   8. Newport, *Apocalypse and Millennium*, 210, states: "It is a simple and telling fact that almost all Branch Davidians, including of course David Koresh himself, had been Seventh-day Adventists and continued to see themselves as such after accepting the Branch Davidian message." Others, including Branch Davidians themselves, might nuance this statement by claiming that the Branch Davidian message called Seventh-day Adventists to a more pure and faithful embrace of Scripture's truth. However, I am convinced that SDAs must not ignore Newport, *Apocalypse and Millennium*, 217, when he observes: "Despite first appearances, appearances which the Seventh-day Adventist Church, for good reasons, has been keen to stress, it simply will not do to describe the success of Koresh (and [his lieutenant] Schneider) in recruiting Seventh-day Adventists to the Branch Davidian cause as an act of unfathomable (if not satanic) intellectual deception. The Seventh-day Adventist ground provided fertile soil for the Branch Davidian seed." Samples, *Prophets of the Apocalypse*, 182, records more of Richard Abanes's interview with Diana Ishikawa (pseudonym). When asked, "Did

theologian says of his initial reaction to the news of David Koresh: "I heard about a man who had Revelation solved.... The man, and most of his followers, had once belonged to Adventist churches. Many in these churches thought—think!—that we have Revelation solved."[9] Not only does this attitude reflect an elitism that places the community (whether Mount Carmel or Adventism) above others, it assumes a view of the book of Revelation as a puzzle to be solved or a code to be broken. Another SDA theologian describes the dangerous effects of approaching the imaginative language of Revelation using a "wooden literalism" that proposes to solve the book.[10] Koresh assumed that each scriptural symbol or image could be decoded by making reference to other biblical texts.[11] Once the passage under consideration was definitively interpreted for his audience, Koresh moved the group on to the next biblical phrase or symbol or image. In such an approach, the decoded final words of the book of Revelation conclude the process of interpretation and, presumably, the book's message. Koresh not only had ethical problems, he had hermeneutical problems. And, sadly, such an approach to interpretation is currently shared by many Seventh-day Adventists who, in their eagerness to make sense of the challenging passages of the book of Revelation, consider the book a code that anticipates a single, consistent, and final

---

being a Seventh-day Adventist prepare you in any way for his [Koresh's] teachings?" Ishikawa answered, "Oh yes. Definitely." When Abanes asked, "How?" Ishikawa replied, "Adventists believe heavily in prophecy. Adventists continually study prophecy."

9. Scriven, "Fundamentalism Is a Disease," 45. Teel, "Kissing Cousins," 48, heard a frightening echo between Koresh as a "keeper of the text" and the attitude of many Adventists about the theological superiority of the SDA denomination.

10. Teel, "Kissing Cousins," 48.

11. Newport, *Apocalypse and Millennium*, 212, gives the following example of Koresh's methodology having listened to hours of tape recordings of Bible study sessions at Mount Carmel: "Koresh will read Revelation looking all the time for the verbal clues, the 'stitch-words,' as scholars would call them in another setting, that relate the passage under consideration to its (generally Old Testament) context. The clues Koresh discovers are often very subtle. Thus, for example, he notes that Rev. 10.3 states that the angel there depicted 'cried . . . as a lion roars.' For Koresh this is part of the code; lions 'roar' but eagles 'cry'; therefore the one who wants to interpret this part of Revelation will need to look for another place in scripture where a lion and an eagle are linked in one symbol. The only one, says Koresh (and he is as usual correct on this biblical detail), is the symbol used to depict Babylon or Nebuchadnezzar. He clearly has Dan. 7.4 in mind. By this somewhat circuitous route he arrives at the conclusion that the angel of Rev. 10.3 will lift up his voice against 'Babylon' (understood as a symbol of the apostate Church)."

meaning.¹² Such readers search for the message of Revelation, a monologic truth in code, by uncovering it bit by bit.

Monologic truth is an idea which proposes to be expressed and comprehended by a single consciousness. Many who seek monologic truth assume that meaning is best articulated as a proposition separate from any specific context and thus made universally relevant. Such an approach assumes that meaning can be stabilized, and therefore closed.¹³ Koresh approached the book of Revelation assuming and finding such monologic truth.

In conversations with many SDAs after the tragedy at Waco, I heard frequent criticisms of Koresh's *particular* interpretation, but rarely a challenge to his approach to interpretation as a process of decoding texts. One prominent Seventh-day Adventist theologian, William Shea, wrote that the key theological difference between the traditional SDA interpretation of Revelation and that of Koresh was Koresh's futurist emphasis. According to Shea, Koresh placed Revelation's judgment scenes in the imminent future, while SDAs understand the judgment sequences as reflecting various eras in (primarily past) human history. Shea states: "He [Koresh] said that he and he alone knew what the seven seals mean. . . . They lie in the immediate future and are of catastrophic magnitude for the inhabitants of the earth. . . . Seventh-day Adventists have also said that they know what the seals represent, but they have put them back in past history."¹⁴ For many, such a "distinction" actually suggests methodological affinity.

Of course, Koresh had an ethics problem. And, of course, his method of teaching, of not allowing other people to speak, should have been suspect by his followers. However, his approach reflected his understanding of truth as an abstract and finalized proposition expressed by a single voice. Koresh could hold thoughtful people captive, both for hours in Bible study and literally inside a surrounded compound, in part because most of them had grown up hearing similar approaches to the

---

12. Bursey, "In a Wild Moment," 50, notes the increasing estrangement among Seventh-day Adventists who approach the book of Revelation in different ways. He calls it a "new standoff." Bursey continues: "This time within Adventism . . . [the standoff is] between those who see current events confirming Adventist interpretation of Revelation and those who see events like the Waco holocaust as confirming suspicion over the whole apocalyptic enterprise that has defined Adventism."

13. Newsom, "Bakhtin, the Bible, and Dialogic Truth," 292, identifies three features of monologic truth: it is a "separate thought"; it gravitates toward a system; and it can be grasped by a single consciousness.

14. Shea, "How Should SDAs Respond?," 44.

book of Revelation by probably less charismatic and able Bible teachers.¹⁵ While the events surrounding the tragedy at Waco emit complexity, Koresh's approach to the book of Revelation is important for this study. His approach exposes some of the limitations and dangers of reading monologically. This present book challenges Koresh's approach and all monologic approaches to the book of Revelation. Instead of approaching the hermeneutical task as the search for Revelation's monologic truth, this book argues for an approach that reflects the dialogic nature of language and meaning. The work of Mikhail Mikhailovich Bakhtin (1895–1975) will be helpful in this journey.

MIKHAIL BAKHTIN AND MEANING AS DIALOGIC

Mikhail Bakhtin spent his lifetime in dialogue with people and their ideas. First with his older brother Nikolai as they grew up in pre-revolutionary Russia,¹⁶ and later with circles of teachers and colleagues and students in the new Soviet Union, Bakhtin explored philosophy, art, language, literature, and the social sciences. Even in his final years, Bakhtin relished conversation with a new generation of students.¹⁷ The actual experience of conversation embodied Bakhtin's conviction that meaning, like language, is dialogic or relational. Language as dialogic requires a minimum of two consciousnesses reflected in their respective voices. These voices exchange utterances, the building blocks of dialogue, which are always located points of view. Utterances take place within particular contexts

---

15. See my interview with Seventh-day Adventist Norman Martin, the brother of one of Howell's recruits, Wayne Martin, a Harvard-educated lawyer who died along with his four teenage children in the fire. Haloviak, "One of David's Mighty Men," 39–42.

16. From his birth (16 November 1895) until the age of nine, Mikhail Bakhtin lived with his family in Orel, south of Moscow. Between 1904 and 1910, the family lived in Vilnius, the capital of Lithuania, a place rich in diverse peoples, languages, and traditions. When Mikhail was 15 years old, his family moved to Odessa, a city linking czarist Russia and southern Europe. After one year at Odessa University, Mikhail transferred to Petersburg University in 1914, where he graduated in 1918. For more on Bakhtin's early years, see Clark and Holquist, *Mikhail Bakhtin*, 16–34.

17. Vadim Valerianovich Kozhinov, Sergey Georgievich Bocharov, and Georgi Dmitrievich Gachev are the three students credited with reintroducing Bakhtin to the wider scholarly community after meeting with him at Ogarev University of Mordovia (earlier the Polezhaev Pedagogical Institute of Mordovia) in Saransk. See Felch and Contino, "Feeling for Faith," 2.

which can never be exactly repeated or completely finished.[18] Bakhtin's dialogism challenges the very notion that monologic truth articulated in abstract terms by a single voice exists.[19] In contrast, language as dialogic requires a particular embodiment in order to be meaningful.

During the middle period of Bakhtin's writing career (mid-1920s to early 1950s), he considered the degree to which literary works reflect the dialogic qualities of language. Bakhtin was particularly drawn to the generic history of the novel culminating, he believed, in the novels of Dostoevsky. Bakhtin claimed to discover a new type of artistic thinking in Dostoevsky's novels. In them, Bakhtin identified polyphonic heroes. Such characters reflected the dialogic relationships between unpredictable consciousnesses involved in the language of real life. Bakhtin suggested that if polyphonic novels reflect the dialogic quality of language, other genres reflect other perspectives on life and language.[20]

Bakhtin's consideration of genres as ways of thinking is important for this book. This understanding of genre considers it a strategy that is inseparable from its ideological perspective on the world. As such, genre is never merely form but is inseparable from meaning itself. This understanding of genre considers the social and historical nature of language, since ideologies are located in people and societies from particular places and times. Bakhtin's genre also provides a way to consider the liturgical elements, especially the hymns, in the book of Revelation.

Communities and commentators who interpret Revelation as a message to be decoded typically ignore or pass quickly over the many hymns within the narrative.[21] For monologic approaches, the hymns are almost intrusions into the narrative. Assumed to be projections beyond

---

18. See Bakhtin, *Problems of Dostoevsky's Poetics*, 166, for his conviction that dialogic meaning is open, which is often remembered through his statement: "*Nothing conclusive has yet taken place in the world, the ultimate word of the world and about the world has not yet been spoken, the world is open and free, everything is still in the future and will always be in the future.*"

19. Green, *Mikhail Bakhtin*, 59, states: "There is simply no permanent, universal, natural, or inherent meaning in literary language."

20. Jackson, *Dialogues with Dostoevsky*, 271, states: "For Bakhtin, the real message of the Dostoevsky novel is the author's means of representing the multileveled, multi-voiced, nonfinalized, dialogical nature of all character, idea, human experience, life itself." Booth, introduction to *Problems of Dostoevsky's Poetics*, xiv, says that in Dostoevsky, Bakhtin finds art "loaded with ideology," the very ideology that is critical to his understanding of cognition, ethics and aesthetics. Dostoevsky's novels are themselves formed ideologies.

21. For examples, see essays in Holbrook, *Symposium on Revelation*.

earthly time and space, they do little to decode Revelation's message for contemporary readers trying to unlock its mysteries. Yet, as Leonard Thompson observes: "Throughout the book resurrection, judgment, and especially the kingship of God over the cosmos are affirmed in the form of hymnic liturgies."[22] These hymnic liturgies within the narrative provide excellent textual locations from which to consider some of Bakhtin's reading strategies.[23]

Most commentaries on the book of Revelation begin with a definition and discussion of apocalyptic literature,[24] various suggestions regarding the social situation which produced this particular apocalyptic text, suggestions on authorship, and an appreciation of the many echoes from the Hebrew Bible heard throughout the work.[25] Additionally, some commentaries include a brief history of interpretation and the continued appeal of apocalyptic literature within sectarian faith communities (marginalized from mainstream Christianity) as well as contemporary society (particularly the world annihilation images in movies and music). The commentator often suggests the textual referents in their historical context as restrictions on potential misreadings of this complex and highly symbolic text.

While the discoveries and insights of apocalyptic studies profoundly enhance current readings of Revelation, the discussion often remains at the level of author, genre, historical context, and textual referents. The question "*What* does this text mean?" guides the scholarship. Is this work prophetic or apocalyptic? What happens if we read Revelation as a letter? How is one to interpret the beast imagery? Did the Christians of Asia Minor experience real persecution, or was it merely perceived persecution?

22. Thompson, "Hymns in Early Christian Worship," 470. Thompson continues: "Hymnic liturgies in the Revelation of John are the means by which the author realizes the kingship of God and his just judgment prior to the realization of these realities in narrative form" (ibid.). Thompson, "Cult and Eschatology," 330–50, shows in more detail the relationship between the worship scenes in the book of Revelation and the unfolding eschatological drama.

23. Aune, *Revelation 1–5*, 314–17, identifies sixteen hymnic utterances within the narrative of the book of Revelation: 4:8c, 11; 5:9b–10, 12b, 13b; 7:10b, 12; 11:15b, 17–18; 12:10b–12; 15:3b–4; 16:5b–7b; 19:1b–2, 3, 5b, 6b–8. See also Harris, "Literary Function of Hymns," 4–16.

24. This discussion typically includes the ways Revelation deviates from other apocalyptic literature, and its internal claims or clues concerning other genres, including the epistolary (1:4–9; 22:21) and prophetic (1:3; 22:19) genres.

25. Peterson, *Reversed Thunder*, 23, finds 518 references to earlier Scripture in the 404 verses of Revelation.

Was persecution a construct of the author to move his readers to specific actions? If so, what actions did he want the Christians to embrace or to resist? These questions remain crucial to anyone serious about the book of Revelation. However, the question "*How* does this text mean?" remains. After the best scholars reach a consensus concerning author, genre, historical context, and textual referents the work of interpretation remains. Meaning as dialogic denies that interpretation is ever finished. Meaning as dialogic suggests that every new reader enters the text from a particular context and, with the text, creates meaning.

The dialogic nature of the hymnic utterances in the book of Revelation invites readers to experience dialogic meaning, rather than to decode monologic truth. Hymns assume the presence of a plurality of consciousnesses, including the many voices of the choir, and the voice(s) of those receiving praise. Hymns, like all utterances, take place in particular contexts. Who is singing? What experiences do such singers bring into the event? What perspectives on life are present? How are different perspectives wrestling with and complementing each other? The hymns reflect the dynamic qualities of experiencing meaning, as the hymns remain open to new insights and future choir combinations. Unlike a monologic approach whose goal is to shut down conversation about the book's meaning, a dialogic approach assumes that meaning is only possible within contextualized dialogic activity. This book will attempt to notice, with Bakhtin's help, dialogic relationships between competing and collaborating genres in the book of Revelation. Especially in Revelation's hymns, apocalyptic, prophetic, and Christian liturgical elements interact dialogically. In the book of Revelation, the apocalyptic genre is not allowed complete dominance, but reflects and aids the interpretive enterprise as it dialogizes with other genres and generic contacts. The argument here is not that the book of Revelation is like Dostoevsky's polyphonic novels. It certainly is not. Rather, Bakhtin's notion of genre as a way of thinking makes a careful reader of Revelation more sensitive to the dialogic relationships between different ideologies and the choices readers must make when reading such a generically complex book.

Bakhtin explored genres further by considering the ways different genres represent the related concepts of time and space. He used the term "chronotope" (literally *time-space*) to refer to this dynamic within texts that provides the field of possible actions and events for the activity of literary characters. Not surprisingly, Bakhtin favored the chronotopes which best represent the time and space of real life. Within such chronotopes, actions make a difference, present time is of most value, and the future is open. Bakhtin's insight into the sense of time and space within literary works is useful for reading the book of Revelation, whose sense of eschatological future time and other-worldly space conflicts and collaborates with its representation of present experience and earthly space. This chronotopic complexity is particularly evident within the hymns of the book of Revelation. When such temporal and spatial tension occurs, the tension works to pull readers into the narrative.[26] In the hymns, different representations of time and space, and the human actions possible in them, compete and complement. In scenes of worship, the redeemed community experiences the eschatological end before it arrives within the narrative.[27] A monologic time line of events will not do. In the book of Revelation, liturgical and eschatological elements work together. Thus, one cannot carefully consider Revelation's eschatology while ignoring the book's liturgy. Thompson states: "The future with which the early Christian prophet was concerned impinged upon the present."[28]

In Bakhtin's early adult years following university he wrote on key philosophical issues to which he returned again and again. Philosophers had long asked how to encompass the realm of the mind and the world of matter. Bakhtin and his conversation partners considered this and related questions in the context of the new Soviet Russia.[29] Bakhtin was able to bridge the self-world, self-other, and author-creation distinctions through his related concepts of "outsideness" and answerability. He

---

26. Ladin, "Fleshing Out the Chronotope," 212–36, considers Bakhtin's understanding of chronotopes.

27. Thompson, "Cult and Eschatology," 342.

28. Ibid., 347. Thompson concludes: "The writer of the Apocalypse used hymnic liturgical materials as they were used by prophets in the worship life of the Christian community: to realize in the present realities otherwise apprehended only as future eschatological events" (348–49).

29. Almost a century and a half earlier, Immanuel Kant's groundbreaking *Critique of Pure Reason* had suggested boundaries to theoretical knowledge, a critique of reason divorced from the real world. For Kant, the mind could not know a "thing-in-itself" but only in relationship to experience. He proposed a "synthesis" of mind and experience. During Bakhtin's day, the Neo-Kantianism of the popular Marburg School understood this synthesis as occurring in the realm of the mind. This was supported by Kant's "categorical imperative," his proposal that the ground for ethical action is achieved *a priori*. The "universality of the ought" assumed a position outside of experience, apart from specific cases in real life. In his move from cognition to ethics (from pure reason to practical reason), Kant had grounded ethics in the realm of theoretical knowledge. Bakhtin would ground his own view of ethics in the realm of knowledge *as dialogic*.

believed that each entity was different from, yet always in relationship to, the other. Each was located in a particular place which provided a "surplus of seeing" when compared to other locations. And each entity's unique location warranted a responsibility or answerability in life. In a variety of ways, Bakhtin's dialogism shaped his understanding of existence, ethics, and aesthetics. Michael Holquist says this about Bakhtin: "Dialogue is an obvious master key to the assumptions that guided Bakhtin's work throughout his whole career: dialogue is present in one way or another throughout the notebooks he kept from his youth to his death at the age of 80."[30]

To exist, a body must respond to, and therefore be in a relationship with, its environment. Katerina Clark and Michael Holquist give an example of this by saying that an organism showing "no signs of life" is one that no longer reacts to its environment, and is pronounced dead. The opposite state of "responding to the environment, being able to answer it, is life itself."[31] The self is distinct from, but never out of relationship with, its environment.

For Bakhtin, the same was true when considering ethics. A self must respond to others from the self's uniquely located position in life. Unlike the self who was actually a "pretender"—performing the abstract obligations of Kant's "categorical imperative"—Bakhtin's self acted within an ethical event that was loaded with the dialogic qualities of real life.[32] For Bakhtin, the self's situatedness outside the other eliminated the possibility of opting out of responding (or claiming an alibi in being).[33] Confronted

---

30. Holquist, *Dialogism*, 15. Bakhtin, "Toward a Reworking," 293, states: "The dialogic nature of consciousness, the dialogic nature of human life itself. The single adequate form for *verbally expressing* authentic human life is the *open-ended dialogue*. Life by its very nature is dialogic. To live means to participate in dialogue: to ask questions, to heed, to respond, to agree, and so forth. In this dialogue a person participates wholly and through his whole life: with his eyes, lips, hands, soul, spirit, with his whole body and deeds. He invests his entire self in discourse, and this discourse enters into the dialogic fabric of human life, into the world symposium."

31. Clark and Holquist, *Mikhail Bakhtin*, 66.

32. Bakhtin considered the ethical realm and Kant's "categorical imperative" as eliminating the specific, local experience from morality. Bakhtin, *Toward a Philosophy*, 25, stated: "The categorical imperative determines the performed act as a universally valid law, but as a law that is devoid of a particular, positive content." In Bakhtin's view, this left both the moral self and morality in the abstract. In contrast, Bakhtin shifted the focus to a model of the self located *in* experience, that is, in the act itself, thus filling the "ought" with real content.

33. Bakhtin, *Toward a Philosophy*, 40–41.

by an other, who was also a uniquely positioned self, the interaction was a morally charged event.[34] The self must answer in some way. When true engagement takes place, the self returns to its own space partially shaped by the interaction with the other.

Like the ethical act, the creative act is also a response by a uniquely positioned self to an other. Bakhtin stated: "An aesthetic event can take place only when there are two participants present; it presupposes two noncoinciding consciousnesses."[35] Since, for Bakhtin, readers, like authors, helped to create meaning, readers also reflected an "outsideness" that called for answerability. This state of affairs made it possible for readers to experience a real engagement with literary art. Each bringing a surplus of seeing, readers "live into" their interpretations with their lives.[36]

Located outside the book of Revelation, a contemporary reader brings a surplus of seeing to the interpretive enterprise.[37] Because of the reader's crucial role, the reader's self is important not only after reading, but prior to the experience. The reader of the New Testament Apocalypse enters into a dialogic relationship with the work's unique evaluation of the world. In this book, such an evaluation is described within the discourse of "moral vision." A responsible reader engages the text as an other, attending to its moral vision by getting as close as possible to it, and then returns to the reader's own location. Unable to claim an alibi in interpretation, a reader is invited to respond to the vision with the reader's life.

Bakhtin's understanding of meaning as dialogic shifts the interpretive enterprise from the search for monologic truth, to an experience of meaning as dialogic. Bakhtin's insights into genre and chronotope provide

---

34. Green, *Mikhail Bakhtin*, 34, states: "I incline toward an other, live into his or her experience. I enter as deeply as I am able the space of the other—their particularity—perceive it to some extent with their eye or ear—and then return to my own space, remembering and marking—integrating—what I have experienced."

35. Bakhtin, "Author and Hero," 22. Bakhtin explored the relationship between artists and their literary characters (ibid., 4–256). Bakhtin, *Problems of Dostoevsky's Poetics*, considered the representation of polyphonic characters as the ultimate literary reflection of an artist treating characters as others outside of self while remaining answerable to them.

36. Green, *Mikhail Bakhtin*, 191, states: "A responsible reader will need to sign her interpretation with her life in some way."

37. Reddish, introduction to *Apocalyptic Literature*, 37, writes: "No one situation can exhaust the full meaning of apocalyptic images. They continue to be reapplied in new situations whenever the forces of evil seem overwhelming and hope recedes into the distance."

new ways of reading the book of Revelation. Revelation's hymns are key textual locations for hearing the ideology of this complex apocalyptic text. The unique sense of time-space in the hymns works to pull readers into the narrative in order to grasp its evaluative position, or moral vision, of the world. It is a moral vision to which readers are answerable.

GOALS FOR THIS BOOK

The primary goal for this work is to read the book of Revelation in a way that is sensitive to *how* the text means, and thus provide an alternative to monologic readings that claim to uncover *what* the text means. This goal is significant both for my own faith tradition following the tragedy at Waco, and for others who read the book as a message to be decoded. I am convinced that all monologic approaches are doomed to fail for they ignore the very nature of language and meaning. Related is my conviction that approaches that attend to the dialogic nature of language provide ways to recover the book for thoughtful Christians who have (in essence) excised it from the living canon of the Christian church. A text so rich in resources for the moral life of the Christian community should not be ignored or avoided.

Chapter 2 considers the genre debate among scholars of apocalyptic literature as they wrestle between "genetic" and "generic" approaches to the texts. Bakhtin's understanding of genre as a way of thinking provides a useful resource within the debate. His understanding of genre emphasizes the social and historical aspects of language, which are explored in the context of the book of Revelation as an apocalyptic text having both generic contacts to Hebrew prophetic literature and ideological reformations due to Christian convictions. The second half of the chapter attempts a reading of the first five hymns of the book of Revelation (the narrative's first throne room scene in Revelation 4–5) noting the ideological medley present within the hymns. Since the hymns contain a variety of perspectives from different contexts, readers must make careful choices while exploring these sections of the narrative.

The third chapter considers the representation of time and space with its realm of possible activity present in the book of Revelation. While New Testament theologians typically make assumptions concerning the type of eschatology (imminent future time-space) and ethics (an "interim" ethics) reflected in the book, Bakhtin's understanding of chronotope provides a fresh way to consider the complex time and space represented within the hymns. It follows that the realm of possible human activity in such time-space is also complex. The second half of the chapter attempts to read the hymns found in the middle section of the narrative (Rev 7–16) by attending to its complex chronotope. Rather than the typical representation of time-space in apocalyptic literature, the book of Revelation's complex genre, particularly noticeable during the hymns, creates a tension between chronotopes that works to pull readers into the scenes of worship. The chronotopes of readers add to this kaleidoscope of interacting times and spaces.

The fourth chapter explores a possible role for the book of Revelation in Christian ethics by suggesting that its imaginative language provides a moral vision or framework for ethical discourse. The liturgical aspects of the book, especially the hymns, invite readers to embrace an evaluative position on the world, that is, a moral vision to which readers are invited to respond with their lives. The second half of the chapter considers the final four hymns in the book of Revelation (19:1–10) in light of the work's moral vision and the reader's answerability to it.

After Waco, readers of the book of Revelation have a "surplus of seeing" unimagined by the text's author. Contemporary readers bring that (and much other) "surplus" to the text. Readers and text participate in the dialogic process of creating meaning. Such a joint venture calls readers to answer with their lives.

The book of Revelation provides the Christian community with an ethical discourse of moral vision where throne and Lamb imagery depict a God whose cosmic existence invites worship and whose presence in history calls for faithful witness. An apocalyptic text with many liturgical moments, the book's narrative draws readers into its vision through its hymnic utterances. Having engaged such a vision, readers return to their own contexts and to the possibilities for worship and witness within their own contexts. Having engaged this apocalyptic vision, readers are invited to respond with their lives.

The final chapter summarizes the main points of this book and concludes with a reading of the book of Revelation that is very different from that of David Koresh and his followers. The book of Revelation understood as the New Testament Psalter, rather than code to be deciphered, moves readers to respond in worship and witness.

2

Hymns to an Immanent Creator and a Transcendent Lamb

Genre and the Book of Revelation

MOST COMMENTARIES AND STUDIES of the book of Revelation written in the last few decades begin with a discussion of the book's genre. New Testament scholars know that many misreadings of the canonical apocalypse can be attributed to misunderstandings of apocalyptic literature.[1] An extreme example of such a misunderstanding of the apocalyptic genre is reflected in the hermeneutics of David Koresh. Koresh interpreted the symbolic language found in Revelation not as one of many first-century Jewish and Christian apocalyptic works, but as the ultimate code book "by which one might unlock all other parts of scripture."[2] Questions concerning sections of Revelation were referred back to often obscure

---

1. Bauckham, *Theology of the Book of Revelation*, 1, begins his book with the following paragraph: "What kind of book is Revelation? It is important to begin by asking this question, because our answer determines our expectations of the book, the kind of meaning we expect to find in it. One of the problems readers of the New Testament have with Revelation is that it seems an anomaly among the other New Testament books. They do not know how to read it. Misinterpretations of Revelation often begin by misconceiving the kind of book it is."

2. Newport, *Apocalypse and Millennium*, 212. Koresh also stated: "The book of Revelation contains all the books of the bible. All the books of the bible meet and end there. This is what we have learned over the years." Newport transcribes these comments from a tape by Koresh entitled "Judge What I Say" (ibid.).

passages from the Old Testament. Likewise, Old Testament passages were clarified through the "unveiling" of Scripture's "final chapter." In essence, Koresh treated the entire Bible as one huge book. Neglecting any distinction between Hebrew prophetic works and Christian apocalyptic texts, he also neglected any distinctions concerning socio-historical location and literary context. His method did not warrant any discussion of the form, content or function typical of apocalyptic works. He felt that there was no need to consider how first readers of the book of Revelation might have heard its overall narrative and embedded epistles. Koresh was and is not alone. Many readers of this final book of the Christian Scriptures have attempted interpretations without heeding Richard Bauckham's caution: "Misinterpretations of Revelation often begin by misconceiving the kind of book it is."[3]

So, what kind of book is Revelation? The question is not an easy one to answer. During the past century, scholars have proposed two major approaches to interpreting the book of Revelation specifically and to apocalyptic literature generally. The first major approach is to consider the sources of literature considered "apocalyptic." The second major approach is to consider common characteristics of apocalyptic works, including form and content (and some would add function).

THE BOOK OF REVELATION AND THE QUESTION OF GENRE

The "Genetic" Approach

John J. Collins calls the first approach the "genetic" approach.[4] It asks: from where does Revelation, as an apocalyptic work, get its "genes"? Several major biblical scholars of the first half of the twentieth century considered Hebrew prophetic oracles as the primary genetic source for apocalypses.[5] Gerhard von Rad challenged this position by suggesting wisdom literature as the primary source.[6] Later scholars, led by Hermann Gunkel, expanded the horizon of apocalyptic studies by considering a

---

3. Bauckham, *Theology of the Book of Revelation*, 1.
4. Collins, *Apocalyptic Imagination*, 14–21.
5. Charles, *Critical and Exegetical Commentary*; Rowley, *Relevance of Apocalyptic*; Russell, *Method and Message*.
6. von Rad, *Old Testament Theology*, 301–15.

multiplicity of non-Israelite sources, including mythology discovered in Canaanite-Ugaritic, Babylonian, Persian, and Hellenistic texts.[7]

This major approach to interpreting apocalypses included searching for the source of the sources; in other words, the specific people living in particular social situations who, perhaps influenced by a variety of literary forms and religious ideas, produced the first (and later) apocalyptic works. Of course, each scholar's assumptions concerning sources led in a particular direction. Paul Hanson, convinced of the prophetic "genes" of apocalyptic, identified "proto-apocalyptic" texts in the Hebrew Scripture's prophetic literature, and then described the creators of the texts as members of a marginalized prophetic community living in post-exilic Israel.[8] Stephen Cook challenged Hanson, suggesting that apocalyptic texts emerged from a variety of social locations including that of the Israelite priestly establishment.[9] Those scholars emphasizing non-Israelite sources considered a variety of traditions and peoples as key to interpreting apocalypses.

Cook's work and other recent studies focusing on the social environment(s) of apocalyptic works continue this "genetic" approach. They suggest that to interpret the book of Revelation one needs to go beyond the text itself to consider the social situation of the author and his first audience. The majority of studies assume an environment of harsh persecution for both the author and his original audience. Others argue that historical sources do not support such an analysis,[10] or that any such crisis was a perceived crisis on the part of the author and/or his original audience,[11] perhaps due to the growing affluence and complacency of the Christian communities. A statement by Adela Yarbro Collins summarizes the quest for those approaching the book of Revelation genetically: "The logic, the sense of a text, is discovered only when it is read in terms of a specific culture, specific historical circumstances, a particular point of view."[12]

---

7. Malina, *On the Genre and Message of Revelation*, is one example, as his work suggests that Greco-Roman astrological myths influenced the Seer's choice of form for the book of Revelation. Cohn, *Cosmos, Chaos, and the World to Come*, argues that the roots of apocalyptic literature are best located in ancient Persian myths. Cohn proposes that the book of Revelation's depiction of a divine warrior who quiets the forces of chaos is a myth found in Zoroastrianism (212–19).

8. Hanson, *Dawn of Apocalyptic*.

9. Cook, *Prophecy & Apocalypticism*.

10. Thompson, *Book of Revelation*. See also, Thompson, *Revelation*, 19–44.

11. Yarbro Collins, *Crisis and Catharsis*.

12. Ibid., 20. Yarbro Collins continues: "If this point of view is not a reconstruction

The "Generic" Approach

The second major approach to interpreting the book of Revelation has been called the "generic" approach.[13] This approach considers the common characteristics of apocalyptic literature in order to suggest a definition of the genre. While indebted to scholars like Klaus Koch who created lists of characteristics common to most apocalyptic works,[14] the Apocalypse Group of the Society of Biblical Literature Genres Project sought a comprehensive list that would include all extant apocalypses.

John J. Collins and the Apocalypse Group began their work at a time when most studies embraced the "genetic" approach. They noted that the "genetic" approach tended to break an apocalyptic work into sections in order for each section to be analyzed separately. While providing a wealth of information about possible sources and cultural influences on each section, the approach neglected seeing apocalyptic works as completed wholes. The Apocalypse Group attempted to rectify this lack by shifting from a study of the historical origins of the literature to identification of the constitutive elements of apocalyptic works. Using an inductive approach, members of the Apocalypse Group "provide a comprehensive survey of all the texts which might be or have been classified as apocalypses and can be dated with any plausibility in the period 250 BCE–250 CE, with the purpose of establishing how far they can purposefully be regarded as members of one genre."[15] Based on their work, the Apocalypse Group proposed the following definition:

> "Apocalypse" is a genre of revelatory literature with a narrative framework, in which a revelation is mediated by an otherworldly being to a human recipient, disclosing a transcendent reality which is both temporal, insofar as it envisages eschatological salvation, and spatial insofar as it involves another, supernatural world.[16]

---

of the original context of the text, it will inevitably be the cultural perspective of the interpreter, perhaps as shaped by some powerful interpretation between the author's and the interpreter's time.... It must be clear by now that I regard careful attention to the original historical context as the essential foundation of the interpretation of any text" (ibid.).

13. Collins, *Apocalyptic Imagination*, 1–14.

14. Koch, *Rediscovery of Apocalyptic*, 23–33.

15. Collins, preface to *Semeia* 14, iii. The study included works that are Jewish, Christian, Gnostic, Greek, Latin, and Persian in origin.

16. Collins, "Towards the Morphology," 9.

After determining the above definition as inclusive of all the literature, the Apocalypse Group noted several key differences among these apocalyptic works both in their manner of revelation and in their eschatological content. In some works, the apocalypticist (the seer or the recipient of the vision) receives the revelation while on a journey in otherworldly space. Such works emphasize an "unveiling" of the cosmic realm. Other works do not include such a journey, remaining more focused on the earth. Therefore, the Apocalypse Group separated apocalypses into Type I (without a journey) and Type II (with a journey). In addition, the eschatological content fell into three different categories: (a) *ex eventu* prophecy of history[17] concluding in eschatological crisis; (b) cosmic or political eschatology without mentioning *ex eventu* prophecy of history; or, (c) eschatology as only personal in character. The first category emphasizes an unveiling of the earthly realm where all epochs of human history are in the apocalypticist's temporal present.

Collins observed that pre-Christian apocalypses did not combine other-worldly journeys (Type II) with *ex eventu* prophecy of history (a).[18] It seemed that some apocalypses emphasized an unveiling of *spatial* realities beyond human experience, while others emphasize an unveiling of *temporal* realities beyond human experience. Collins stated: "It would seem that there are two strands of tradition in the Jewish apocalypses, one of which is characterized by visions, with an interest in the development of history, while the other is marked by other-worldly journeys with a stronger interest in cosmological speculation."[19] In contrast to early Jewish apocalypses, a single Christian apocalyptic work can incorporate both an other-worldly journey and *ex eventu* prophecy of history.[20] However, the book of Revelation, maintaining a key generic tie to Jewish apocalypses, does not include an *ex eventu* prophecy of history along with its (atypical) journey into the heavenly realm.

From the start of the project, Collins admitted that the functional and socio-historical aspects of the genre of apocalyptic are left out of this

---

17. *Ex eventu* prophecy (prophecy after the fact) of history is best understood as a historical overview presented within a vision that includes a prediction of the future.

18. Collins, "Towards the Morphology," 16. The only possible exception is the relatively late Jewish apocalyptic work entitled the "Apocalypse of Abraham," believed to be a first- or second-century CE text. See Rubinkiewicz, "Apocalypse of Abraham."

19. Collins, *Apocalyptic Imagination*, 6.

20. Collins, "Towards the Morphology," 15–19.

particular study and that these factors are necessary for interpretation.[21] However, he also stated that "while a complete study of a genre must consider function and social setting, neither of these factors can determine the definition."[22] Instead, while "the study of apocalypses, even from a literary point of view, must eventually address the history and social functions of the genre . . . these questions are consequent to the purely literary description and identification."[23] In his later work, Collins stated his approach more forcefully: "The study of the apocalyptic genre rejects the genetic orientation of previous scholarship and places its primary emphasis on the internal coherence of the apocalyptic texts themselves. It is apparent that the apocalypses drew on various strands of tradition and that the new product is more than the sum of its sources."[24] Collins then restated his proposal for a generic, rather than genetic, approach to the study of apocalyptic literature. That is, an approach that seeks "the internal coherence of the apocalyptic texts themselves" rather than solely the sources for the origins of apocalyptic.[25]

David Hellholm challenged the Apocalypse Group's definition of apocalyptic because Hellholm believed that any definition of genre must take function into consideration.[26] Hellholm proposed the following addition to the definition of apocalypse: "intended for a group in crisis with the purpose of exhortation and/or consolation by means of divine authority."[27]

21. Collins, preface to *Semeia* 14, iii.
22. Collins, "Towards the Morphology," 1.
23. Ibid., 4. Collins repeatedly states that the work of the group is not complete without a discussion of socio-historical issues. However, he credits the literary description with being the foundation on which further work on "this genre must necessarily be built."
24. Collins, *Apocalyptic Imagination*, 21.
25. Ibid.
26. Hellholm, "Problem of Apocalyptic Genre," 26–27.
27. Ibid., 27. Collins, *Apocalyptic Imagination*, 41, challenged Hellholm by stating that, while it is true for most Jewish apocalypses, to describe apocalyptic literature as emerging from a "group in crisis" is not appropriate for *all* apocalypses. Collins continued: "Whatever the underlying problem it is viewed from a distinctive apocalyptic perspective. This perspective is framed spatially by the supernatural world and temporally by the eschatological judgment. The problem is not viewed simply in terms of the historical factors available to any observer. Rather it is viewed in the light of a transcendent reality disclosed by the apocalypse. The transcendent world may be expressed through mythological symbolism or celestial geography or both. It puts the problem in perspective and projects a definite resolution to come. This apocalyptic

The Interdisciplinary Nature of Contemporary Approaches

In recent years interdisciplinary approaches to the book of Revelation dominate the literature emerging from the Society of Biblical Literature. Scholars frequently cross over between "genetic" and "generic" approaches. In addition, from traditional categories emerge new possibilities.[28] Given this current situation in Revelation studies, a literary critic who considered genre as a way of thinking, with all its ideological and contextual implications might be a helpful conversation partner.

Mikhail Bakhtin would applaud the move by Collins and the Apocalypse Group to consider apocalyptic works as completed wholes, for they function as works, not as separate sections. However, Bakhtin would also challenge the strict "generic" approach for its assumption that forms exist in isolation from social contexts and ideological convictions. While providing a detailed description of apocalyptic works in their entirety, the descriptions alone do not address their meaning.[29] Typically, such studies cease before suggesting what these (whole) works mean to real people in real social situations who read and hear them. While a book like Revelation is certainly "more than the sum of its sources," the environmental influences—issues concerning functional and socio-historical aspects of the literature—are critical. For Bakhtin, an understanding of "genre" separate from these influences was a misunderstanding of the term and of its inherent resources for interpreting texts.

Therefore, Bakhtin would also applaud approaches that carefully consider "genetic" sources which are in the process of being modified generically. For Bakhtin, a genre always emerged from a specific social situation. A genre was not merely form, but ideology, a way of thinking. Since ideologies were always located within particular social locations, the traditional focus on past historical influences and events must not

---

technique does not, of course, have a publicly discernible effect on a historical crisis, but it provides a resolution in the imagination by instilling conviction in the revealed 'knowledge' that it imparts. The function of the apocalyptic literature is to shape one's imaginative perception of a situation and so lay the basis for whatever course of action it exhorts" (41–42).

28. For example, considering the book of Revelation as a drama provides new possibilities for interpretation. See Barr, "Apocalypse of John," 243–56.

29. Beale, *Book of Revelation*, 41, lists a group of scholars who criticize "the hermeneutical profit of recent genre research." For other biblical scholars who agree, see Beale, *Book of Revelation*, 41n24. It seems that Bakhtin might join them in wondering what such an approach has (thus far) yielded in interpretive insights.

be neglected. However, socio-historical insights were not ends in themselves. When one was confronted with a particular genre, one met an ideology with a history *and* with a future. Genre as ideology implied the possibility of new readings emerging from a given work.

This book suggests that Bakhtin's understanding of genre aids current studies of the book of Revelation by affirming aspects of both the "genetic" and "generic" approaches, thus providing new possibilities for interpretation. Some of these possibilities will be explored by looking at the first five hymns found in the book of Revelation.

The hymns of the book of Revelation provide excellent textual locations from which to consider the compelling nature of genre for the interpretation of this literary work. Each hymn allows a reader to recognize it as a separate utterance, a "simple" genre that now only exists within the "complex" genre of the apocalypse.[30] Also, the hymns have been the site of previous "genetic" versus "generic" scholarly debates,[31] and so to study the hymns underscores the impossibility of considering one without the other. The hymns, like all good liturgical elements, hold both the past and the present, both the traditions of the old and the possibilities of the new. Therefore, these moments in the narrative contain rich resources for interpreting the book of Revelation.

In an essay on the liturgical elements of Jewish apocalyptic texts, James Charlesworth posed a challenge: "We need to examine why many of the Jewish apocalypses are intermittently punctuated by hymns and prayers."[32] The book of Revelation, a Christian apocalypse, has an unusually large number of hymns and other liturgical elements, making Charlesworth's challenge even more pertinent. If hymns within an apocalyptic narrative contain a medley of generic contacts, to study them in the context of this whole rich utterance is to explore fascinating possibilities for interpretation.

---

30. Bakhtin, "Problem of Speech Genres," 61–62, discussed the difference between "simple" or "primary genres," and "complex" or "secondary genres." A hymn (like Bakhtin's example of a letter inside a novel) "enters into actual reality" only through the book of Revelation as a whole.

31. Shepherd, *Paschal Liturgy*, 77–84, suggested that the sources for the hymns in Revelation were the common liturgical practices of the Christian communities at the time the Seer wrote. Bauckham, *Climax of Prophecy*, 140, suggested a more generic/ideological reading: "Arguments that the heavenly liturgy of the Apocalypse reflects an earthly liturgy practiced in John's churches can probably not be sustained.... But the worship of Christ in the Apocalypse is nevertheless 'highly suggestive of the devotional attitude of the Asiatic Church... towards the Person of Christ.'"

32. Charlesworth, "Jewish Hymns," 422.

BAKHTIN'S INSIGHTS INTO GENRE

Typically the genre of a particular literary work is considered its type or form of writing. In biblical studies, for example, distinctions are made among narratives, prophetic oracles, epistles, parables and prayers. Since one reads a story differently from a letter, ascertaining the forms found within a given work is an important step in determining textual meaning. Lengthy studies carefully list the various characteristics of each type of writing in order to aid the reader in interpreting texts.[33] Bakhtin found this understanding of genre inadequate. Instead of *a step* on the way to textual meaning, Bakhtin understood genre as the *embodiment* of meaning itself, the shape that a particular idea takes. For him, any and all textual meanings were incomprehensible apart from a work's genre.

Bakhtin, with his conversation partner P. N. Medvedev,[34] believed that humans make sense of reality not through a "string of words and sentences," but through a series of internal genres which are constantly evaluating individual utterances.[35] Bakhtin stated: "Each separate utterance is individual, of course, but each sphere in which language is used develops its own *relatively stable types* of these utterances. These we may call *speech genres*."[36] Human experiences are not expressed randomly, but in particular forms that are already bearing a good deal of meaning.[37] In a

33. Aune, *New Testament in Its Literary Environment*, is one example.

34. Among Bakhtin scholars there is much debate concerning the authorship of three books possibly written by Bakhtin under other names. Medvedev, *Formal Method*, is one of the debated works. At the very least, Bakhtin and Medvedev seem to have been collaborating at the time the work came into existence. For further discussions of the authorship question, see Clark and Holquist, *Mikhail Bakhtin*, 146–70; Morson and Emerson, *Mikhail Bakhtin*, 101–19; and, Steinglass, "International Man of Mystery," 33–41.

35. Bakhtin, "Problem of Speech Genres," 71, identified an "utterance" as a unit of speech communication bounded on each side by a change of speaker. For Bakhtin, the utterance implied language in action; that is, language involved in real life communication and exchange. In the same essay, Bakhtin stated: "To ignore the nature of the utterance or to fail to consider the peculiarities of generic subcategories of speech in any area of linguistic study leads to perfunctoriness and excessive abstractness, distorts the historicity of the research, and weakens the link between language and life" (63).

36. Ibid., 60.

37. Bakhtin, "Response to a Question," 5, said: "Shakespeare, like any artist, constructed his works not out of inanimate elements, not out of bricks, but out of forms that were already heavily laden with meaning, filled with it. We may note in passing that even bricks have a certain spatial form and, consequently, in the hands of the builder they express something."

work on the topic, Bakhtin/Medvedev said: "We think and conceptualize in utterances, complexes complete in themselves."[38] Therefore, any particular perspective on human experience can only exist as an expression within a known form.[39] Because humans think in genres, humans can experience meaning. Imaginations existing in rich, ideological environments have ready access to innumerable genres.

Given these convictions, Bakhtin considered genre as a way of visualizing reality, that is, as "forms of thinking."[40] For him, meaning could only occur through contemplation of the entire creative work as a particular form which embraced a particular perspective on human experience. Thus, genre was an intricate and inseparable part of each creation, perhaps best defined as "form-shaping ideology."

Gary Saul Morson and Caryl Emerson begin to unpack this understanding of genre in the following description: "A genre, understood as a way of seeing, is best described neither as a 'form' (in the usual sense) nor as an 'ideology' (which could be paraphrased as a set of tenets) but as 'form-shaping ideology'—a specific kind of creative activity embodying a specific sense of experience."[41] The relationship between form and ideology emphasized by this description underscores the inadequacy of considering one without the other.

---

38. Bakhtin/Medvedev, *Formal Method*, 134. Bakhtin, "Problem of Speech Genres," 78–79, wrote: "To learn to speak means to learn to construct utterances (because we speak in utterances and not in individual sentences, and, of course, not in individual words). Speech genres organize our speech in almost the same way as grammatical (syntactical) forms do. We learn to cast our speech in generic forms and, when hearing others' speech, we guess its genre from the very first words." Morson, "Bakhtin, Genres, and Temporality," 185, adds: "In acquiring language, we learn genres and therefore learn ways of shaping and evaluating experience." Morson, "Introduction to Extracts," 89, also states: "Children learn genres from their earliest experiences with language. Because the social relations that are crystallized in specific genres change, so do the genres themselves."

39. Bakhtin, "Problem of Speech Genres," 78–79, explained: "If speech genres did not exist and we had not mastered them, if we had to originate them during the speech process and construct each utterance at will for the first time, speech communication would be almost impossible."

40. Morson and Emerson, *Mikhail Bakhtin*, 280.

41. Ibid., 282–83.

The Genre Debate: Form vs. "Form-Shaping Ideology"

Through his understanding of genre, Bakhtin/Medvedev challenged his contemporaries, particularly the literary theorists known as Formalists,[42] who considered genre a collection of literary devices merely holding the various elements of a work together. For Formalists, meaning was located within the individual elements, not the completed work, making overall genre practically incidental to literary analysis. Bakhtin/Medvedev turned this view of genre on its head. Instead of literary theory that focused on *parts* or individual *elements* of a work, Bakhtin suggested that analysis must first consider each work *as a whole*, that is, as a genre. Morson and Emerson consider the ramifications of this view of genre by stating: "A 'whole work' is a specific conceptualization of the world and a genre is an overall way of conceiving it, a starting point for a particular conceptualization. The selection of specific elements, devices, or themes is a consequence of the work's 'vision.'"[43] Each part of a work can only be properly grasped in relationship to the ideological perspective made accessible by and inseparable from its genre.

So, instead of working with individual literary elements in textual interpretation, Bakhtin *began* with genre.[44] Similarly, studies on sections of the book of Revelation should first consider the genre of this particular literary work. When attempting to interpret the hymns found in this work, it is critical to note their embeddedness in a larger literary utterance. The entire book of Revelation is a creative act whose form and ideology are inseparably linked. Any expression of its ideology in a different genre would be a different ideology. Bakhtin/Medvedev was convinced: "If we approach genre from the point of view of its intrinsic thematic relationship to reality and the generation of reality, we may say that every genre has its methods and means of seeing and conceptualizing reality,

---

42. The view of genre expressed by Bakhtin/Medvedev also challenges contemporary biblical scholars who embrace Formalist approaches to texts.

43. Morson and Emerson, *Creation*, 272. Bakhtin/Medvedev, *Formal Method*, 129, states: "Poetics should really begin with genre, not end with it. For genre is the typical form of the whole work, the whole utterance. A work is only real in the form of a definite genre. Each element's constructive meaning can only be understood in connection with genre."

44. Genre as "form-shaping ideology" demanded that a discussion of genre, the form in which language was actually experienced, must be the starting point of literary theory. This approach also allowed for a wider analysis of genres, including non-literary genres.

which are accessible to it alone.... Every significant genre is a complex system of means and methods for the conscious control and finalization of reality."[45] Therefore, one cannot discuss apocalyptic literature without considering the unique portrait of reality created through the genre. Such "form-shaping ideology" is not only critical for interpretation, it is the point from which all other interpretive endeavors take place.

In addition to the inadequacy of genre as merely a collection of literary devices, it is also inadequate to excerpt generic observations in order to ground ideological propositions. Various views of reality presented by literary genres cannot be expressed apart from their literary forms. Morson and Emerson state: "Genres are neither lifeless collections of formal features nor abstract combinations of philosophical premises, although critical descriptions may involve both."[46] The following caution is extremely important: "So long as one does not confuse transcribed propositions for the essence of the genre, they can be helpful."[47] Thus, genre as "form-shaped ideology" emphasizes the work as a completed whole—its literary composition, its conceptualization of the human experience, and the relationship between the two.

This understanding of genre as inseparable from ideology assumes historical contexts for all genres. Ideas do not appear out of nowhere. Genres, as utterances, work in life. Actual authors of utterances consider actual recipients. These moments are located within time and space. The utterances are spoken by particular ideological tongues, and are heard by

---

45. Bakhtin/Medvedev, *Formal Method*, 133. Ibid., 134, continued: "The process of seeing and conceptualizing reality must not be severed from the process of embodying it in the forms of a particular genre. It would be naive to assume that the painter sees everything first and then shapes what he saw and puts it onto the surface of his painting according to a certain technique. In real fact, seeing and representation merge. New means of representation force us to see new aspects of visible reality, but these new aspects cannot clarify or significantly enter our horizon if the new means necessary to consolidate them are lacking. One is inseparable from the other.

"The same is true in literature. The artist must learn to see reality with the eyes of the genre. A particular aspect of reality can only be understood in connection with the particular means of representing it. On the other hand, the means of expression are only applicable to certain aspects of reality. The artist does not squeeze pre-made material onto the surface of the work. The surface helps him to see, understand, and select his material."

46. Morson and Emerson, *Creation*, 283.

47. Ibid. Morson, "Bakhtin, Genres, and Temporality," 176, discusses "the 'surplus' of wisdom beyond transcription."

ideological ears.[48] This understanding of genre shifts the historical quests of much biblical scholarship from the search for historical referents, to the nuancing of texts through the exploration of their inherent ideologies which have been shaped by historical situations. At some point, the entire work of Revelation was spoken, heard, experienced. The work as a whole created a response which was more than the sum of the various literary devices. Real choices were made by all who were involved at each stage of the process. Something genuinely new was created. Meaning was possible because the utterance was a speech act within a particular socio-historical context.[49] Bakhtin's sense of genre highlights the actual expression and experience of an utterance.

Genre as utterance assumes an audience. For Bakhtin, utterances were always oriented toward a listener. The author and audience form some type of relationship. Irreducible to formal qualities, a work's genre is a communicative act that is mindful of its audience.[50] Each utterance is always directed to someone, a real someone with particular perspectives. Immediately, the reader has a responsive attitude towards the utterance. Bakhtin said: "Alive utterance, is inherently responsive. . . . Any utterance is a link in a very complexly organized chain of other utterances."[51] An utterance anticipates future utterances. Genres anticipate future "form-shaping ideologies."

The Book of Revelation as an Apocalyptic Text

Given Bakhtin's understanding of genre, discussing the book of Revelation as apocalyptic literature must begin with how the book *thinks*

---

48. Bakhtin/Medvedev, *Formal Method*, 131, said: "Thus the work enters life and comes into contact with various aspects of its environment. It does so in the process of its actual realization as something performed, heard, read at a definite time, in a definite place, under definite conditions." According to Morson and Emerson, *Creation*, 272, this highlights another reason for the priority of genre: "For Medvedev, the first topic was the work as a social fact oriented toward an audience, which for him meant that the forms of whole utterances—their genre—must be the starting point."

49. Bakhtin/Medvedev, *Formal Method*, 132.

50. Ibid. They continued: "It is the whole utterance and its forms, which cannot be reduced to any linguistic forms, which control the theme. The theme of the work is the theme of the whole utterance as a definite sociohistorical act. Consequently, it is inseparable from the total situation of the utterance to the same extent that it is inseparable from linguistic elements."

51. Bakhtin, "Problem of Speech Genres," 68–69.

apocalyptically. Apocalyptic as a "form-shaping ideology" allows for a study of genre that brings together the best of both "genetic" and "generic" insights, and an admission that one cannot be adequately studied without the other. Precisely through its form, the book of Revelation embodies an ideology, a particular way of envisioning human experience. That ideology or vision shapes every other literary element. For the seer[52] to write using the apocalyptic genre was to write in an already value-laden form.[53] It was to see with the genre's vision and "to exploit the potential of that vision to express something genuinely new and valuable."[54] The seer was simultaneously embracing a tradition that made it possible for him to comprehend his ideas, and he created something new with that tradition. This understanding of genre is truly language-in-action. Form-shaping ideology is "appraising reality," while reality is simultaneously "clarifying genre."[55] The seer used apocalyptic because he had to; it was the best way to grasp and articulate his world view. The seer's creation also made possible a new view of reality. As an artist, the seer lived on the boundaries. While "literature is an inseparable part of culture and it cannot be understood outside the total context of the entire culture of a given epoch,"[56] it is also an evaluation of culture from a particular ideological perspective. Thus, rather than reading the book of Revelation as simply a window on Christian life in Asia Minor at the end of the first century CE, the book is an evaluation of that Christian experience from a particular perspective. By using the apocalyptic genre in his evaluation, the seer also embraced a perspective from generations earlier.

Beginning no later than the second century BCE, Jewish apocalyptic literature evaluated the experience of terrible persecution against Judaism and the Jewish people under Antiochus IV.[57] Antiochus aggressively persecuted those who refused to renounce their faith. Jews who

---

52. For the purposes of this project, "seer" refers to the author/artist who created the book of Revelation. "John" refers to the narrative's implied author, the recipient of the vision. Several times within the narrative, the "narrator" will identify himself as "John." As will be shown below, the narrator will sometimes become a character within the narrative.

53. Bakhtin, "Response to a Question," 5.

54. Morson and Emerson, *Creation*, 276.

55. Bakhtin/Medvedev, *Formal Method*, 136.

56. Bakhtin, "Response to a Question," 2.

57. Russell, *Apocalyptic*, 9–12, gives a brief summary of life under Antiochus during 175–164 BCE.

remained faithful to God often paid for their loyalty with their lives. Second-century apocalypticists wrote of the stark contrast between the oppressed and their oppressors. In the future, the transcendent God would judge all people according to their actions. God would punish the violent persecutors and vindicate their innocent victims.

The ideology emerging from this particular social context took literary shape by including specific elements. Jewish apocalyptic literature carried a pessimistic view of the human situation, whose only hopes for societal justice was divine intervention. Thus, apocalyptic literature emphasized the transcendent realm and a future break in history. Setting itself to be the true reality "unveiled" for the lucky few who could "see," apocalyptic literature was intrigued with strange symbolism, celestial geography, and future epochs. The human visionaries within the narratives were constantly reminded that the world of apocalyptic was far from their own. The canvas for apocalyptic literature was the entire cosmos. Apocalyptic ideology was vast in scope, claiming spatial and temporal comprehensiveness.

From the vantage point of the transcendent, apocalyptic literature considered the whole of human history. The visionaries, suddenly unlimited by temporal existence, could see the past and future as clearly as the present. In order to capture the whole of human history, apocalyptic literature had to include the end of human history as currently experienced. Thus, this genre anticipated a future punctuated by a radical break from what was currently and historically known.

Apocalyptic literature also expressed a heightened sense of good and evil. Ambiguity was minimized. Good and evil were given supernatural force through their embodiment in mythic figures and events. The loyal were not described by their nation or culture, but by their choices for God in the midst of oppressive affluence and persecution. In apocalyptic literature human social history was on the decline. From all earthly perspectives, evil appeared to be winning the day. Faithlessness and accommodation, deceit and violence ruled the affairs of the earth. However, the greater, revealed reality affirmed the ultimate defeat of evil and all those who attached themselves to it. Apocalyptic literature concluded that while only divine interaction into human history could eradicate evil and its consequences and vindicate the loyal, such action— a type of eschatological judgment—*would indeed* occur. And the resulting radical break would be so pervasive that individual human bodies, cities, entire civilizations, and the cosmos would be transformed. Even people who had died would be able to experience this transformation through resurrection.[58]

This apocalyptic perspective on human existence shaped the various compositional elements found in particular apocalypses.[59] Here it will be helpful to recall the widely embraced definition by the Apocalypse Group:

> "Apocalypse" is a genre of revelatory literature with a narrative framework, in which a revelation is mediated by an otherworldly being to a human recipient, disclosing a transcendent reality which is both temporal, insofar as it envisages eschatological salvation, and spatial insofar as it involves another, supernatural world.[60]

Resisting the temptation to consider these features as merely formal devices, Bakhtin's understanding of genre suggested that each feature was shaped by the ideology of apocalyptic literature.[61] For example, even the name "apocalypse" suggests a perspective that requires some revelatory action beyond the earthly experience of the human visionary. The assumption of such literature is that the most important aspects of reality cannot be seen by humanity and need unveiling. This idea is underscored by the presence of an other-worldly being, usually an *angelus interpres*, who guides both the human's interpretation of the vision and his journey. The human's abilities are inadequate to the task. He requires outside help. The gap between what is human and what is transcendent remains stark.

In addition, the narrative structure of apocalyptic texts creates the work's forward movement. There is a beginning, middle, and end. The

---

58. Collins, "Apocalyptic Eschatology," argues that the possibility of an afterlife, the transcendence of death, was a major theological contribution of apocalyptic eschatology. Hanson, "Biblical Apocalypticism," 6, states: "It was this kind of ultimate trust in God's sovereignty that fostered belief in the resurrection of the godly among those who witnessed the martyrdom of many of their most revered leaders and beloved sisters and brothers in the faith. Resurrection faith, in other words, arose within apocalyptic circles as the natural extension of the confession in a divine power and grace that was so dependable as not to be foiled by evil or restricted by the limits of human existence."

59. For discussions of the ideology of apocalyptic literature, see Russell, *Method and Message*, 104–57, and Koch, *Rediscovery of Apocalyptic*, 18–35.

60. Collins, "Towards the Morphology," 9.

61. Charlesworth, introduction to *Old Testament Pseudepigrapha*, 3, considers the two ways that scholars typically discuss apocalyptic literature. The first way is as a genre, the second is as a historical movement. Bakhtin, of course, suggested that these two aspects of genre cannot be separated.

concept of an abrupt end requires the clear edges of a narrative. There must also be deliberate movement in a direction that is temporally future. A narrative structure provides this as well. While there are often features that challenge or at least deflect the forward movement,[62] such features must be understood in light of the narrative framework of the apocalyptic text as a whole.

The seer expresses these theological convictions as he considers his own context and the context being carried by the apocalyptic genre. The seer's literary creation located in a particular time and place takes on a dialogic relationship with the times and places of past apocalyptic texts. By the time the seer created the book of Revelation, the apocalyptic genre had already carried for two hundred years the world view of the era in which the genre coalesced.[63]

If Bakhtin is correct that genres carry the world view of the era in which they crystallized,[64] the seer's use of the apocalyptic genre pulled the hopes of second-century believers into the experience of Christian communities of faith. Thus, the seer created an apocalyptic utterance for Christian Jews at the end of the first century CE that carried the ideology of earlier apocalyptic utterances. As the seer considered the transformation of the world, he did so remembering the people persecuted under Antiochus who had glimpsed a world where peace was possible and the faithful martyrs would live again.

The seer, guided by a view of human experience that was best articulated through apocalyptic, created the book of Revelation. In turn, his creative act suggested a way to understand reality anew. While the players had different faces and circumstances, the same drama continued in a new time and place. In order to create apocalyptic literature, the seer had to see apocalyptically.

---

62. Schüssler Fiorenza, *Book of Revelation*, 170–73, discusses the techniques of interludes and intercalation as interrupting the forward movement of the narrative.

63. The consensus among scholars concerning the birth of Jewish apocalyptic literature is during the first half of the second century BCE. Collins, "From Prophecy to Apocalypticism," 147, says: "The first major cluster of Jewish apocalyptic writings originated in the period shortly before and during the Maccabean revolt."

64. Bakhtin, "Discourse in the Novel," 390. Morson and Emerson, *Creation*, 288, state: "Artists create potentials for the future by exploiting the resources of the past."

Genre as Form-Shaping Ideology with a History and a Future

If every genre was a form-shaping ideology that lived and flourished in a particular context, then the critical study of a genre must also include the study of the context in which the genre lived. This meant that genres were able to give readers a glimpse into earlier social situations. Bakhtin did not stop here. Not only were genres formed in particular contexts, they also remembered their previous uses and contexts, carrying world views from past eras into new ones. In this way genres acted as links between past ideologies and their contexts, and later social situations as people search for ways to articulate their own observations on human experience. Since, theoretically, artists only have access to already existing genres, the artist must rely on those genres in order to express an assessment or particular view concerning some aspect of human experience. In choosing a particular genre, an artist acknowledges some sort of relationship between the artist's world and the context in which the genre was formerly used.

Bakhtin explored the history of genres in several essays written in the 1940s,[65] and then in his revision of the Dostoevsky book.[66] The majority of these works highlighted the ideological links between different eras which are carried by genre. For Bakhtin, the best genres were those that depicted the reality in which human life occurs. He followed such genres and their culmination in novels by Dostoevsky.[67] In Dostoevsky's novels, daily life occurred in real time and in specific and distinct locations. In addition, characters exchanged ideas in conversations that challenged points of view and that moved the narrative forward. As they do in real life, characters in novels acted in surprising

---

65. Bakhtin, "From the Prehistory"; Bakhtin, "Epic and Novel."

66. Bakhtin, *Problems of Dostoevsky's Poetics*.

67. Bakhtin carefully studied the historical development of the novel from its ideological roots in Mennipean satire to its culmination in novels by Dostoevsky. See esp. chap. 4, "Characteristics of Genre and Plot Composition." Bakhtin stated: "For our purposes it was important to trace only the basic lines of the tradition. We emphasize again that we are not interested in the influence of separate individual authors, individual works, individual themes, ideas, images–what interests us is precisely the influence of the *generic tradition itself* which was transmitted through the particular authors. Throughout this process the tradition is reborn and renewed in each of them in its own way, that is, in a unique and unrepeatable way. This constitutes the life of the tradition. What interests us—we use a comparison here—is the discourse of a *language*, and not its *individual use* in a particular and *unrepeatable context*, although, of course, the one cannot exist without the other. . . . We are interested only in the tradition itself" (ibid., 159).

ways and articulated diverse, often troubling, perspectives on human experience. Most importantly, the conversations were never finished. For these reasons, the novel reigned supreme in Bakhtin's hierarchy of genres. In Bakhtin's view, apocalyptic literature was the opposite of the novel as it emphasized grand moments outside the human experience of time and space. Its characters were often more like pawns than real people, typically being acted upon, rather than acting decisively for themselves. And, probably most troubling of all for Bakhtin, apocalyptic literature's sense of a determined future eliminated the possibility of dialogue, surprise, and moral action.

In Bakhtin's work on the history of genres, he emphasized the ongoing relationship, a dialogic relationship,[68] between the ideological shaping of form and the creation which shapes ideology. For example, the time was right for Dostoevsky when he created his polyphonic novels, and his novels also created a way of viewing human experience in all its delightful messiness. Dostoevsky's creation of the polyphonic novel mirrored an ideological shift in authorial position, and the novel, in turn, further "loosened" the author from the hero. Therefore, genres not only carried world views from one era to another, they also participated in shaping those eras. Genres were not only "ideologies shaping form," they were formed ideologies shaping ideologies.

While Bakhtin often turned to literary history to see genres remembering the ideology of other eras even when artists might not, he clearly expressed the conviction that past expressions of genres "do not dictate new creation."[69] All expressions of genres in a new environment were new creations. While utterances had meaning because they occurred in learned ideologically-shaped forms, these forms quickly responded to new situations calling for their formal-ideological qualities. Past artistic creations reflecting on human experience provided the means to express new reflections on human experiences. In this way, Bakhtin's insights into genre merged tradition with the act of creation.

Remembering required re-forming. As remembering assumed a new environment from which to remember, it required a new formation

---

68. Bakhtin, *Problems of Dostoevsky's Poetics*, 142, stated: "The essence of every genre is realized and revealed in all its fullness only in the diverse variations that arise throughout a given genre's historical development. The more accessible all these variants are to the artist, the more richly and flexibly will he command the language of the given genre (for the language of a genre is concrete and historical)."

69. Morson, "Bakhtin, Genres, and Temporality," 185.

of all that was carried into the present context. As an artist prepared to create, he or she must reshape previous ideologies within a new (the artist's own) context. When a genre was carried into a new context, the genre also must be modified since, like life, the creative event was not merely discovered, but shaped. Dostoevsky created art, something new, even as his art remembered aspects of past generic traditions of multi-voiced, multi-layered reality. In turn, his art made possible a new kind of human experience as well as thinking about that experience, which also made possible the creation of yet more new genres.

For Formalists, new forms were created by clever, innovative combinations of older forms. Bakhtin did not see that as anything really new. Instead, for Bakhtin, new forms expressed new experiences and ways of thinking about those experiences: "New genres reflect changes in real social life."[70] Humans quickly learn how to reformulate genres or to create new ones. New ways of understanding life require the creation of new genres. Rather than new combinations of literary devices in already existing genres, rather than mechanical manipulation, Bakhtin believed that ideological changes demanded new literary forms. Thus, there was the real possibility of surprise and newness. Genres carry potential as they themselves are carried to new situations and re-formed, or new genres created.[71] As a new vision of reality emerges, so does a new genre. The process is a slow one. According to Bakhtin it takes place over "great time."[72] But the creation of new genres is possible since "authors intend their works to mean more than their intended meanings."[73]

---

70. Morson and Emerson, *Creation*, 277. They then add that "genres respond to social experience."

71. Bakhtin, "Problem of Speech Genres," 63–88; 95–100.

72. Bakhtin, "Response to a Question," 4, wrote: "Great literary works are prepared for by centuries, and in the epoch of their creation it is merely a matter of picking the fruit that is ripe after a lengthy and complex process of maturation. Trying to understand and explain a work solely in terms of the conditions of its epoch alone, solely in terms of the conditions of the most immediate time, will never enable us to penetrate into its semantic depths. Enclosure within the epoch also makes it impossible to understand the work's future life in subsequent centuries; this life appears as a kind of paradox. Works break through the boundaries of their own time, they live in centuries, that is, in *great time* and frequently (with great works, always) their lives there are more intense and fuller than are their lives within their own time . . . . If it [the work] had belonged entirely to today (that is, were a product only of its own time) and not a continuation of the past or essentially related to the past, it could not live in the future. Everything that belongs only to the present dies along with the present."

73. Morson and Emerson, *Creation*, 286. See also Bakhtin, "Discourse in the

This understanding of genre *expected* readers to see in new ways. Morson and Emerson state: "Genres convey a vision of the world not by explicating a set of propositions, but by developing concrete examples. Instead of specifying the characteristics of a world view, as philosophical theories might, they allow the reader to view the world in a specific way."[74] Therefore, new understandings of human experience and new social experiences yield new genres. Morson and Emerson conclude: "Literary forms change not because devices wear out, but because real people create new ways to understand their changing lives."[75]

The Book of Revelation as a Christian Prophetic-Apocalyptic Text

Given Bakhtin's understanding of genre, apocalyptic literature is a form-shaping ideology with a history and a future. In order to study the history of the genre, one must examine the social context in which apocalyptic ideology flourished and in which apocalyptic literature was first formed. In addition, one must consider the ways the sources of apocalyptic were being modified generically, maintaining links to previous contexts while being re-formed in new contexts. For Bakhtin, such analysis was critical in order to articulate a genre's potential for new creations in future social situations.

Many scholarly studies have explored possible historical contexts for the origin of apocalyptic texts. While Julius Wellhausen dismissed apocalyptic, considering it greatly inferior to prophetic literature,[76] Paul D. Hanson argued that prophetic literature contained the earliest sources of apocalyptic literature. In his pivotal work, *The Dawn of Apocalyptic*, Hanson reported his observation of an ideological transition between prophetic works like Isaiah, Ezekiel and Jeremiah, and those of Second Isaiah (Isa 40–55), and even more so Third Isaiah (Isa 56–66) and Second Zechariah (Zech 9–14). Hanson suggested that the earlier prophetic works combined their visionary encounters with historical realities, while the later works kept their visions separate from reality. After

---

Novel," 421; and, Bakhtin, "Epic and Novel," 37, for a discussion of the "surplus" of potential in great works.

74. Morson and Emerson, *Creation*, 282.

75. Ibid., 277.

76. Collins, *Apocalyptic Imagination*, 1. Koch, *Rediscovery of Apocalyptic*, 36–56, surveys the negative view of apocalyptic literature in the biblical scholarship of the twentieth century.

identifying what he called "proto-apocalyptic" texts in Third Isaiah and Second Zechariah, Hanson proposed a social context for the creation of these texts. He argued that the "proto-apocalyptic" texts were created by post-exilic prophets marginalized by the Zadokite priestly establishment.

According to Hanson, as the Israelite religion sought to redefine itself after the exile, the priestly establishment won out over the visionary, prophetic communities. Given their precarious social situation, the prophets shifted their ideological perspective from the traditional prophetic focus on the present, earthly realm, to a future time when God would break into history and vindicate the loyal. By the second century BCE, as the entire Israelite community experienced severe persecution, the views previously expressed by those on the margins of Israelite society were embraced by the community as a whole. As members of an oppressed community, Israel's apocalypticists wrote in a style that heightened the gap between the cosmic vision and earthly reality, emphasizing their ultimate victory through God's judgment of social injustice at the end of human history. Thus, in Hanson's thesis, the "apocalyptic" perspective came to fruition in texts that moved even further away from traditional prophetic literature. Hanson states: "Prophetic eschatology is transformed into apocalyptic at the point where the task of translating the cosmic vision into the categories of mundane reality is abdicated."[77] In Hanson's view, the apocalyptic genre was born when writers emphasized a *discontinuity* with prophetic literature.

Similar to Bakhtin's sense of a genre, Hanson acknowledged the importance of ideological perspective and historical context in the creation of a genre. Even if one is not convinced of Hanson's thesis, his argument provided a heuristic sketch of how a particular genre contained a view of human experience growing out of a particular social situation. In Hanson's view, Hebrew writers of the second century BCE expressed their view of the world by using some of the form-shaping ideologies of the post-exilic prophets. As the earlier works had been shaped by their contexts, so full-blown apocalypses were shaped by the social locations of the apocalypticists. In turn, the apocalyptic works shaped how people viewed their contemporary world.

The problem with Hanson's work, in light of Bakhtin's insights into genre, is his sharp distinction between prophetic and apocalyptic works. Bakhtin frequently suggested that genres remembered their earlier

---

77. Hanson, "Old Testament Apocalyptic Reexamined," 49.

contexts. Hanson's emphasis on the discontinuity between apocalyptic and prophetic neglected consideration of any continuity between the two genres. While Hanson argued that readers needed to grasp the historical and ideological "dawning of apocalyptic" in order to properly read later apocalypses, he left readers without strategies to consider the generic links between apocalyptic texts and their generic ancestor, Hebrew prophetic literature. For Bakhtin, such links were crucial for understanding the works themselves, and their potential for future genres.

Bakhtin's understanding of a work's "generic contacts"[78] demanded consideration of the earlier contexts remembered and carried by the genre. If apocalyptic literature did indeed find such contacts in Hebrew prophetic literature, then apocalyptic held onto, as well as reshaped, the wisdom and world views of earlier eras. Apocalyptic literature embraced, as well as reconsidered, perspectives on human experience articulated by prophetic literature. In creating apocalyptic works with generic contacts to prophetic literature, apocalypticists shaped a genre that acknowledged some sort of relationship between the apocalypticist's world and the context in which the genre was formerly used.[79] These insights provide a tremendous resource for reading the book of Revelation, an apocalypse that maintains numerous generic contacts with Hebrew prophetic literature. With Bakhtin's help, careful readers of the book of Revelation can explore the form-shaping ideologies and social contexts of Hebrew prophetic texts as they are remembered and recreated in this particular apocalyptic work.

Many Revelation scholars who emphasize a relationship between prophetic and apocalyptic literature can aid in this endeavor. David E.

---

78. Bakhtin, *Problems of Dostoevsky's Poetics*, 157–59.

79. Ibid., 157, is helpful: "In order to master this [a given genre's] language, that is, in order to attach himself to the . . . generic tradition in literature, a writer need not know all the links and all the branchings of that tradition. A genre possesses its own organic logic which can to a certain extent be understood and creatively assimilated on the basis of a few generic models, even fragments. *But the logic of genre is not an abstract logic.* Each new variety, each new work of a given genre always enriches it in some way, aids in perfecting the language of the genre. For this reason it is important to know the possible generic sources of a given author, the literary and generic atmosphere in which his creative work was realized. The more complete and concrete our knowledge of an artist's *generic contacts*, the deeper can we penetrate the peculiar features of his generic form and the more correctly can we understand the interrelationship, within it, of tradition and innovation." (Italics in original. While this statement is in the context of talking about carnivalistic generic tradition, it is applicable for other genres as well.)

Aune argues: "Apocalyptic literature is historically and genetically derived from the various revelatory media of ancient Israel, of which classical prophecy was the most important exemplar."[80] Aune continues: "Most scholars regard apocalyptic as the offspring of Israelite prophecy, and this view is certainly correct."[81] Elisabeth Schüssler Fiorenza assumes a connection between the book of Revelation and prophetic literature, since she holds that the book is an example of Christian *prophecy*.[82] G. K. Beale begins his lengthy discussion of the book of Revelation's genre by stating: "Too much distinction has typically been drawn between the apocalyptic and prophetic genres."[83] While there are definite differences between prophetic and apocalyptic, the generic contacts must not be overlooked. Such contacts exhibit the inherent potential within literary works for creative activities in future contexts.

According to Bakhtin, great writers have a sense of "creative understanding." That is, they sense that each creation contains both a specific meaning for its particular time and place, and also the potential for meaning in future times and places. The best readings of texts are those that appreciate this "creative understanding."[84] Stated Bakhtin: "Great writers—Shakespeare, Dostoevsky—have a special relation to tradition. More fully than others, they intuit the rich resources of the past carried by genres; they imagine the potential uses, both past and possible, to which those resources could be put; and they plant more potentials for unexpected development in the future."[85] Like Shakespeare and Dostoevsky, the author of the book of Revelation took, consciously or unconsciously,[86] the ideology of Hebrew prophetic literature, and allowed its perspective on human experience to enrich the narrative of his apocalypse.

80. Aune, *Prophecy in Early Christianity*, 114.

81. Ibid.

82. Schüssler Fiorenza, *Justice and Judgment*, 133–56, includes a lengthy argument on the book of Revelation's claim to be a prophetic revelation. Schüssler Fiorenza states: "Rev., therefore, should not be misunderstood as an only slightly Christianized form of Jewish apocalyptic theology but must be valued as a genuine expression of early Christian prophecy whose basic experience and self-understanding is apocalyptic" (140).

83. Beale, *Book of Revelation*, 37.

84. Morson, "Bakhtin, Genre, and Temporality," 186.

85. Morson and Emerson, *Creation*, 297.

86. Bakhtin, *Problems of Dostoevsky's Poetics*, 121, argued that the genre remembers even if the artist does not.

The next section of this chapter shows that the hymns in the book of Revelation are moments within the narrative that are rich with generic contacts to Hebrew prophetic literature. The hymns remember the form-shaping ideology of the prophets, even as they help to form an apocalyptic text. The hymns are places in the apocalyptic narrative where the prophetic genre's previous contexts are being remembered, while the genre is being modified for a new time and place. Remembering requires re-forming, and the hymns are constantly doing both.

The act of remembering assumes a new context full of new experiences, ideological shifts, and new visions. Such situations require new creations, new literary forms, new genres. The seer's social situation was certainly such a new context. Like the contexts of his literary ancestors (the second-century BCE apocalypticists) which required the re-forming of the prophetic genre into something new, the social situation of the seer required a re-forming of the Jewish apocalyptic genre. As a Christian living at the end of the first century CE, the seer was located physically and ideologically in a very different place from other Jewish apocalypticists. The seer used the apocalyptic genre which, like all genres, remembered and re-formed what had gone before.

The Christian conviction that the Messiah had already arrived within human history in the person of Jesus of Galilee demanded a new literary form. Such an ideological shift required a new genre that remembered its past, but from a dramatically new and unique perspective. The whole book of Revelation as an utterance contained a vision of human existence after Christ that shaped every other element within the narrative, including the numerous hymns. Norman Perrin stated: "A major contribution of apocalyptic was that in Judaism it provided the successor to prophecy and in Christianity the vehicle for the return of prophecy."[87] Perhaps Bakhtin would nuance Perrin's statement by suggesting that Christian apocalyptic did not return to prophecy, as much as it remembered its own generic history from the vantage point of the Christian faith.

This understanding of genre goes beyond merely an interest in the formal features shared by the book of Revelation and prophetic literature (such as prophetic oracles and call visions). Rather, this perspective emphasizes the ideological and contextual contacts present, and the importance of such elements for interpretation. Even characteristics seemingly

---

87. Perrin, "Apocalyptic Christianity," 127.

discontinuous between prophetic and apocalyptic literature have to be reevaluated. When apocalyptic ideology exists next to prophetic ideology, then there remains some sort of dialogic relationship between the two. For example, apocalyptic literature's view of a restoration of justice only at a future radical break in human history had to be re-formed when the apocalypticist believed that the future had arrived in the historical figure of Jesus the Christ. Something significant had *already* happened *within* human history. Certainly the present could not be ignored. The genre had to wrestle with this ideological tension, exploring new possibilities, and being modified in the experience. Apocalyptic literature's future focus began a dialogic dance with prophetic literature's emphasis on present, earthly realities. The Christian literary landscape was suddenly exploding with temporal and spatial possibilities.[88]

In the book of Revelation worship moments, especially hymns, hold these diverse temporal and spatial possibilities, these colliding and collaborating genres. In the hymns the apocalyptic genre's vast cosmic scope remembers the experience of Isaiah, his call and convictions, and the social context in which he formed his literary creations. Revelation's scenes of heavenly worship remember the prophetic call to proper worship and social justice as all of creation sings before the throne. At its most "apocalyptic" moments, the book of Revelation remembers its generic links to Hebrew prophetic literature. Revelation remembers the prophetic works and holds onto them, creating a new masterpiece out of their ideas and contexts now being celebrated from a new perspective, a new place.

The new place was the Christian community of the late first century CE. In the book of Revelation worship moments, especially the hymns, hold the Christian convictions concerning Jesus Christ.[89] In this apocalyptic text, the Christ figure is not presented in terms of the historical Jesus, but in terms of apocalyptic and prophetic expectations—one like the son of man, the lion of the tribe of Judah, the root of David, the slaughtered Lamb, the rider on a white horse. The seer "constructed his works not out of inanimate elements . . . but out of forms that were

---

88. These possibilities will be explored later in the context of Bakhtin's understanding of "chronotope" and subsequent hymns within the book of Revelation's narrative.

89. See Rev 15:3; 16:7; 19:2. Morson and Emerson, *Creation*, 293, observe that "when oral genres penetrate written ones, the interactions may be especially complex." See also, Bakhtin, "Problem of Speech Genres," 66.

already heavily laden with meaning."⁹⁰ And this prophetic-apocalyptic Christ figure—a Lamb in the throne room scene of chapter 5's hymns—is worshiped by the created beings of the cosmos.

The seer's audience, people in relatively small Christian communities within large cities of the Roman Empire, worshiped Jesus. They experienced new ways of seeing and responding to human existence, which required new ways to articulate their experiences. The Christian apocalyptic genre was born. States Collins: "The worship of Jesus, and the way in which divine imagery is applied to him, marks perhaps the most fundamental point at which Revelation departs from Jewish precedent."⁹¹ Amos Wilder speaks about the creation of the gospel genre in a similar way: "Behind the particular New Testament forms lies a particular life-experience and a language-shaping faith."⁹²

In this Christian apocalypse, liturgical moments within the narrative became places of ideological feasts. As apocalyptic literature, the book of Revelation was able to express the cosmic ramifications of the appearance of the Christ. And, in light of Christ, in the context of worshiping him, the book of Revelation remembered prophetic ideas and re-formed the Jewish apocalyptic genre into a Christian apocalypse.

HYMNS BEFORE THE THRONE: REVELATION 4-5

The task of this section is to consider the first five hymns of the book of Revelation in light of Bakhtin's insights into genre. As an apocalyptic text, the book of Revelation is the result of a particular "form-shaping ideology" having both a generic past and potential futures. The hymns present in this apocalypse provide key textual locations for exhibiting the importance and possibilities of generic considerations when interpreting this complex work. This will be demonstrated through close attention to the first five hymns, and the narrative surrounding them.⁹³

---

90. Bakhtin, "Response to a Question," 5.
91. Collins, *Apocalyptic Imagination*, 274.
92. Wilder, *Early Christian Rhetoric*, 9.
93. At times it will be important to illustrate observations by including the Greek text in brackets. Throughout my reading of the book of Revelation, I have used Nestle-Aland, *Novum Testamentum Graece*.

The hymns in Revelation are located within an apocalyptic work which maintained a distinct perspective concerning human experience.[94] In apocalyptic literature, the transcendent or divine realm, that is, the realm beyond human experience, takes center stage. Unlike Bakhtin's descriptions of novels with their prosaic, messy, and irreverent portraits of human existence, in apocalyptic literature human existence can never be adequately comprehended without going beyond the prosaic. In order to truly grasp life's earthly drama, humanity must glimpse into the heavens. After all, the visible, daily, earthly existence was full of suffering and persecution and injustice and death. Apocalypticists declared that such earthly realities were definitely not the whole story. An apocalyptic perspective described a future when earthly existence was transformed for the better by divine intervention.

Bakhtin suggested that after identifying the work's overall vision then smaller units and compositional techniques should be considered in light of the work's vision. Thus, the individual hymns embedded within the book of Revelation are then read for how they nuance the work's form-shaping ideology. As utterances themselves, the hymns imply a located speaker and audience. While some scholars explore possible sources behind Revelation 4–5, including synagogue liturgy and ancient Christian church liturgy,[95] the approach taken by this present book is to consider possible *generic* contacts, rather than formal associations or sources. Whether or not a group of people sang these hymns prior to their appearance in the book of Revelation,[96] their creation and place-

---

94. As mentioned above, the hymns are "primary genres" which exist only as part of the apocalyptic work ("secondary genre").

95. Prigent, *L'Apocalypse de Saint Jean*, discusses the book of Revelation as reflective of synagogue liturgy. Mowry, "Revelation 4–5," 75–84; Piper, "Apocalypse of John," 10–22; and Shepherd, *Paschal Liturgy*, consider ancient Christian liturgies and the book of Revelation. Aune, *Revelation 1–5*, 314–17, shows the similarities between Revelation's hymns and Roman imperial hymns. Bakhtin, "Problems of Speech Genres," 62, argued that once an utterance is placed within a narrative, it can only be understood within the narrative as a whole.

96. Most scholars currently hold that the specific hymns in the book of Revelation were created by the author of the narrative, and do not reflect a particular Christian liturgy at the time the book of Revelation was written. Bauckham, *Climax of Prophecy*, 140, says: "Arguments that the heavenly liturgy of the Apocalypse reflects an earthly liturgy practiced in John's churches can probably not be sustained." However, such elements do reflect similar worship experiences. Perrin, "Apocalyptic Christianity," 142, says: "The particular form of John's vision came from the culture he inherited, the scriptures on which he meditated, and the liturgy of the church whose worship was a

ment within the narrative of the book of Revelation highlights a form-shaping ideology that is crucial to all readings of this book. The seer's audience received the hymns as part of the work's larger narrative.

The five hymns are located in the first heavenly throne room scene, which takes place toward the beginning of the narrative. These hymns enter the narrative immediately following the letters to seven churches (Rev 2–3), and they lead readers into the first judgment sequence (Rev 6:1–8:1).[97] Since the series of unsealings (6:1—8:1), trumpets (8:2—11:19), and bowls (16:1—18:24) form relationships with each other within the narrative,[98] the invitation into the heavenly throne room (4:1) can actually be understood as introducing the entire narrative prior to the parousia (4:2b—19:10). This is further supported by the similarities between the description prior to receiving an invitation into the throne room in 4:1, "behold a door in heaven opened" (ἰδοὺ θύρα ἠνεῳγμένη ἐν τῷ οὐρανῷ), and the declaration which introduces the parousia in 19:11, "Then I saw heaven opened" (Καὶ εἶδον τὸν οὐρανὸν ἠνεῳγμένον). There is a repetition of the word "heaven" (οὐρανός) and the verb "to open" (ἀνοίγω). Additional compositional elements also tie this throne room scene with the narrative as a whole. For example, the characters described in this scene (four living creatures, elders, angels) will play key roles in the rest of the narrative. Another example is the "jasper stone" (λίθῳ ἰάσπιδι) helping to describe the throne scene in 4:3, which shows up again at the end of the narrative as a description of the New Jerusalem (21:11, 18, 19). Any generic reading of a particular hymn must be aware of connections with the rest of the book, including the hymn's placement within the larger narrative.[99]

Bakhtin's works invite a consideration of a genre's history. The previous journeys of apocalyptic literature are rich with interpretive resources. Various statements within the book of Revelation itself argue for some

---

central aspect of his life."

97. Just prior to the final judgment scene, another series of five hymnic utterances are included in the narrative (Rev 19:1–2, 3, 4b, 5, 6b).

98. These three sequences of seven gradually increase in scope and magnitude the judgments issued from the throne. Most scholars note a relationship between them. For example, as the seventh unsealing takes place (8:1), seven angels prepare to sound the seven trumpets (8:2). It is also seven angels who receive seven bowls filled with the final plagues or judgments issued from the temple (15:7–8).

99. Harris, "Literary Function," 29–30.

connection to the prophetic tradition.[100] An even greater argument is found in the presence of ideological contacts between this particular apocalypse and Hebrew prophetic literature. By incorporating throne room visions and liturgical elements, the book of Revelation remembers prophetic perspectives on human experience, and historical contexts where prophets call people to proper worship and social justice. In the book of Revelation, the transcendent realm so often overshadowing all activity in apocalyptic literature, maintains a dialogic relationship to a sense of the immanent realm, that is, the realm of human experience. Similarly, in the book of Revelation the future eschaton so often the focus of apocalyptic literature, maintains a dialogic relationship with the present experience of those in worship before the throne of God. Careful readings observe this textual complexity, a complexity that can be best understood through this apocalypse's generic contacts to prophetic literature.

Remembering a generic history from the perspective of a new location requires a re-forming of the genre. Bakhtin emphasized that each generic creation is a new creation. The hymns of the book of Revelation remember the throne room experiences of the prophets from the perspective of Christian communities at the end of the first century CE. The seer's convictions as a Jewish Christian shaped his creation. For these reasons, his was an apocalyptic text that is unique from other Jewish apocalypses. Careful readings of the book of Revelation notice how the seer's social situation made it possible to reformulate a centuries-old genre. The book of Revelation, an apocalyptic text, includes Christian symbols and images and declarations, particularly surrounding Jesus Christ.[101] Such convictions re-form the genre. Thus, the book of Revelation is a new creation, a new way of thinking, a new genre. It remembers a rich past and makes possible the creation of something really new and surprising.

Contemporary readers of the book of Revelation enter this work with its complex generic qualities requiring ears attuned to the ideological medley made audible particularly in the hymns. Literary products are

---

100. Statements at the beginning and end of Revelation (1:3; 22:7, 10, 18, 19) refer to it as a "prophecy." John's task is described as "prophesying" in 10:11. See Aune, *Prophecy in Early Christianity*, 174–288; Schüssler Fiorenza, *Justice and Judgment*, 133–56; and Aune, *Revelation 1–5*, lxx–lxxi. Aune calls Revelation a "prophetic apocalypse" (*Revelation 1–5*, lxxxix).

101. Collins, *Apocalyptic Imagination*, 273, states: "The distinctively Christian character of Revelation derives not from its view of history but from the central role of Jesus Christ."

cultural products. Therefore each literary work must be considered within an era's entire culture, including the ever-increasing knowledge of that culture.[102] In addition, all great works possess interpretive possibilities for future eras. Therefore, interpretations of the book of Revelation, for Bakhtin co-authorings of the book, have occurred in every era since its composition. Readers today bring new cultures, new questions, and new convictions to this work. When the book of Revelation is approached with "creative understanding,"[103] it can reveal to us "its new aspects and new semantic depths."[104]

Holy is the Creator: The *Trisagion* (Rev 4:8c) and its Antiphon (Rev 4:11)[105]

The beginning of Revelation 4 sounds a lot like any good apocalyptic text, complete with the assumption of a three-tiered universe,[106] movement into the heavenly realm through an open door,[107] and a throne room vision report that includes God enthroned and surrounded by otherworldly beings.[108] While not a full-blown other-worldly journey,[109] Rev-

---

102. This is a paraphrase of a statement by Bakhtin in "Response to a Question," 3. Bakhtin later considers the growing knowledge of epochs "through archeological excavations, discoveries of new texts, improvement in deciphering them, reconstruction, and so forth" (6).

103. Ibid., 7. This is a phrase used by Bakhtin to depict a sense of one's own social location as outside the culture of a given text. The two do not merge, but encounter each other, and so "are mutually enriched."

104. Ibid.

105. Aune, *Revelation 1–5*, 315, places the hymns of Revelation into seven antiphonal units. Only the hymn in Rev 15:3–4 stands alone. Units include: 4:8–11; 5:9–14; 7:9–12; 11:15–18; 16:5–7; 19:1–4, 5–8.

106. A typical feature of apocalyptic literature, the book of Revelation also hints to this view in describing the one like the son of man having the keys to the door of the underworld (1:18). The earthly and heavenly realms fill out the rest of the three-tiered universe. For examples, see Isaac, "1 (Ethiopic Apocalypse of) Enoch"; Stone, "Greek Apocalypse of Ezra"; and Sanders, "Testament of Abraham."

107. Aune, *Revelation 1–5*, 281, discusses this open door as a typical feature of apocalyptic denoting a scene of revelation. For example, see 1 Enoch 14:14b–15, in Isaac, "1 (Ethiopic Apocalypse of) Enoch," 20–21.

108. For examples, see 1 Enoch 14 and 71, in Isaac, "1 (Ethiopic Apocalypse of) Enoch," 20–21, 49–50; and Testament of Levi 2:6; 5:1, in Kee, "Testament of the Twelve Patriarchs," 788–95.

109. Yarbro Collins, "Early Christian Apocalypses," 71, says: "John is not led from

elation 4 does narrate movement of the character John from an earthly location, through an open door into the heavens (4:1a). For John the narrator, time is more ambiguous. Earlier he describes himself in 1:10 as "being in the spirit on the LORD's day" (ἐγενόμην ἐν πνεύματι ἐν τῇ κυριακῇ ἡμέρᾳ), which has had a variety of interpretations,[110] and it is unclear whether that location in time ever changes.[111] Then John states that the voice telling him to move upward through the open door is the same trumpet-like voice as at the start of the vision in 1:10. John reports in 4:1b that the voice said: "Come up here, and I will show you what must take place after this" (ἀνάβα ὧδε, καὶ δείξω σοι ἃ δεῖ γενέσθαι μετὰ ταῦτα). This voice shares a message similar to the earlier statement of the "one like the son of man" who said to John in 1:19: "Now write what you have seen, what is, and what is to take place after this" (γράψον οὖν ἃ εἶδες καὶ ἃ εἰσὶν καὶ ἃ μέλλει γενέσθαι μετὰ ταῦτα). This voice which promises to unveil things that will take place in the future, along with the upward movement and out-of-this-world imagery of this scene, creates certain expectations in any reader familiar with apocalyptic texts. Readers expect to hear and to see into events far beyond human experience and comprehension. Whether a journey to other worlds or a review of the history of their own world, the experience from the perspective of heaven requires explanations and clarifications from an other-worldly guide interpreting on behalf of the visionary.

Even the additional description of the throne room heightens the expectation for unveiled knowledge. The throne is not empty. Present is one who defies description, as stated in 4:3, "the one seated there looks like jasper and carnelian." The ever-increasing concentric circles around the throne underscore that "the one seated on the throne" is located at the very center of the universe.[112] A human visionary has entered the realm

---

region to region in the beyond as is typical in works of the journey type."

110. Bauckham, "Lord's Day," understands the "LORD's Day" as a day of worship that celebrates the resurrection of Jesus Christ. Maxwell, *God Cares*, 82–85, considers the "LORD's Day" as the day of worship that celebrates the Jewish Sabbath. Shepherd, *Paschal Liturgy*, 11–15, explores the "LORD's Day" as referring to the parousia. While the narrator moves "in the spirit" through space and time, his body remains on Patmos during the "LORD's Day." This will be discussed further in the context of Bakhtin's concept of "chronotope."

111. While some approaches to this book rely on it as a blueprint of future eras, others suggest that the entire vision gives a glimpse into the parousia on the "day of the LORD"; that is, during one twenty-four-hour period for the author.

112. There is repeated use of the words translated as "around" or "circling"

HYMNS TO AN IMMANENT CREATOR AND A TRANSCENDENT LAMB   47

of the transcendent. Expecting to hear a review of the epochs of human history culminating in a radical end of time, John instead hears singing "day and night without ceasing" (4:8b).[113] Expecting the overthrow of evil in society, John instead sees a worship scene. While a Jewish apocalyptic text emphasizes either a journey into the divine realm or a review of history, and while Rev 4:1 hints at both possibilities, neither actually occurs. Instead, the spatial movement and anticipated temporal revelation takes John into a divine worship service where other-worldly creatures sing:

> Holy, holy, holy [ἅγιος ἅγιος ἅγιος],
> the LORD God, the Almighty [κύριος ὁ θεὸς ὁ παντοκράτωρ],
> the one who was and is and is to come [ὁ ἦν καὶ ὁ ὢν καὶ ὁ ἐρχόμενος]
> (4:8c).

Typically apocalyptic literature emphasizes the huge gap between the divine or heavenly realm and humanity. Almost every compositional element in apocalyptic literature stresses this distance, including out-of-this-world imagery, strange spatial and temporal realities, a cosmic canvas that includes bizarre creatures and holy beings, and the end as a radical break from present social-historical realities. Whether a tour of other worlds or a review of history, the visionary's limitations are punctuated by the strange discord between everyday life and the experience of the vision. The human, an onlooker to the events, usually requires a guide or intercessor or translator in order to even minimally grasp the visual images.

Yet, the book of Revelation does not include a review of history.[114] It does not describe a journey through distant worlds.[115] It does not even

---

(κυκλόθεν, κύκλῳ 4:3, 4, 6, 8). The throne is surrounded by a rainbow (4:3), by twenty-four thrones with elders upon them (4:4), and by four living creatures described as having eyes all around (4:6b–8). Other descriptions of images and beings surrounding the throne room include: lightning, rumblings and peals of thunder (4:5a), seven torches (4:5b), a sea of glass (4:6a), a host of angels (5:11), and finally all living things (5:13). The same Greek word will be used in 7:11 to describe another scene of worship.

113. Aune, *Revelation 1–5*, 303, notes that the only other example of ceaseless praise found in an apocalyptic work is Testament of Levi 3:8.

114. It certainly does not include one in Revelation 4–5. Although some interpreters of the book of Revelation base their entire reading of the book on a review of the epochs of human history (specifically, and in different ways, the historicist and futurist approaches to Revelation), I agree with John J. Collins and the Apocalypse Group that the book of Revelation does not include a historical review.

115. While this is certainly a visit into the heavenly realm, it is not the beginning of a tour of celestial places like most Type II apocalypses.

involve an other-worldly guide who interprets what is going on.[116] Instead, it is the figure of the exalted Christ who first interprets for John. The one who in 1:17–18 calls himself "the first and the last and the living one," who "was dead," but is "alive forever and ever," says to John: "As for the mystery of the seven stars that you saw in my right hand, and the seven golden lamp stands: the seven stars are the angels of the seven churches, and the seven lamp stands are the seven churches" (1:20). This same figure then continues by dictating to John the letters to the seven churches (2:1—3:22). The exalted Christ is the other-worldly guide. This is a fascinating generic re-formation. In these first three chapters, there is no intermediary between John and transcendent divinity. Thus, the gap between the heavenly and earthly realms, between divinity and humanity, is softened. Instead of the vast distance typical of the form-shaping ideology of apocalyptic literature, John actually ends up a part of the worship scene (5:4–5, 13a).

These unusual features of this particular apocalyptic text are hints disclosing for readers the work's generic contacts to prophetic literature. The writer of the book of Revelation repeatedly revisits the generic ancestors of apocalyptic literature. By taking the main human character into the heavens and landing him before the throne, the seer recalls encounters with the divine in throne room vision reports where the culmination of the experience was worship, not other-worldly journeys; where the human bowed before holiness, not history. In short, he recalls the narrative's links to Hebrew prophetic literature. The only place in the entire Hebrew Scriptures where one finds the phrase "holy, holy, holy," is in another throne room vision report, when Isaiah sees the embodiment of God's glory in the context of Judah's temple. In the narrative account, no intermediary—neither human priest nor angelic being—stands between Isaiah and the LORD. After a brief description of the throne room, one of the winged beings proclaims:

> Holy, holy, holy [Ἅγιος ἅγιος ἅγιος],
> is the LORD of hosts [κύριος σαβαωθ],
> the whole earth is full of his glory [πλήρης πᾶσα ἡ γῆ τῆς δόξης αὐτοῦ]
> (Isa 6:3, LXX).

---

116. Some suggest that there is never an *angelus interpres* (interpreting angel) as in typical apocalyptic texts. An elder will provide some guidance in 5:5; 7:13–17, and an angel, eager to avoid being worshiped by John, will give some direction to him in 19:9–10; 21:9–14; 22:1a, 6, 8–9. But they never actually interpret for John (5:5; 17:1).

As in Isaiah's vision, John's includes other-worldly creatures giving praise to God. This praise with its inclusion in the larger vision is remembered in Revelation 4, not only formally and linguistically, but ideologically. The cultural values of the writer of Isaiah and the entire epoch that shaped those values enter, along with John, through the "door standing open in heaven." The first five chapters of the book of Isaiah portray Judah as a people who no longer worship God faithfully. There are false idols in the land which are the creations of human hands.[117] Revelation's narrative revisits these ideas in the context of Jewish Christians living in the Roman Empire. Images from Isaiah 1–5 pulled into this Apocalypse bring the prophetic genre (and its "form-shaping ideology") into this apocalyptic work. For example, Judah tramples God's courts (Isa 1:12; Rev 11:2), Jerusalem acts like a whore (Isa 1:20; Rev 17), people worship the work of their own hands (Isa 2:8; Rev 9:20–21), therefore they hide themselves in rocks and caves and caverns from the presence of God (Isa 2:10, 19, 21; Rev 6:15–16). Judah acts like Sodom (Isa 3:9; Rev 11:8), placing material goods above all else (Isa 3:18–23; Rev 18:9–24), even human lives (Isa 3:14–15, 5:8–23; Rev 18:13b). Having been created as God's own vineyard (Isa 5:1–7; Rev 14:14–16), Judah ignores the ways of her Creator, and becomes a vineyard of wild grapes, that is, of bloodshed and injustice (Isa 5:7; Rev 14:17–20). Therefore, the wicked will be devoured by the sword (Isa 1:20; Rev 19:15), and then the city will again be called "the city of righteousness" (Isa 1:26; Rev 21:1–5a). It will be located upon Mount Zion (Isa 2:3, 4:2–6; Rev 14:1). There the inhabitants will be called holy (Isa 4:3; Rev 22:11), and God will be present day and night on Mount Zion (Isa 4:5; Rev 7:15–17; 21:3–5a), providing shade from the heat (Isa 4:6; Rev 7:15–17) for all who are on God's holy mountain. The book of Isaiah's image-shaping theology (view of God) and image-shaping ideology (view of human existence) enter into the book of Revelation.[118]

The vision of the throne room recorded in Isaiah 6 carries much more than a hymn into the book of Revelation. It carries a way of thinking about humanity's relationship to a holy God. God's own people, God's creation, turn away from God. They worship the work of their own hands, instead of the one whose hands shaped all of creation. For prophetic literature, such false worship typically rises from and results in social injustice. The false worship of human hands always link to hands

---

117. Isa 2:8.

118. These motifs from Isaiah are all from material just prior to (in anticipation of) the throne room scene and Isaiah's encounter with divinity in chap. 6.

that commit bloodshed in society. Over and over again, the writer identifies Judah's sins as idolatry and injustice, specifying the latter as ignoring and oppressing the poor, the orphan, and the widow (Isa 1:16–17, 23; 3:14–15; 4:8–23). Inherent within prophetic works is the conviction that the earthly realm must *not* be the only reality if justice is to prevail. Holiness is necessary for social wholeness.

Then Isaiah encounters holiness. It is in the human encounter of the holy that Isaiah experiences the depth of Judah's evil, and the hope for Judah's renewal. The vision of a holy God moves Isaiah to acknowledge the gap between himself and divinity, proclaiming in Isaiah 6:5: "Woe is me. I am lost, for I am a man of unclean lips, and I live among a people of unclean lips; yet my eyes have seen the King, the LORD of hosts." Yet, in the moments that follow, Isaiah accepts God's invitation, saying: "And I heard the voice of the LORD saying whom shall I send and who will go for us? And I said, 'Here I am, send me'" (Isa 6:8).

In the presence of the holy, Isaiah embraces God's earlier invitation for the people of Judah to offer themselves as sacrifices: "Though your sins are like scarlet, they shall be like snow; though they are red like crimson, they shall become like wool" (Isa 1:18). For Isaiah's writer and for the seer, a worship scene within prophetic literature invokes much about human experience. It carries a way of thinking about a holy God, and proper responses to that God. In contrast to Judah stands the Isaiah character. Instead of Judah's idolatry and injustice, Isaiah worships God's holiness and is willing to accept God's call and act on behalf of God's people (Isa 6:9a). Within the book of Isaiah, this worship scene witnesses to everything that Judah should have been and to all that God already was. This particular prophetic work portrays human existence as moved by the divine to immediate action in the earthly present. All of the earlier accounts concerning proper worship and moral action (Isa 1–5) are present in the experience of Isaiah before the heavenly throne (Isa 6).

In this first hymn of the book of Revelation, readers can notice generic contacts to Hebrew prophetic literature. Careful readers of the hymn sense the presence of earlier ideologies and their former contexts. While expressing his apocalyptic view of human experience, the seer includes a perspective on human experience from a prophetic context.[119] The seer and his first-century social location is joined by a fellow traveler,

---

119. Aune supports this further by interpreting the repeated phrase "in the Spirit" (1:10; 4:2; 17:3; 21:10), as "in a prophetic trance." See Aune, *Revelation 1–5*, 283; and Caird, *Revelation of Saint John*, 59.

the writer of Isaiah of generations earlier. The seer's apocalyptic view of the ultimate transcendent reality includes the prophetic encounter with an immanent divinity. As the seer created an apocalyptic work with heavenly beings in continuous praise to God, generic contacts to prophetic literature pull the prophet Isaiah and the nation of Judah into the scene. In order to read the book of Revelation alert to genre issues, one must see like John *and* like Isaiah, must hear living creatures *and* seraphs singing. The scene of apocalyptic praise in the transcendent is also an encounter with an immanently present God who calls all heavenly and earthly beings to worship and social justice.

This dialogic activity between genres is multidirectional. The transcendent realm takes on the ideology of prophetic throne room encounters and the throne room visions of prophets are given cosmic significance in the context of the book of Revelation. The seer changes the *Trisagion* from "holy, holy, holy, LORD of hosts" (Isa 6:3), to "holy, holy, holy, the LORD God, the Almighty" (Rev 4:8c). This is an example of how the seer takes the prophetic view of God and humanity and expands them across time and space. The "LORD of hosts," or "LORD of armies" (κύριος σαβαωθ), connotes the heavenly LORD of a localized, earthly realm. The seer changes this description to "the LORD God, the Almighty" (κύριος ὁ θεὸς ὁ παντοκράτωρ) which expands God's authority to a universal domain, including supernatural beings and powers. While the writer of Isaiah portrays a God concerned with the future of Judah, the seer's apocalyptic canvas involves *all* of humanity from all times and places. The use of ὁ παντοκράτωρ declares this conviction.

The hymnic lines that follow each *Trisagion* are also important. In Isaiah the hymn concludes: "the whole earth is full of his glory." The seer changes it to: "the one who was and is and is to come" (ὁ ἦν καὶ ὁ ὢν καὶ ὁ ἐρχόμενος). While some suggest that the seer changes the phrase because the chapters that follow in Revelation will portray a world *devoid* of God's glory,[120] it seems more reasonable that the hymn's presence in a new genre requires such a modification. In apocalyptic, the earth, even the *whole* earth, is not a large enough realm! Apocalyptic literature expands the scope of the vision to involve the entire cosmos. "The whole earth" is too limited. The God who cannot be confined by space, is also located throughout all time: ὁ ἦν καὶ ὁ ὢν καὶ ὁ ἐρχόμενος. Divinity permeates all locations in space and time.

---

120. Harris, "Literary Function," 88–89.

If the reader had not already heard a version of this phrase twice earlier in the book of Revelation (1:4, 8), it would be shocking, as it contains an unusual formula that shifts from time to space. Since the first two sections of the description "who was and is" denote existence in time, readers expect the phrase to conclude "and will be." Instead, the description, the first Christian use of this divine description,[121] ends with: "and *is to come.*" The LORD God Almighty, the recipient of this praise, will be described with similar language throughout the book of Revelation (1:4, 8; 4:8; 11:17; 16:5).[122] In the first appearance of the divine title, the one "who is and who was and who is to come" (ὁ ὢν καὶ ὁ ἦν καὶ ὁ ἐρχόμενος) is the source of "grace and peace," along with the seven spirits and Jesus Christ (1:4–5). In the second appearance, the voice of the LORD God declares, "I am the Alpha and the Omega" (1:8a), which is then followed by the further identification of the speaker, "who is and who was and who is to come, the Almighty" (ὁ ὢν καὶ ὁ ἦν καὶ ὁ ἐρχόμενος, ὁ παντοκράτωρ).

It is interesting that this declaration and description follow directly after the description of the parousia in 1:7 where the word "to come" (ἔρχομαι) is also used: "Behold he is coming with the clouds; every eye will see him, even those who pierced him; and on his account all the tribes of the earth will wail" (Ἰδοὺ ἔρχεται μετὰ τῶν νεφελῶν, καὶ ὄψεται αὐτὸν πᾶς ὀφθαλμὸς καὶ οἵτινες αὐτὸν ἐξεκέντησαν, καὶ κόψονται ἐπ᾽ αὐτὸν πᾶσαι αἱ φυλαὶ τῆς γῆς). In verse 7, the figure of Jesus Christ "is coming." In verse 8, the LORD God Almighty is the one "who is to come." It seems that the seer's Christian convictions concerning the divine nature of the exalted Christ and his proximity to God allow him to blur the descriptions of the two here and throughout the book of Revelation.

Later in the narrative, during another hymn (11:15b), loud voices in heaven declare that "the kingdom of the world has become the kingdom of our LORD and of his Messiah, and he will reign forever and ever" (ἐγένετο ἡ βασιλεία τοῦ κόσμου τοῦ κυρίου ἡμῶν καὶ τοῦ χριστοῦ αὐτοῦ, καὶ βασιλεύσει εἰς τοὺς αἰῶνας τῶν αἰώνων). Then immediately the twenty-four elders sing to the "LORD, God the Almighty, who is and who was, for you have taken your great power and begun to reign" (κύριε ὁ θεὸς ὁ παντοκράτωρ, ὁ ὢν καὶ ὁ ἦν, ὅτι εἴληφας τὴν δύναμίν σου τὴν μεγάλην καὶ ἐβασίλευσας). Once again the descriptions of the Messiah figure and the LORD, God the Almighty are similar, as both are referred to as reigning.

---

121. Aune, *Revelation 1–5*, 303.

122. Bauckham, *Theology of the Book of Revelation*, 28–30, includes a fascinating discussion of these phrases.

In addition, the obvious absence of the phrase "is to come" in this part of the narrative (in contrast with the earlier descriptions in 1:4, 8; 4:8c) suggests that the arrival of God, and the reign of the Messiah and God Almighty have already begun!

There is one final account of this title found during the third bowl plague. In the "solo song" in 16:5b, an angel cries out: "You are just, who is and who was, the holy one, for you have judged these things" (δίκαιος εἶ, ὁ ὢν καὶ ὁ ἦν, ὁ ὅσιος, ὅτι ταῦτα ἔκρινας). Later voices respond using some of the language found in the *Trisagion* for the One seated on the throne: "Yes, LORD God, the Almighty, your judgments are true and just" (ναὶ κύριε ὁ θεὸς ὁ παντοκράτωρ, ἀληθιναὶ καὶ δίκαιαι αἱ κρίσεις σου). However, within the narrative, it is the Christ-figure who judges (19:11); that is, he who is called "the word of God" (19:13b) and "king of kings and LORD of LORDS" (19:16b). Christian convictions re-form apocalyptic visions. Filled with Christian ideology, the apocalyptic genre is never the same again.

The narrative continues with additional descriptions of the throne room and the worship participants, followed by the first antiphon, or responsive hymn. This further description of the throne room and the hymn contains major linguistic similarities which are highlighted by the arrangement of 4:9–11 below:

> And when/whenever [ὅταν] the living creatures will give
> > glory [δόξαν]
> > and honor [τιμὴν]
> > and thanksgiving [εὐχαριστίαν]
> > > to the One seated on the throne [τῷ καθημένῳ ἐπὶ τῷ θρόνῳ],
> > > who lives forever and ever [τῷ ζῶντι εἰς τοὺς αἰῶνας τῶν αἰώνων],
>
> the twenty-four elders
> > will fall [πεσοῦνται]
> > > before [ἐνώπιον] the One seated on the throne [τοῦ καθημένου ἐπὶ τοῦ θρόνου]
> > and will worship [καὶ προσκυνήσουσιν]
> > > the one who lives forever and ever [τῷ ζῶντι εἰς τοὺς αἰῶνας τῶν αἰώνων];
> > and will cast their crowns [καὶ βαλοῦσιν τοὺς στεφάνους αὐτῶν]
> > > before [ἐνώπιον] the throne singing:
>
> You are worthy [ἄξιος εἶ], our LORD and God to receive
> > glory [δόξαν]
> > and honor [τιμὴν]

and power [δύναμιν]
because you created [ἔκτισας] all things
and by your will they existed [ἦσαν]
and were created [ἐκτίσθησαν]
(4:9–11)

This section of the passage is recorded here in its entirety to highlight some important elements. First, the description and antiphon are placed in the narrative immediately after the four living creatures sing the *Trisagion*. Some scholars suggest that the "glory, honor and thanksgiving" mentioned in 4:9a refer back to the *Trisagion*. These scholars, including Beale, translate the Greek word ὅταν as "whenever," making this cycle of praise and adoration a continuous heavenly occurrence, since the *Trisagion* is repeated "day and night without ceasing" (4:8b).[123] Aune argues that ὅταν should be translated as "when," denoting a specific time of occurrence, not an on-going experience. He then suggests that the actual doxology[124] is absent from the narrative, with the "glory, honor and thanksgiving" described, but not performed until 5:13. R. H. Charles proposes that the antiphon does occur at various future times throughout the narrative, identified by the twenty-four elders falling down before the throne.[125] Like Aune, Charles emphasizes not continual action, but deliberate, specific action at particular times. In both views, this second hymn (4:11) maintains a close relationship to the *Trisagion*, as the worship scene describes first the four living creatures (4:8–9), and then the responsive actions and song from the twenty-four elders (4:10).[126] Perhaps the description is supposed to be ambiguous, including both "whenever" and "when." After all, this is a hymn located within an apocalypse. Perhaps it is meant to be both continuous and punctuated. Perhaps that is part of

---

123. Beale, *Book of Revelation*, 334.

124. Aune, *Revelation 1–5*, 307, discusses the features of a doxology and notes that this hymnic summary has these features, including the identification of a deity usually in the dative case, "One seated on the throne," a listing of attributes, especially "glory," usually in the nominative case, and a formula describing the length of reign as "forever and ever."

125. Charles, *Critical and Exegetical Commentary*, 127.

126. Other connections between the *Trisagion* and the description prior to the antiphon include the involvement of the four living creatures (4:8a, 9), the emphasis on God's everlasting existence (4:8c, 9, 10), and the focus of praise upon the "One seated on the throne" (4:9, 10).

HYMNS TO AN IMMANENT CREATOR AND A TRANSCENDENT LAMB   55

the power of a worship scene within an apocalypse. In the "beyond" God is praised continually, *and* at particular moments.

The twenty-four elders are described as falling (πεσοῦνται) before the One seated on the throne[127] and then as throwing or casting (βαλοῦσιν) their crowns also before the throne. They throw themselves and then their crowns in the same direction. These two actions directed to the throne take place just before and immediately after the twenty-four elders' act of worship (προσκυνήσουσιν) which is also directed to the one on the throne, this time described as "the one who lives forever and ever" (τῷ ζῶντι εἰς τοὺς αἰῶνας τῶν αἰώνων).[128] Within the narrative just as the verbs "will fall" and "will throw" surround the word "will worship," so all the elders' actions surround the throne itself and the one seated upon it. They simultaneously fall and worship and cast their crowns and sing, perhaps continuously. Apocalyptic literature allows for scenes that are physically impossible within the earthly realm. In the book of Revelation's worship scenes, space and time are flexible and open. Living creatures and elders and songs and colors and crowns and a rainbow can all simultaneously surround a throne. The One seated on the throne receives worship for being the center of the cosmos, for living forever and ever, for creating everything, for willing everything, and for creating everything (stated a second time for emphasis? honor? future creation?). This is no ordinary antiphon. This is an apocalyptic antiphon.

A lot of action takes place between the living creatures' doxology of "glory and honor and thanks," and the twenty-four elders' antiphon, with its modified trilogy: "glory and honor and power." With so many phrases repeated in these few verses, the change from "thanksgiving" (εὐχαριστίαν) to "power" (δύναμιν) has the effect of emphasizing God's power. The actions described in this scene express a reality beyond daily, earthly existence, which also reshape John's perception of earthly reality. To see into the "beyond," to glimpse the transcendent, is not to perceive unending circles of worlds or epochs, but circles whose center is an occupied throne, whose power is praised by the very creatures surrounding it. The one seated upon it receives continuous and punctuated praise from other-worldly creatures, all of whom owe their very existence to

---

127. This is the first description of the recipient of the four living creatures' doxology (4:9).

128. This is the second description of the recipient of the four living creatures' doxology (4:9).

the everlasting creative power and life of the Creator. No being can really exist outside of the circles surrounding the throne.

In the seer's social location, the ultimate place of power rested at the Caesar's throne. All circles of earthly existence (economic, social, religious, military, political) found their authority at the seat of the Roman empire. As scholars learn more about the seer's cultural context, the throne room scene in Revelation 4 gains further significance. Instead of fire brought before the emperor, a custom which "was an integral feature of imperial ceremonial" practices probably as early as 30 BCE,[129] seven flaming torches burn before God's throne (4:5). Instead of praising an inanimate statue—"Zeus was, Zeus is, Zeus shall be; O mighty Zeus"[130]— *living* creatures sing to the One seated on the throne, "who was and is and is to come." By describing God's heavenly throne room within an apocalypse, the seer presents an unambiguous interpretation of Rome's seat of power: either one bows before Rome's throne or God's. To worship Rome means embracing Roman power and its system of violent oppression of people (described as beastly powers later in the narrative). The seer clearly distinguishes the two kingdoms. Readers must choose one or the other.

When first-century readers chose to join the circles of elders and creatures bowing down before God, they embraced a different reality than the one that encompassed every aspect of their daily lives. Instead of the Caesar who had conquered all creatures, the book of Revelation records scenes of worship to the One who creates all life, *including* the life of the Caesar. All earthly rulers must bow before the Christ, "the beginning of God's creation" (ἡ ἀρχὴ τῆς κτίσεως τοῦ θεοῦ). This description of the exalted Christ in 3:14b suggests a connection between the Creator seated on the throne and Jesus Christ. Similar to the prologue of the fourth gospel account,[131] the book of Revelation presents Christ as intimately involved in the creation of life. As the *Trisagion* and its antiphon conclude this section of the throne room scene, the ability to create all things dominates the description of the divine, and anticipates a God who is able to re-create everything anew (21:1–5a).[132]

129. Aune, *Revelation 1–5*, 295.

130. Ibid., 31.

131. John 1:1–18, esp. 1:1–4.

132. Bauckham, *Theology of the Book of Revelation*, 51, states: "The eschatological hope of Revelation actually has its basis, not only in the understanding of God as Creator, but also in the belief in the Creator's faithfulness to his creation. If faith in

These first two hymns, the *Trisagion* and its antiphon, acknowledge a holy God, who *is ὁ παντοκράτωρ*, that is, the one with universal domain. This God is worthy of worship and praise because God creates everything. As Isaiah had been a witness and participant in a throne room vision scene, so John, and the seer's audience witness worship as the true reality at the center of the cosmos. Such worship is itself a witness to the Creator of all living beings. Different eras collide in this timeless throne room. Judah, and Isaiah, and returning exiles, and the persecuted under Antiochus, and the Jewish Christians of the seer's day, all bring their various social values and their understandings of worship from different times and places. When readers worship, they join the timeless scene, full of so many different times. They welcome a prophetic tradition that unites honor of God and justice to the poor. They embrace an apocalyptic tradition that gives loyalty to the transcendent God whose domain is the cosmos. And they believe in the incarnate Creator, "the beginning of God's creation."

Worthy Is the Lamb:
Songs of the Exalted Christ (Rev 5:9b–10, 12b, 13b)

The throne room scene continues in 5:1 with the phrase "Then I saw . . ." (Καὶ εἶδον). This phrase, found throughout the book of Revelation, denotes a change in focus, without a change of scene (5:2, 6, 11, 13; 6:1). Other phrases, "after this I saw" (Μετὰ τοῦτο εἶδον) (7:1; 15:5; 18:1) and "after these things I saw" (Μετὰ ταῦτα εἶδον) (4:1; 7:9), suggest a more dramatic scene shift. The object of praise from the two earlier hymns remains the focus of the narrative as additional description includes a scroll or book (βιβλίον) in the figure's right hand. The narrative leaves out any clear explanation as to the book's origin or purpose. With symbolic attributes it is described in 5:1b as "written on the inside and on the back, having been sealed with seven seals" (γεγραμμένον ἔσωθεν καὶ ὄπισθεν κατεσφραγισμένον σφραγῖσιν ἑπτά). In this apocalyptic scene of the transcendent realm, the One at the center of the cosmos holds a mysterious book.

Such books are common features of apocalyptic literature.[133] They are an ideal vehicle for conveying special or secret knowledge formerly

---

God as Creator raises the possibility of new creation, it is trust in his faithfulness to his creation which gives hope for new creation."

133. Dan 7:10b and 1 Enoch 93. Examples from prophetic literature include Isa

unknown by the human visionary, and partially or fully disclosed in the visionary's encounter with the transcendent realm. Here John continues to experience events far removed from ordinary human existence. Additional elements highlight the extended worship scene as apocalyptic in its composition and ideology: the continued focus on the throne at the center of the cosmos, symbolic numbers which help to describe key characters and recurring objects, and other-worldly beings, specifically elders and angels.

In 5:2 one angel in particular, a "strong" or "mighty angel" (ἄγγελον ἰσχυρὸν), cries out a critical question with a loud voice (φωνῇ μεγάλῃ) which is presumably heard throughout the cosmos: "Who is worthy to open the scroll and break its seals?" (τίς ἄξιος ἀνοῖξαι τὸ βιβλίον καὶ λῦσαι τὰς σφραγῖδας αὐτοῦ;).[134] This question reverberates throughout the heaven, the earth, and even under the earth (5:3). While the scene's backdrop has expanded to the cosmos, the question reminds readers once again of Isaiah's vision of the throne room, and God's call, "Whom shall I send, and who will go for us?" (Isa 6:8). Aune discusses this as a heavenly council scene, where heavenly beings request the commissioning of an emissary. A question goes out: "Whom shall I send?" "Who will go for us?" "Who is worthy?" In this way, Aune connects the angel's question in Revelation 5 with the question by the LORD's voice in Isaiah 6.[135] However, instead of commissioning someone to move outward from the heavenly throne room to the earth, the scene in Revelation 5 requests someone to move inward. Someone is needed to go to the One seated on the throne, and to take the book in his right hand.[136] Once again, the book of Revelation exhibits an interaction between the apocalyptic genre and its contacts to prophetic literature.

John reports in 5:3 that "no one was able [ἐδύνατο] in heaven or on earth or under the earth to open [ἀνοῖξαι] the book or to look [βλέπειν] into it." This description is interesting, since the angel's question uses the

---

29:11 and Ezek 2:9–10.

134. The narrative includes a total of three strong angels (5:2; 10:1; 18:21).

135. Aune, *Revelation 1–5*, 373, also includes the question in 1 Kgs 22:20: "Who will entice Ahab?" in this category. Aune concludes that the seer's description "generally tallies with conventional OT and Jewish traditions of epiphanies of God and visions of the heavenly throne room" (313).

136. There are biblical similarities to a sealed document which is unreadable (Isa 29:11), and a scroll with lamentation and mourning written on the front and on the back (Ezek 2:9–10).

adjective "worthy" (ἄξιος) in its search for someone "to open" (ἀνοῖξαι) the book and "to loose" or "to break" (λῦσαι) its seals, while John reports that no one in all the cosmos (the three-tiered universe) is "able" (ἐδύνατο) "to open" (ἀνοῖξαι) or "to look" (βλέπειν) into the book. The different adjectives and infinitives in the narrative associate worthiness with ability and the breaking of the seals of the book with the opportunity to look into it. This observation challenges any interpretation of the book as one in which partial reading is possible without unsealing it.[137] However one understands the writing on the book which was "written on the inside and on the back" (γεγραμμένον ἔσωθεν καὶ ὄπισθεν), the narrative implies that its contents are inaccessible unless someone is found worthy and able to break the seven seals.

The import of this moment is underscored through repetition as John, in a first-person account recorded in 5:4, states that he started to weep with heart-wrenching grief (ἔκλαιον πολύ) because in all the cosmos: "no one was found worthy to open the book or to look into it" (οὐδεὶς ἄξιος εὑρέθη ἀνοῖξαι τὸ βιβλίον οὔτε βλέπειν αὐτό). As John weeps, the seer's readers sense the enormity of the moment. The entire cosmos watches. Without explaining exactly what is at stake, all sense that at some level everything is. Given the scene's strong generic links to the prophets, John joins a long line of believers who weep while waiting for the Messiah to save them from persecution.[138] Rachel weeps (Jer 31:15). The prophet Jeremiah weeps (Jer 9:1). All of Jerusalem weeps (Lam 1:2). John weeps (Rev 5:4a).

The next spoken word in the narrative comes from one of the twenty-four elders: "Do not weep" (μὴ κλαῖε). Although elders will speak several times throughout the narrative (7:13; 17:1; 21:9), in the book of Revelation they do not act like the typical other-worldly interpreters of apocalyptic encounters. This is another generic connection to prophetic literature, where God speaks directly to the prophet, rather than through an intermediary. The elder continues, "Indeed the Lion of the tribe of Judah, the root of David [ἡ ῥίζα Δαυίδ] has conquered [ἐνίκησεν] so that he can open the book and its seven seals" (5:5). The verb "to conquer" (νικάω; here ἐνίκησεν) typically involves an object signifying what has been conquered. Without an object, the conquering remains open and unlimited in scope. The description here proclaims that the Lion's

---

137. Aune, *Revelation 1–5*, 341–43, discusses this as a "doubly written legal document." This is suggested by some interpretations of the unsealing sequence.

138. Aune, *Revelation 1–5*, 373.

"victory is unlimited and absolute."[139] This complete victory makes it possible for the book to be opened, which was the original call by the mighty angel (5:2), and John's hope (5:3, 4). However, the action of unsealing and opening the book is paused for further description of the Lion of Judah.

In the book of Amos, the first literary prophet of the Hebrew Scriptures, the lion is used as a description for God. Immediately following the book's introduction, the voice of the prophet declares: "The LORD roars from Zion, and utters his voice from Jerusalem" (Amos 1:2a). After seven oracles against nations that were surrounding Israel, the voice of God pronounces punishment on Israel as well, since those who are living there "sell the righteous for silver, and the needy for a pair of sandals—they who trample the head of the poor in the dust of the earth, and push the afflicted out of the way" (Amos 2:6b–7a). Further descriptions of a lion (Amos 3:4a, 4b, 8 12) depict images of doom for Israel including the horrendous image of a shepherd pulling pieces of the lion's prey from its teeth (Amos 3:12). In the next major section, the writer of the book of Amos describes the gifts of goods and protection granted by God, "yet you did not return to me, says the LORD" (Amos 4:6b, 8b, 9b, 10b, 11b). The final reference to a lion occurs in the description of the "day of the LORD" (Amos 5:18–24). On the day of the LORD, no one will be able to escape its "darkness" (Amos 5:18b, 20b). Even Israel's worship will be rejected by God, since worship without social justice is not true worship (Amos 5:21–24). In contrast to Israel's social injustice, God calls for justice to "roll down like waters, and righteousness like an ever flowing stream" (Amos 5:24). Since prophetic forms and images carry prophetic values, the lion of Revelation's throne room scene can remind readers acquainted with the Hebrew prophets of the just God who roars in judgment on the "day of the LORD." In prophetic literature, eschatological hope means that God will act within history on behalf of the oppressed. In apocalyptic literature, the restoration of justice will occur only in a future which breaks into and disrupts human history. At this point in the narrative, the seer maintains a tension between these two eschatological viewpoints.

Then, to add yet another layer of eschatological complexity, the seer resolves the tension by suggesting that the day of the LORD has already arrived! The Lion "*had* conquered" (past tense, ἐνίκησεν). The hope of

---

139. Ibid., 349.

the messiah from the line of David, that is, the "root of David" is present.[140] In the book of Revelation, John looks to see the Lion previously announced by the elder (5:5), and instead sees a Lamb "standing as if it had been slaughtered" (ἑστηκὸς ὡς ἐσφαγμένον). These two images, side by side within the narrative, illustrate the medley of traditions coming together to create a new way of thinking about God and the eschaton. The prophetic tradition of a warrior-messiah who delivers God's people, joins another prophetic tradition of a suffering-servant. The Christian conviction that Jesus embodied both traditions on a cosmic scale re-forms the two prophetic traditions in the context of a new creation, the book of Revelation.[141] The Lion roaring for justice is also the suffering Lamb. The day of the LORD that ended oppression, *includes* suffering. The Lamb is a divine *sufferer*, Jesus the Christ of the Christian faith, who conquered.[142] David Barr expresses it this way: "Rather than the lion who tears his prey (Ps 17:12), Jesus is the torn lamb."[143] Given its placement in an apocalyptic text, the victory of the torn Lamb has universal implications, which will be highlighted during the next hymn and through the repetition of the word "slaughtered" (ἐσφάγης) in 5:9. Rather than a lion devouring Israel's immediate neighbors and Israel for social injustices, the Lamb of the book of Revelation defeats cosmic forces of evil and injustice.

The Lamb is described in an unusual position. First, the Lamb was "in the middle of the throne and the four living creatures" (ἐν μέσῳ τοῦ θρόνου καὶ τῶν τεσσάρων ζῴων). Does this suggest that the Lamb is located *between* the throne and the four living creatures (5:6a)? Probably not, given that the four living creatures are themselves located "in the midst of the throne" (ἐν μέσῳ τοῦ θρόνου) and also "surrounding the throne" (καὶ κύκλῳ τοῦ θρόνου) (4:6b). The description of the Lamb in chapter 5 depicts his close proximity to both the living creatures, and

---

140. Aune, *Revelation 1–5*, 350, discusses this as a messianic term found in Hebrew prophetic literature (Isa 11:1, 10). This idea resurfaces at the end of the book of Revelation, as the voice of Jesus speaks: "I am the root and the descendant of David" (22:16b).

141. Ibid., 373, states: "The striking contrast between the two images suggests the contrast between the type of warrior messiah expected by first century Judaism and the earthly ministry of Jesus as a suffering servant of God (see Matt 11:2–6 = Luke 7:18–23)." On this traditional messianic imagery, see Caird, *Revelation of Saint John*, 73–74; and Yarbro Collins, *Apocalypse*, 39–40.

142. If they are all messianic figures, the Lamb will also come in judgment as one like the son of man (14:14–20), and as the rider on a white horse (19:11–21).

143. Barr, *Tales of the End*, 70. Along with Ps 17:12, Amos 5:12 depicts a lion consuming its prey.

to the one "seated on the throne" who has been the center of the throne room description since 4:2. Has the Lamb been there all along? Has the "One seated on the throne" *become* the Lamb? This very apocalyptic description leaves open various possibilities, some of which are physically impossible within the earthly realm. Second, the Lamb is "in the midst of the elders" (καὶ ἐν μέσῳ τῶν πρεσβυτέρων). Once again the description highlights the ever-widening circles surrounding the throne, and now the Lamb figure. All that is proclaimed in the two previous songs can now be sung (and will soon be sung) to the Lamb. The repeated phrase "in the midst of . . . " (ἐν μέσῳ) is problematic in any other world than the world of apocalyptic literature. Here the circles simultaneously focus the reader inward to their center, and outward into the cosmos. They take readers beyond mere formal description to the ideology shaping the description. The narrative thus far prepares the reader for the cosmic worship to come when the worthy Lamb takes the strange book, and all the beings of the universe respond in praise.

The judgment of the seven cities and nations surrounding Israel in the book of Amos[144] expand to Israel and to Isaiah's Judah, to Ezekiel's Jerusalem,[145] and to the seven churches of Asia Minor mentioned at the beginning of the book of Revelation.[146] Then apocalyptic literature takes the scene to the cosmos, where all created beings surround the throne.[147] All eyes are upon the seven-eyed Lamb, who is also a lion, an ancestor of David, a slaughtered creature with seven horns, whose seven spirits fill the earth. Unlike Isaiah 6, no human anywhere in the cosmos can step forward and accept this invitation. No one but this strange Lamb from the transcendent realm can go forward.[148] This first act by the Lamb within the narrative is highlighted in two ways. First, the narrator repeats

---

144. The seven cities and nations are: Damascus, the capital of Syria; Gaza, in the land of the Philistines; Tyre, a Phoenician city; Edom, Ammon, and Moab of the Jordan region; and Judah (Amos 1:3, 6, 9, 11, 13; 2:1, 4).

145. In the prophetic work attributed to the prophet-priest Ezekiel, a similarly strange book, with "writing on the front and on the back" (γεγραμμένα ἦν τὰ ὄπισθεν καὶ τὰ ἔμπροσθεν) (Ezek 2:10, LXX) contained "lamentations and woes" because of God's judgment on Jerusalem.

146. Ephesus, Smyrna, Pergamum, Thyatira, Sardis, Philadelphia, and Laodicea (Rev 1:11; also 2:1, 8, 12, 18; 3:1, 7, 14).

147. In Rev 20:11–13 all people are placed before the throne in judgment.

148. Aune, *Revelation 1–5*, 332–35, argues that this is a scene of "investiture" of the Lamb rather than the history-of-religions approach to the Lamb's "enthronement." The Lamb is affirmed in a status already held.

for emphasis the act of taking the book. The earlier focus on "opening" (ἀνοίγω) and "loosing" (λύω) and "looking" (βλέπω) is replaced by the act of "taking" (λαμβάνω) the book. Even this *preliminary* action is heralded. The phrase in 5:7, "He came and took from the right hand of the One seated on the throne" (καὶ ἦλθεν καὶ εἴληφεν ἐκ τῆς δεξιᾶς τοῦ καθημένου ἐπὶ τοῦ θρόνου), is followed by: "And when he took the book" (Καὶ ὅτε ἔλαβεν τὸ βιβλίον), in 5:8a. The second way the narrative highlights the Lamb's action is by describing the cosmic reaction to his action. Such a response underscores the importance of this act of taking the book, although readers are yet to discover exactly what the book contains.

At the moment that the Lamb takes the book, the Lamb also takes the place of the One seated on the throne, at least within the description of the worship scene. Immediately, the twenty-four elders, who had previously fallen (verb πίπτω, in 4:10 πεσοῦνται which is future tense) "before the One seated on the throne" (ἐνώπιον τοῦ καθημένου ἐπὶ τοῦ θρόνου), now fall (again the verb πίπτω, in 5:8 ἔπεσαν which is aorist) "before the Lamb" (ἐνώπιον τοῦ ἀρνίου). The worship description also includes items in the hands of the elders and the four living creatures which are critical in future sections of the narrative. Each elder and creature holds a harp (κιθάραν) and golden bowls full of incense "which are the prayers of the saints" (5:8b).

These items hint to the reader that the next scene will be another worship scene, since both the harp and the bowls of incense were used in liturgical settings. Liturgical music was accompanied by the harp (κιθάρα).[149] The noun form of κιθάρα is found in several places in the book of Revelation (5:8; 14:2; 15:2). In each instance the harps accompany either a new song (5:9; 14:3), or the song of "Moses and the Lamb" (15:3). In one of these scenes, which is found in Rev 14:2b, the word is used in its verbal form translated "playing" or "harping" (κιθαριζόντων). And in two instances the word is used as a noun denoting harp players, or harpists (κιθαρῳδῶν). The first example of the use of "harpists" is also found in Revelation 14: "The voice I heard was like the sound of harpists harping on their harps" (ἡ φωνὴ ἣν ἤκουσα ὡς κιθαρῳδῶν κιθαριζόντων ἐν ταῖς κιθάραις αὐτῶν). The other instance is found in Revelation 18 at the destruction of Babylon where the mighty angel says to the fallen city: "The sound of harpists [φωνὴ κιθαρῳδῶν] and minstrels and of flutists and trumpeters will be heard in you no more" (18:22). Throughout the

---

149. Ibid., 355–56, lists the following references: Pss 33:2–3; 43:4; 57:7–9; 71:22; 81:1–3; 92:1–3; 98:4–6; 108:1–3; 147:7; 150:3–5; 1 Mc 4:54; T Job 14:1–3.

narrative, harps and harpists either involve worship of the one on the throne and the Lamb, or else they will never be played again. Thus the image of the harps is associated with both celebration and judgment. The harps mediate a mixture of ideas, much like the "day of the LORD," and much like the golden bowls.

The bowls (φιάλας), also elements of both liturgy and judgment, will return later in the book of Revelation. While in chapter 5 they are associated with the prayers of the saints, in other places within the narrative the contents of the bowls are more frightening. Following another worship scene, the bowls are "full of the wrath of God" (15:7), and are then emptied upon the earth (16:1, 2, 3, 4, 8, 10, 12, 17). Even the prayers of the saints, in chapter 5 connected with the bowls, will have a destructive force as they are sent to heaven on the gold altar (8:3–4), and then judgment language immediately follows with "peals of thunder, rumblings, flashes of lightning, and an earthquake" (8:5).[150] Thus, throughout the book of Revelation, liturgical moments hold praise and celebration, but also the potential for judgment and destruction. The world view of the prophets concerning humanity's relationship to holiness on the "day of the LORD," expands to fill the entire cosmos, the spatial dimensions of apocalypses. Would the "day of the LORD" be a day of wrath or celebration, judgment or harping? When John describes a transcendent Lamb taking the book from the One at the center of the universe, he proclaims a new way of understanding humanity's relationship to holiness. And, as is often the case in Hebrew literature, the new relationship requires a new song.

The writer of Second Isaiah records a similar situation. It follows one of the "servant songs" (Isa 42:1–9), which celebrates hope in a future servant of God who will "bring forth justice to the nations" (Isa 42:1b), who will "faithfully bring forth justice" (Isa 42:3b), and who will "not grow faint or be crushed until he has established justice in the earth" (Isa 42:4). It is certainly clear that the servant of God will be concerned about social justice. Then the voice of God calls for the servant of righteousness (Isa 42:6a), to be a "light to the nations" (Isa 42:6b), to "open the eyes of the blind" (Isa 42:7a), to "bring out the prisoners from the dungeon" (Isa 42:7b), and the prisoners from the darkness (Isa 42:7c). At last, all things will become new again. The voice of God says: "See, the former things have come to pass, and new things I now declare; before they spring forth, I tell you of them" (Isa 42:9). Then the narrative shifts into praise

---

150. Peterson, *Reversed Thunder*, 87–101, emphasizes the relationship between the prayers of the Christian community and the divine judgments upon the earth.

as the writer declares: "Sing to the LORD a new song, his praise from the end of the earth!" (Isa 42:10a). The servant of God will bring the end of oppression and the beginning of justice. The servant of God transforms existence. In such a situation, a new song issues forth in celebration. The prophetic hope expressed in Second Isaiah is carried into an apocalyptic scene where a transcendent Lamb is worthy to approach the throne and take the book. The Lamb acts as the ultimate servant of God bringing forth justice, and a new existence, and a new song.

Revelation's narrative breaks forth: "Then they sing [ᾄδουσιν] a new [καινὴν] song [ᾠδὴν]" (5:9a). The new song is sung by a group, since the plural form of the noun "to sing" (ᾄδω, here ᾄδουσιν) is used. But which group is doing the singing? Most commentaries assume that it is the group of elders and living creatures which were mentioned in Revelation 5:8. However, the last reference in Revelation 5:8 is to the saints (τῶν ἁγίων), whose prayers are contained as incense in the golden bowls. In later scenes of singing with harps, it will be the "saints" described as the one hundred forty-four thousand (14:1–5) and as "those who had conquered the beast and its image" (15:2) who will do the singing. Perhaps the same choir sings here in Revelation 5. Later, in Revelation 14, the redeemed sing "before the throne *and* before the four living creatures and the elders" (emphasis supplied, 14:3b), for it was only the one hundred forty-four thousand who could even *learn* the song (14:3c). The description in Revelation 14 is interesting, as the scene uses the language which earlier describes the situation of the sealed book. In 5:3 the narrator said: "No one was able in heaven or on the earth or under the earth to open the book or to look into it." The phrase "no one was able" (οὐδεὶς ἐδύνατο) is exactly repeated in the worship scene of Revelation 14: "no one was able [οὐδεὶς ἐδύνατο] to learn the song." The phrase in 5:3 which describes part of the three-tiered universe where the mighty angel attempts to find someone worthy, "on the earth" (ἐπὶ τῆς γῆς), will be slightly but significantly modified in 14:3, where the redeemed will be described as redeemed "from the earth" (ἀπὸ τῆς γῆς). Thus, those redeemed *from* the earth who are able to sing the new song remind the reader of the only one *on* the earth (or heaven, or under the earth) who is found worthy and able to take the book. The Lamb and the saints/redeemed are connected even before they sing of the Lamb's work of redemption. "And they sing a new song singing":

You are worthy [ἄξιος εἶ]
> to take [λαβεῖν] the book and
> to open [ἀνοῖξαι] its seals, for
> you were slaughtered [ἐσφάγης] and
> you purchased/redeemed [ἠγόρασας] for God by your blood [ἐν τῷ αἵματί σου]
>> from every tribe [φυλῆς] and
>> tongue [γλώσσης] and
>> people [λαοῦ] and
>> nation [ἔθνους]
> and you have made [ἐποίησας] them
>> a kingdom [βασιλείαν] and
>> priests [ἱερεῖς] to our God and
>> they will reign [βασιλεύσουσιν] upon the earth [ἐπὶ τῆς γῆς]
> (5:9–10).

The Greek verb σφάζω means "to slaughter," as sheep are slaughtered.[151] When this verb refers to people, it implies terrible violence like a massacre.[152] This same word is used of the Lamb in 5:6, 12 and 13:8. It is also the word used in reference to the mission of the red horse (σφάξουσιν) (6:4), the earthly end of the souls under the altar (ἐσφαγμένων) (6:9), the beast (ἐσφαγμένην) (13:3), and the victims of Babylon (ἐσφαγμένων) (18:24). In both this hymn and in its antiphon (5:9, 12), the Lamb is worthy (ἄξιος, ἄξιόν) because it was slaughtered (ἐσφάγης, ἐσφαγμένον). The Lamb was not shielded from the violence embodied by the red horse and unleashed upon humanity (6:4). The Lamb had met a violent death, yet that very death made him worthy of the saints' anthem.

This violent verb in the completed past (aorist) tense is followed by two more aorist verbs: "to purchase" or "to redeem" (ἀγοράζω) and "to make" (ποίεω). First, the hymn states that the Lamb was able to redeem (ἠγόρασας) through his blood (ἐν τῷ αἵματί σου), people from around the

---

151. Bauer et al., *Greek English Lexicon*, 795.

152. Ibid., 796. Schüssler Fiorenza, *Justice and Judgment*, 73–76, suggests that the seer is associating Jesus with the Paschal lamb and theologically interpreting his death with the Exodus. She also connects the other two aorist verbs to the Exodus: the "purchasing" of people enslaved, and the "making" of them a new kingdom or nation. The writer of 1 Peter shares a similar conviction: "You know that you were ransomed from the futile ways inherited from your ancestors, not with perishable things like silver or gold, but with the precious blood of Christ, like that of a lamb without defect or blemish" (1 Pet. 1:18–19).

world. The qualifying phrase associated with this verb again emphasizes the violent death of the Lamb. Readers recall the beginning of the book, when Jesus Christ was described as the one "who loves us and freed us from our sins by his blood" (ἐν τῷ αἵματι αὐτοῦ) (1:5b). When Babylon finally falls at the end of the narrative (Rev 18:2–24), those who watch the city's demise are reminded that in Babylon "was found the blood [αἷμα] of prophets and saints and all who have been slaughtered [ἐσφαγμένων] on the earth" (ἐπὶ τῆς γῆς). The Lamb and his own are connected within the larger narrative. Those who sing the new song (5:9; 14:3; 15:3), who are redeemed *from* the earth by the Lamb's sacrifice (5:9; 14:3; 15:2), also include those who themselves were slaughtered *on* the earth (6:9; 18:24). Because of their close association with the Lamb, these people are made to be a kingdom, priests serving God, and people who will reign *on* the earth (5:10). Several aspects of the description of Jesus early in the narrative (1:5–6) are repeated in this first hymn to the Lamb:

and from Jesus Christ,	You are worthy [ἄξιος]
the faithful witness [ὁ μάρτυς, ὁ πιστός],	to take [λαβεῖν] the book
	and to open [ἀνοῖξαι] its seals
the firstborn [ὁ πρωτότοκος] of the dead	for you were slaughtered [ἐσφάγης]
and the ruler of the kings of the earth	
To him who loves [ἀγαπῶντι] us	
and freed [λύσαντι] us from our sins *by his blood* [ἐν τῷ αἵματι αὐτοῦ],	*and by your blood* [ἐν τῷ αἵματί σου]
	you purchased [ἠγόρασας]
	from every tribe
	and language
	and people
	and nation,
and made [ἐποίησεν] *us*	*and made* [ἐποίησας] *them*
to be *a kingdom* [βασιλείαν],	*a kingdom* [βασιλείαν]
priests [ἱερεῖς] *to his God* and Father,	and *priests* [ἱερεῖς] *to our God*,
to him be glory	and they will reign [βασιλεύσουσιν]
and dominion forever and ever.	upon the earth (5:9b–10).
Amen (1:5–6).	

When the phrases are placed side by side, several observations can be made. First, both the introduction to the book, and this first hymn to the Lamb focus on the figure of Jesus, the Christ. Second, both refer to the death of Jesus (firstborn of the dead, one who was slaughtered). Third, his blood is specifically mentioned. In the first instance, Jesus' blood acts to free humanity from its sins. In the second instance, Jesus' blood ransoms or purchases or redeems global humanity. Fourth, in both sections redeemed humanity is made into a kingdom. In contrast to the earthly kings who persecute people, a new kingdom is created. Fifth, in the new kingdom every member of the new kingdom is a priest to God. Instead of needing an intermediary between God and individual human beings, each person has direct access to divinity. Finally, in the first scene God's dominion goes on forever and ever. In the hymn scene, it is the new kingdom which reigns upon the earth. Together, these scenes anticipate some of the final scenes in the book of Revelation where God and humanity jointly reign (20:6; 22:5). John sees that humanity living in the transformed city will not need light for "the LORD God will be their light," and then concludes: "and they [God and the redeemed] will reign forever and ever" (22:5b). These brief observations suggest that the ideology found within this third hymn is similar to the ideology of the book of Revelation as a whole. From the unique epistolary form at the start of this apocalypse (1:4–8), to its more traditionally apocalyptic elements, the genre is re-forming because it must, because its way of viewing the world is undergoing re-forming too.

Elisabeth Schüssler Fiorenza highlights the *differences* between the descriptions in 1:5–6 and the hymn in 5:9–10. She suggests that the changes are socio-political in nature. She argues that the Exodus imagery associated with the three aorist verbs (slaughtering of the Paschal lamb; redemption of slaves; creation of a new kingdom) underscores the political ramifications of the Lamb's work. In addition, the language of Revelation 5 suggests a future experience not yet realized, rather than a current state of affairs. It is less individual, and more communal. She states: "As the kingdom for God, the Christian community is understood in political terms as the alternative community to the Roman empire."[153] But it has not yet become the kingdom that encompasses the world.

This book argues that the Lamb's work as described in this throne room scene has political ramifications not only because it uses words

---

153. Schüssler Fiorenza, *Justice and Judgment*, 75.

associated with the Exodus, but because this apocalyptic text maintains its strong generic links to prophetic literature. It is impossible to do a careful reading of the book of Revelation without hearing the voices of Amos and Isaiah and Ezekiel. And, if one hears their words, one hears the genres in which their ideas took shape. If one hears the genres, one hears ideologies, that is, ways of understanding human experience. These passages are political because they are prophetic. The Christian communities of the seer's day who live in seven Roman cities, already live as prophetic communities, in contrast to communities who worship the violent works of their own hands. In addition, these passages have global implications because they are apocalyptic. Christian communities around the globe, throughout all space and time, stand in opposition to all systems of violence and oppression and injustice. When the apocalyptic tendency toward dualism—the stark contrast between forces of good and forces of evil—is no longer applied to entire nations (literal Israel "good," literal Babylon "bad"), but to systems of good (ideal "Israel," or Christian communities of faith and justice) and systems of evil (symbolic "Babylon," or systems of violence, oppression, injustice), the communal nature of existence is heightened. In apocalyptic literature, communities must decide which kingdom to embrace, who to worship, and how to treat others.

The narrative continues with John describing more of the throne room scene just prior to the antiphonal hymn. It begins in 5:11, "Then I looked . . . ," but instead of describing what he sees, John describes what he hears. The concentric circles expand. Suddenly around the throne, and the four living creatures, and the elders is a huge group of angels. In anticipation, readers wait, expecting to hear the number of this heavenly choir. Instead of a specific number, readers learn that there can be no number that encompasses the angels, for there are "myriads of myriads and thousands of thousands" (μυριάδες μυριάδων καὶ χιλιάδες χιλιάδων). This is the same description used in a throne room scene in the book of Daniel. Daniel 7 contains a throne with one seated on it described in much the same way as the "one like the son of man" is described in Revelation's first chapter. Daniel 7 also contains books which, unlike the one in Revelation 5, are already opened. Similarly, there are "a thousand thousands" (χίλιαι χιλιάδες, LXX) serving before the throne, and "ten thousand times ten thousand" (μύριαι μυριάδες, LXX) in attendance. The scene is described as a court in judgment, immediately followed by the phrase "and the books were opened" (Dan 7:10b).[154] After the destruction of the fourth beast, "one like a son of man" comes down from heaven through clouds. The One seated on the throne gives him "dominion and glory and kingship," over a kingdom that is everlasting (Dan 7:14). Along with Isaiah's encounter with the divine, the seer pulls Daniel's revelation of the divine judge into a new literary and social context. The past prophetic works are remembered by Christian communities that celebrate the redemptive act of Calvary. As the scene's concentric rings surrounding the throne move out towards the ends of the earth, so the generic layers create a scene rich in a new form-shaping ideology. The prophetic throne vision meets apocalyptic judgment and Christian salvation, and the universe explodes in song: "Worthy is the Lamb that was slaughtered!" (5:12). A Christian apocalyptic genre is born.

The earlier hymn had already emphasized the universal ramifications of the slaughtered Lamb through the four-fold description of the redeemed: "from every tribe and language and people and nation" (5:9).[155] The responsive hymn from the other-worldly creatures and hosts of heaven affirms the interpretation. The Lamb's sacrifice has global, even cosmic significance. The Lamb—as lion, as messiah,[156] as suffering servant,[157] as sacrifice[158]—establishes justice on earth and throughout the universe. The idolatry and social injustice of Israel and Judah and Babylon and Rome, and all nations, end with the Lamb's victory. The Lamb has conquered *everything* that required conquering. He has cosmic sovereignty because he has provided cosmic salvation.

> Worthy is the Lamb that was slaughtered [ἐσφαγμένον] to receive [λαβεῖν]

---

154. Beale, *Book of Revelation*, 86-99, discusses the importance of Daniel 7 for understanding the book of Revelation.

155. This description will be repeated seven times in the book of Revelation (5:9; 7:9; 10:11; 11:9; 13:7; 14:6; 17:15).

156. For examples of the Lamb as an apocalyptic symbol of a leader, see 1 Enoch 85-90. For a connection between David and a lamb, see 1 Enoch 89:45-46.

157. In addition to the earlier connections made between the Lamb and Isaiah 42, throughout the book of Revelation, the Lamb never speaks. Revelation's Lamb is like Isaiah's description of a suffering servant who, "did not open his mouth; like a lamb that is led to the slaughter, and like a sheep that before its shearers is silent, so he did not open his mouth" (Isa 53:7). In contrast, the beast from the earth (Rev 13:11-18), looks like a lamb, but "spoke like a dragon" (13:11).

158. Throughout Revelation the Lamb is referred to as a sacrifice (1:5; 5:6, 9, 12; 7:14; 12:11).

power [τὴν δύναμιν]
and wealth [καὶ πλοῦτον]
and wisdom [καὶ σοφίαν]
and might [καὶ ἰσχὺν]
and honor [καὶ τιμὴν]
and glory [καὶ δόξαν]
and blessing [καὶ εὐλογίαν]!
(5:12)

This hymn or doxology to the Lamb also begins with the word "worthy" (ἄξιόν). Once again, the reader is reminded of the mighty angel's call and the one figure in all the universe able to take the book from the One seated on the throne. Once again, the song includes the horrendous word (ἐσφαγμένον) that refers to his brutal death. However, given the seer's convictions as a Christian, Jesus Christ is described as "the firstborn of the dead" (1:5a) *before* he is described as the one who saved humanity "by his blood" (1:5b). He is the Lamb "standing" (5:6b), before he is described as the one "slaughtered" (5:6b, 9, 12). While his sacrifice makes him worthy of this cosmic doxology, he does not remain dead or a victim. The Lamb stands because he is resurrected. Later in the narrative, a form of this same Greek word for "standing" (ἑστὸς) will be used again, this time noting his triumphant stance on Mount Zion surrounded by the redeemed of the earth, the one hundred forty-four thousand (14:1). Revelation 14 is the only time Mount Zion[159] is referred to in the book of Revelation, and it is a scene of glorious celebration, with harps and the singing of a new song. In the throne room scene of Revelation 5 it is the innumerable angels who sing aloud a doxology to the Lamb who was slaughtered.

This hymnic utterance has much in common with several introductory descriptions (1:6; 4:9), acclamations (4:11; 5:12), and doxologies (5:13; 7:12; 19:1) found throughout the book of Revelation. The seer's use of similar language and in honor of both God and the Lamb link the two. Throughout this apocalyptic narrative, the seer aligns the One seated on the throne and the Lamb, proclaiming the holiness and divinity of the Lamb. The Lamb is *like* God. The Lamb *is* God!

The similarities between the worship and praise of God and the Lamb in the book of Revelation declare the divinity of Jesus Christ in a

---

159. Aune, *Revelation 6–16*, 803–4, states that in Jewish apocalyptic literature, Mt. Zion is where the messiah would defeat his foes.

way that is unlike any other New Testament book. Christ is to be worshiped. The Jewish Christian faith strongly avoided the worship of any beings other than God, including other-worldly messengers.[160] But the Lamb is not merely a messenger or an actor within the apocalyptic narrative. The one who is slaughtered is worshiped. The final hymn in this throne room scene is set up in such a way that readers are reminded of the unique character of the Lamb. John again reports what he hears: "Then I heard every creature in heaven and on earth and under the earth [ἐν τῷ οὐρανῷ καὶ ἐπὶ τῆς γῆς καὶ ὑποκάτω τῆς γῆς] and in the sea, and all that is in them, singing . . . " (5:13a). Before considering their song, it is interesting to note that the same description was used by John to convey the angel's search for one worthy to open the book. No one was found "in heaven or on earth or under the earth" (ἐν τῷ οὐρανῷ οὐδὲ ἐπὶ τῆς γῆς οὐδὲ ὑποκάτω τῆς γῆς) (5:3). Now, the Lamb who *is* worthy and able to take the book is worshiped by all of the cosmos. A universe of created beings worship their Creator (4:11) and their Redeemer (5:9)[161] together (5:13b) singing:

> To the One seated on the throne and to the Lamb,
>   blessing [ἡ εὐλογία]
>   and honor [ἡ τιμὴ]
>   and glory [ἡ δόξα]
>   and dominion [τὸ κράτος]
>   forever and ever [εἰς τοὺς αἰῶνας τῶν αἰώνων]!
>   (5:13b).

The "One seated on the throne" and the Lamb "in the midst of the throne" are worshiped by every creature in the cosmos.[162] This includes John. Unlike most apocalyptic visionaries, John is not only an observer. More like his counterparts in prophetic literature, John participates. He

---

160. Rev 19:9–10; 21:9–14; 22:1a, 6, 8–9. Bauckham, *Climax of Prophecy*, 118–49, argues that if the Christ figure is only an angel or interpreter, he would not have been worshiped. Those who worship angels are rebuked. Those who worship Christ are considered worshipers of God.

161. Phil 2:9–11 states that "God also highly exalted him and gave him the name that is above every name, so that at the name of Jesus every knee should bend, in heaven and on earth and under the earth, and every tongue should confess that Jesus Christ is LORD, to the glory of God the Father."

162. Harris, "Literary Function," 105, states: "It appears that the message of the hymns are so important that they take on a universal significance, refusing to be relegated to a simple spatial sphere."

weeps. He worships. This fifth hymn in the throne room scene embraces prophetic messianic traditions, apocalyptic imagery, and Christian convictions: the root of David receives cosmic praise as the slaughtered and conquering Lamb. When their song is finished, the four living creatures say, "Amen," and the elders again throw themselves down in worship.

Summary:
Hymns to an Immanent Creator and a Transcendent Lamb

The first five hymns in the book of Revelation are located within the first, and by far the lengthiest, throne room scene. The throne room is apocalyptically described as the center of the cosmos. It is the place where the transcendent realm is farthest away from earthly existence. However, the throne room is also the place where Hebrew prophets encounter divinity within earthly experience. It is the location where divinity is most immanent. Therefore, the hymns are moments in the narrative when the genre appears ideologically complex.

The hymns, as elements within an apocalyptic text, reflect the perspective on human experience carried by the genre: the realm beyond human history is humanity's best hope for the future. As this realm is revealed to John, the reader acquainted with the genre expects accounts of exotic travels and historical epochs. However, this is not a typical apocalypse. Instead of journeys and visions, John is a witness to worship. The book of Revelation frequently deviates from expected apocalyptic elements recalling, especially at those moments, its generic contacts with Hebrew prophetic literature.

In prophetic literature divinity is not so far away. A more immanent God speaks directly to prophets, and agonizes with nations. Will Israel repent? Will Judah live justly? Rather than epochs long gone, or strange eras to come, prophetic literature emphasizes the now of earthly existence.

In the first two hymns, readers attuned to these elements within prophetic literature, sense an apocalyptic work remembering its generic ancestors. The gap between the heavenly and earthly realms, typical of apocalyptic literature, is softened. Even while surrounded by otherworldly beings in physically impossible situations, John is more like Isaiah than an apocalyptic visionary. More importantly, the God who is praised by the first two hymns is a divine being intimately connected to creation.

The generic contacts to prophetic literature allow for a complex portrait of divinity: the LORD of the cosmos is the Creator who is present.

The hymns to the Lamb move in the other direction. Because of the seer's Christian convictions concerning the divinity of Christ, the messiah who brings a new earthly existence is worthy of cosmic worship. The worthy Lamb acts in ways that redeem the earthly realm, but his actions are not confined to earthly realities. His act of sacrifice transcends all earthly limitations. The three hymns of chapter 5 celebrate the cosmic ramifications of his violent death. Christian ideology re-forms the apocalyptic genre. The seer creates an apocalyptic work that remembers the literature of the Hebrew prophets from the perspective of Christian convictions. This Apocalypse includes hymns of worship in honor of the transcendent Lamb.

This reading of the first five hymns in the book of Revelation results in several important findings. First, to consider the apocalyptic genre as a way of thinking makes available new possibilities for interpreting the book of Revelation as an apocalyptic text. As Bakhtin's insights into genres helps readers see, the book of Revelation is a specific view of the world. The book's strategy for conceiving that world is apocalyptic. Yet, it is an apocalyptic strategy holding onto generic contacts with Hebrew prophetic literature and introducing Christian elements which reshape its strategy in important ways. The various elements within the narrative reflect the work's vision. This present book concentrates on the liturgical elements in Revelation, especially the hymns. This chapter attempts to show ways that "seeing and representation merge"[163] in Revelation's first five hymns. The hymns contain dialogic activity between ideologies which reflects a new way of conceiving the relationship between God and humanity. This understanding of genre challenges any analysis of apocalyptic literature that locates meaning in individual literary elements separated from each other and from the apocalyptic text as a whole.

While the "generic" approaches initially held promise with the expressed commitment to begin with a consideration of the work as a whole, such approaches so far fail to consider the whole work as reflecting a contextualized world view. This leads to a second finding.

Genres, like all utterances, are located in particular contexts. Genres emerge from real life situations. While most scholars locate the birth date of Jewish apocalyptic literature as the mid-second century BCE, few

---

163. Bakhtin/Medvedev, *Formal Method*, 132.

scholars actually consider how that particular context remains in a dialogic relationship with all future seers and their apocalypses. The seer of the book of Revelation is located on the boundaries between his culture and an evaluation of his culture. In expressing his evaluation through the strategy of apocalyptic, the seer considers his own context as a Christian in the Roman Empire of the late first century in a dialogic relationship with the evaluations of Jewish apocalypticists living under Antiochus. Genres can remember their previous ideology-shaping contexts.

Genres also remember their generic histories. This is a third important finding from reading the hymns in Revelation's first throne room scene. The hymns in the book of Revelation are the locations of much generic remembering. The cosmic realm of apocalyptic ideology dialogically interacts with the earthly realm of prophetic ideology. The transcendent realm suddenly moves down to the earth, where humans do not merely watch from afar, but respond in acts of worship and social justice. Simultaneously prophetic ideology is expanded by apocalyptic into the cosmos. In the hymns, apocalyptic and prophetic ideologies maintain a dialogic relationship, soliciting restraint on interpretations that would consider one perspective without the other.

A fourth finding underscores the new context from which remembering occurs. As the hymns remember the wisdom of the prophets and earlier apocalypticists, they do so from a new context. This makes possible the creation of something genuinely new. The book of Revelation reflects Christian convictions concerning Christ's work of redemption. Such convictions fill the hymns, interacting with prophetic encounters of divinity and with apocalyptic visions of the cosmos. Small groups of Christians who worship Christ join heavenly choirs and other-worldly beings before the One seated on the throne and before the Lamb. The hymns reflect a combination of ideologies, thus creating a new perspective on divinity and humanity: in Christ (Christian conviction), the God of the cosmos (apocalyptic) is present with humanity (prophetic). The hymns as elements within the text reflect the dialogic activity taking place in the book of Revelation, and within the Christian communities of the late first century. The ideological feast found within the hymns reflects a new ideology, a new genre: the Christian prophetic-apocalyptic genre is born!

The next chapter expands these findings by considering some of the ways different genres in Revelation's hymns represent time and space. Different genres offer different fields of possible human activity. Since the hymns reflect ideologies in dialogic relationship, readers should expect that they also offer competing and collaborating ways to consider time and space, with their varied possibilities for human action. The complex sense of time and space in the hymns reflects the Christian community's understanding of eschatological time and space, and invites readers to enter into worship scenes that both celebrate the work of other-worldly beings, and call for humans to respond in worship and witness.

3

Hymns Celebrating the Presence of the Future

Chronotope and the Book of Revelation

LIKE ALL GENRES, APOCALYPTIC literature embodies a particular perspective on temporal and spatial categories. Some genres reflect a time and space that heightens the role of human activity within the literary work. Other genres sideline such activity. The task of this chapter is to revisit the dialogism in Revelation's hymns by identifying some of the ways different representations of time and space interact. Such a task includes identifying the complex times and spaces within the book itself. As genres collide, so do their temporal and spatial categories. These collisions underscore the choices of readers who become part of the narrative by entering into its scenes of singing. Readers both experience the complexity and contribute to it by bringing their own locations in time and space to the worship scenes. This chapter suggests that the sense of time and space within the New Testament Apocalypse reflects a Christian eschatology that, far from neglecting ethics, *expands* the value of human action. In the book of Revelation, humans respond in acts of worship and witness which take on cosmic significance.

The earliest Christian communities developed as particular responses to a theological environment of Jewish eschatological expectations.[1] While there were diverse ways of articulating such expectations

---

1. Käsemann, "Beginnings of Christian Theology," 40.

(reign of messiah, time of peace and justice, a new exodus, renewal of earth, creation of a new earth, radical divine intervention, end of human history), the Christians' understanding of time was crucial for expressing the new movement's continuities and discontinuities with Judaism. In the Christ-event, something decisive, surprising, amazing had taken place within history—in real time and space. It was expressed in a variety of ways, including the temporal-spatial language of the eschaton.

Discussions continue among scholars concerning the nature of New Testament eschatology. Such discussions remain critical for the quest for the historical Jesus as well as for Christian theology, including ethics. Scholarship observes a relationship between eschatology and ethics, that is, between Jesus' understanding of the ultimate kingdom of God, and his own call to life in the kingdom.[2] Typically, the more imminent or immediate the end, the less contemporarily relevant the ethics.[3] If Jesus is best understood as an eschatological prophet, particularly of the apocalyptic variety, then he expected God to disrupt the affairs of earth and usher in his own kingdom in the near future. Therefore, Jesus' call to discipleship might be best described as "the ethic of the interim."[4] That is, people living in the first century were called to moral behavior in preparation for the imminent divine intervention which would establish the kingdom of God on earth. Such an ethical program hardly seems suitable for people living two millennia later. If, however, Jesus is best understood as proclaiming God's kingdom already present among his followers, his call to discipleship might yield more of a basis for social ethics in contemporary Christian settings. As these two brief alternatives suggest, varying proposals concerning the eschatology of the historical Jesus result in different ethical programs. The book of Revelation, written several generations after the historical Jesus, is typically considered the New Testament document that most emphasizes a radical apocalyptic eschatology.

2. In this project the relationship can be described as an understanding of eschatological time/space and the ethical behavior called for and possible in that time/space. In an essay, Farmer, "Kingdom of God in the Gospel of Matthew," 125, notes that "a term common to the study of both eschatology and ethics is the kingdom of God."

3. Braaten, *Future of God*, 20, criticizes the tendency to embrace ethics at the expense of apocalyptic eschatology: "The impulse to modernize Jesus is still strong, and since modernity is supposedly open to ethics but allergic to apocalypticism, the pictures of Jesus are painted without restraint *à la mode moderne*."

4. Schweitzer, *Quest of the Historical Jesus*, 366.

In the book of Revelation, the present experience of believers living in the Roman Empire is understood in light of the imminent divine judgment upon wickedness that will result in the end of human history. With its sense of urgency and cosmic scope, the book launches readers into the final stages of earth's history, a time which rewards faithfulness and condemns evil as the earth is transformed into the kingdom of God. With such a radical imminent eschatology, most contemporary readers concerned about social ethics turn away from this final work of the Christian canon, unable to find relevance for current social situations.

Such readers can find support for their position by recalling the immoral behavior of some extreme readings of the book of Revelation. David Koresh's ethical program is such an example. Koresh believed that the images throughout Scripture and in particular the book of Revelation depict an imminent apocalyptic eschatology. Such a literal expectation of the near future led him to justify horrendous actions in the interim. In addition to his highly publicized multiple "marriages" with underage girls, Koresh committed other acts of brutal child abuse, even to his own biological children, with the understanding that their imminent future experiences, post-eschaton, assuaged, even warranted all present suffering.[5] Koresh and the Mount Carmel community embodied what many Christians fear about the ethical ramifications of apocalyptic literature—that its eschatology leaves no grounding for ethics. Or, worse yet, that such an eschatology gives a grounding for actions typically renounced by Christian ethics.[6] At best, apocalyptic eschatology provides an ethic for avoiding contact with the world.[7] At worst, it justifies despicable behavior.

---

5. Samples, *Prophets of the Apocalypse*, 58–59, records a conversation with Robyn Bunds, wife number four to Koresh who gave birth to their son, Wisdom. Bunds admits that she spanked her son as Koresh had instructed all adults in the compound: "Children eight months and older ought to be disciplined by having their bottoms beaten with some type of paddle . . . until the child stopped crying. The beatings lasted thirty to forty-five minutes." She is quoted as saying: "Yeah, I spanked him [Wisdom]. . . . I'm not proud of it. . . . There's no way to take it back. But I was told to. . . . All I can say is I was in a certain frame of mind. Vernon said that even if a child died from a spanking they would go to heaven."

6. Mary Ann Tolbert, in response to a paper presented at the Millennium Conference, Berkeley, CA, 20 October 1995, suggested that works like the book of Revelation which contain scenes of violent revenge may actually encourage unethical and immoral behavior.

7. Some historians have commented that the Seventh-day Adventist denomination is an exception to this trend. Hudson, *Religion in America*, 323–24, discusses the

After a brief survey of four major perspectives on New Testament eschatology and the resulting ethical programs, I will explore the dilemma of how to evaluate the book of Revelation. How is the book's eschatology best described? What are the ramifications of its eschatology for ethics? Bakhtin's understanding of "chronotope" will be explored to aid in this study. The "chronotope" section suggests that the complex sense of time and space present in the book of Revelation offers new ways to consider the book's eschatology and therefore its potential for contemporary ethics. This chapter will then consider seven hymns found in the book of Revelation in light of Bakhtin's understanding of chronotope. These hymns include two "solo songs" placed at critical points within the apocalyptic narrative. Although "solo," these songs are not monologic, but reflect the dialogism taking place between generic contacts and chronotopes in all the hymnic utterances. As will quickly become clear, the previous chapter's focus on genre is never far from Bakhtin's discussion of chronotope. Considering the complexity of time and space in the book of Revelation results in new possibilities for eschatology and ethics. This will provide a helpful transition into the next chapter on moral vision and answerability.

THE BOOK OF REVELATION AND NEW TESTAMENT ESCHATOLOGY

The current debate within historical Jesus research struggles with issues that are relevant for all readers of the New Testament, including the book of Revelation. Different pictures of Jesus yield different understandings of what it means to follow him as the Christ of faith. While there is agreement that the historical Jesus spoke of the kingdom of God, the debate lingers as to what kind of kingdom Jesus meant. For the concept of the kingdom of God to be meaningful, it must be located within time and space. So, what type of time and space was to hold this kingdom announced by Jesus? Was this kingdom a present or future reality? Was it

---

SDA church as unusual in its "firm belief in the imminent end of the world" while maintaining a "heavy investment in publishing houses, hospitals, homes for the aged, and especially educational institutions." Hudson's work includes the observation: "Seldom, while expecting a kingdom of God from heaven, has a group worked so diligently for one on earth." Morgan, *Adventism and the American Republic,* carefully follows the history of Seventh–day Adventist involvement in American society from its beginning in the mid-nineteenth century to the present.

external or internal? Did it occur within history or would it arrive after the end of history? Was Jesus' message similar to or different from John the Baptist's message? What were the moral imperatives of Jesus' message? Is Jesus best understood as a sage whose observations on human nature continue to offer words of wisdom in our current pursuits for social justice? Or, does Jesus' strange apocalyptic rhetoric seem to wrench him from relevance in today's global world? One picture minimizes his focus on the future and maintains his wisdom for all possible presents—whether Galilee of the early first century, or America of the twenty-first century. Another portrait makes Jesus so concerned about an imminent future (that still has not arrived) that he seems irrelevant (not to mention, wrong) in both his own present and ours.

While scholars debate which portrait best describes the historical Jesus, few argue over whether or not the book of Revelation portrays apocalyptic eschatology. The assumption is that the New Testament Apocalypse is apocalyptic in its eschatology. The kingdom of God portrayed in its pages must be an imminent future kingdom that will break into and disrupt historical time and space. However, as the last chapter suggested, the work's genre is complex. The book of Revelation contains a mixture of genres—apocalyptic, prophetic, Christian liturgical—collaborating while remaining unmerged form-shaping ideologies. The dynamics of this dialogue of genres involve considering various ways to see reality and to understand the narrative. The tension created within the narrative during the first five hymns—for example, the earthly space of prophetic literature and the cosmic realm of apocalyptic—is not easily resolved. The prophetic genre and the apocalyptic genre collide and collaborate. Christian ideas reshape the genres and complicate their dialogue further. This chapter explores the representations of time and space within the hymns of the central section of the narrative (Rev 6–18) in order to better express the relationship between Revelation's eschatology and ethics.

Apocalypse Soon: Eschatology without Ethics

Albert Schweitzer concluded that, unlike most accounts of the life of Jesus written up to that time (1906), the historical Jesus was really an apocalyptic prophet in the tradition of John the Baptist.[8] As such, Jesus

---

8. Schweitzer, *Quest of the Historical Jesus*, 398–403.

believed that the kingdom of God was an other-worldly reality that would soon break into historical time and space, radically altering human history and eliminating evil and injustice from the world. Future, ahistorical time and otherworldly space overshadowed present, historical time and earthly space. In such a scenario, humanity's greatest act was waiting for God to act. Given such "thoroughgoing eschatology," first-century followers of Jesus were to live "the ethic of the interim" while awaiting the apocalyptic consummation he proclaimed.

For some, such a portrait of the historical Jesus eliminates any relevance to contemporary Christian ethics.[9] In their view John and Jesus were wrong. History kept and keeps moving slowly forward. Suffering remains part of each person's experience. A world without suffering and death remains a fantasy for creative imaginations. Those who take up this particular type of eschatology often separate themselves from this world in preparation for a new one. In the analysis of most scholars, imminent apocalyptic eschatology eliminates social ethics.

Apocalypse Now: Ethics without Future Eschatology

Rudolf Bultmann's groundbreaking work in gospels studies suggests that the New Testament documents are so layered with church traditions that the real historical Jesus is ultimately unable to be isolated.[10] Whatever Jesus believed about the kingdom of God in time and space, his earliest followers and the writers of the New Testament connected his message to their present experience. Each person was confronted with the invitation to enter the kingdom of God and to participate in radical obedience. Therefore, emphasis should be placed upon the experience of the risen Christ in the present lives of believers. Both past historical time and space, and future eschatological time and space are minimized, while the present is relished for all its potential. Bultmann neutralized any temporal tension found in the gospels by proposing an "existential eschatology."

C. H. Dodd's proposal that New Testament eschatology is best understood as "realized eschatology" results in a similar emphasis on the present. The future "end" has already been realized or experienced in the

---

9. Borg, "Jesus Was Not an Apocalyptic Prophet," 48, calls such interim ethics "banal." In another essay within the same work, Borg, "Historical Jesus and Contemporary Faith," 155, states: "The apocalyptic Jesus provides little basis for seeking justice in this world."

10. Bultmann, *History of the Synoptic Tradition*, 368–74.

ministry of Jesus. The future has already begun! Such an eschatological understanding sees ethics as the moral behavior of those who have already entered into the kingdom of God: "It is the hour of decision. It is realized eschatology."[11]

Whether Bultmann's "existential eschatology" or Dodd's "realized eschatology," the result is the opposite of the "Apocalypse Soon: Eschatology without Ethics" category. Rather than eschatology without ethics, the focus on the present proposes ethics without a future eschatology. Ethics is understood as decision-making and radical obedience. Every moment is an eschatological moment, an eternal now. Such interpretations of Jesus' life and call to discipleship minimize, if not eliminate, a future eschatology.

Apocalypse Never: Eschatology Reduced to Ethics

During the past two decades historical Jesus research has focused upon determining the earliest sayings of the historical Jesus and upon sociological insights into Jesus' cultural location. While debates continue, many scholars, particularly those associated with the Jesus Seminar, conclude that the earliest sayings portray Jesus as a philosopher, a teacher of wisdom.[12] Rather than an apocalyptic prophet focused upon an imminent future time and otherworldly space, Jesus the sage emphasized the importance of moral behavior and the challenge to immoral systems within his social world. Only later layers of church redactions created a literary Jesus concerned with apocalyptic eschatological happenings. Jesus the wisdom teacher called his followers to be about creating the kingdom of God on earth as an alternative community. As John Dominic Crossan concludes, rather than an ethic where humanity waits for God to act, the historical Jesus advocates an ethic where God waits for humanity to act.[13] Crossan proposes an "ethical eschatology" where any future apocalyptic eschatology is in essence eliminated.

Jesus as a first-century wisdom teacher remains relevant to all times and places where observations concerning human behavior aid moral dilemmas. In this description, eschatology as "end" disappears altogether.

---

11. Dodd, *Parables of the Kingdom*, 159.
12. Mack, *Lost Gospel*; Witherington, *Jesus Quest*, 58–92, 161–96.
13. Crossan, *Birth of Christianity*, 283–89.

Any tensions between present and future, with the resulting ramifications for ethics, disappears. Ethics wins the debate, hands down.

Apocalypse Now *and* Then: Eschatology and Ethics

Still other scholars wrestle with the temporal tension of New Testament eschatology without completely resolving it. They might say, with Carl Braaten, that the "preaching of the church which does not arise out of the tension between the future of God's kingdom and the present reality of this world is lacking its New Testament credentials."[14] Scholars in this category believe that, while many of the synoptic parables depict a present experience of the kingdom of God, the future aspect of other sayings attributed to Jesus makes it impossible to ignore some type of apocalyptic eschatology in the witness of the historical Jesus and his proposed kingdom. Oscar Cullmann addresses this temporal tension by suggesting a New Testament "inaugurated eschatology."[15] Cullmann proposes that Jesus' life and ministry fell at the "mid-point" of time, the pivotal point in history. Since Jesus, the final stage of earth's history has begun and moves towards completion.

Theologian Jürgen Moltmann proposes that such a consummation will not be annihilation, but transformation.[16] Creation will be completed in time. Such a transformation connotes something new within history, not an interruption in history. Also, if Christianity grew out of a Jewish apocalyptic eschatology, then perhaps Judaism itself contains an understanding of God's eschatological kingdom as both present and future.[17]

Amos Wilder and Norman Perrin reject the limitations typically placed on interpretations of apocalyptic language or descriptions of the kingdom of God. Wilder suggests that Jesus used apocalyptic language because of the pervasive emphasis on eschatology within first-century Judaism, and also because of the symbolic qualities inherent in apocalyptic language. Wilder says: "Jesus, in his eschatology, cast into the form of myth the epoch-making, world-transforming significance of his own

---

14. Braaten, *Future of God*, 119. See also Braaten, *Eschatology and Ethics*, 69–84.
15. Cullmann, *Christ and Time*, 144–74.
16. Moltmann, *Theology of Hope*, 133–38; Moltmann, *Coming of God*, 226–55.
17. Beasley-Murray, *Jesus and the Kingdom of God*, 51.

life, in Jewish terms."[18] Wilder's work opens up the possibility of a variety of temporal interpretations of Jesus' words and ministry. With similar results, Perrin calls for understanding kingdom of God language as a "tensive symbol," whose "meaning could never be exhausted, nor adequately expressed, by any one referent."[19]

While the above description of this fourth category includes many differing views on the historical Jesus, all maintain some type of temporal tension when considering the kingdom of God and eschatology. The relationship between the present and future is in flux. Most positions suggest that this temporal tension of the kingdom of God has ramifications for ethics. It seems to me that this position best reflects the eschatology of the book of Revelation.

Eschatology in the Book of Revelation

As mentioned above, the majority of scholars assume that the book of Revelation, called the "Apocalypse," falls under the first category above, that is, "Apocalypse Soon: Eschatology without Ethics." After all, the book of Revelation graphically describes the final consummation of historical time and space by divine interaction, an action that vindicates the righteous and destroys the wicked. Revelation's picture of the resurrected Christ intensifies the portrait of an apocalyptic prophet like John the Baptist, by making Christ an apocalyptic warrior carrying a two-edged sword and having an attitude of righteous indignation. The faithful are called to "endure," to "hold on a little longer," and to "be faithful unto death." They live in the midst of a world gone awry. Only divine interaction against wickedness will rectify such a scenario. Here is imminent apocalyptic eschatology writ large.

Yet, the book of Revelation also suggests temporal tension in its portrait of eschatological realities. The imminent future does not dismiss all present considerations. The work begins and ends as a letter to believers living within historical time and earthly space.[20] The Christ figure present among them is concerned with their ethical behavior in local congregations and social settings. The members of these congregations are called to change their ways and to remain faithful.

---

18. Wilder, *Eschatology and Ethics*, 35.
19. Perrin, *Jesus and the Language of the Kingdom*, 31.
20. Barr, "Using Plot to Discern Structure," 23–33.

The book of Revelation also significantly modifies two typical features of apocalyptic literature: (1) a pseudonymous writer; and (2) a review of historical epochs. These modifications seem to be related and are crucial for sensing the temporal and spatial complexity of this particular apocalyptic text. As the genre is modified in significant ways, so is the work's representation of time and space.

First, instead of a proposed revered writer from Israel's heritage, the writer of this apocalypse is simply, "John." Much ink has been spilled trying to determine the exact identity of John the seer.[21] However, the crucial point, it seems to me, is that John is presented as a contemporary of his audience. He is living at the same time as those to whom he writes (1:4, 9). This is very different from other Jewish apocalyptic texts where a writer, taking the name of someone from the past, writes in "prediction" of current events. Such authors of apocalyptic texts gain authority through both their remembered and revered "past" roles within Israel's past history, and through their "predictive" accuracy of "future" eras. Since the apocalypticist "saw" up to the present, readers should heed their literary messages. In addition, "future" time is heightened in importance as the apocalypticist from the past "predicts" each epoch of history, concluding with the experience of his readers. Such value of future time is abruptly challenged when the apocalypticist announces that he is a contemporary of his readers and remains within their era throughout the text! Such an authorial twist saturates *the present* with enormous value.

The second modification of apocalyptic is related to the first. The book of Revelation's lack of historical review also heightens the value of the temporal present. Rather than a chain of historical events culminating in the future, the Seer plays with tenses and times, often suggesting the arrival of the future and at other times speaking in anticipation of the future. Time is hard to pin down. The seer of the book of Revelation considers different times and places from the perspective of a Christian living at the end of the first century CE. He gives the sense of living in the most exhilarating time of all. The eras of the past need not be recited. The present experience of the living Christ overwhelms all temporal and spatial categories. Jesus is neither prophet nor sage. He is the Christ, "the living one." Such convictions compel the seer to suggest new language with which to describe this new time and space. The resurrection event

---

21. Ford, *Revelation*, 50–56, argued for the involvement of John the Baptist in the making of the book of Revelation. For a lengthy discussion of introductory issues including authorship, see Beale, *Book of Revelation*, 3–36.

shifts previous eschatological categories. Temporal tension is both a problem and a necessity! Mikhail Bakhtin, a literary critic deeply sensitive to temporal and spatial representation, provides language with which to clarify the complex eschatology of the book of Revelation.

BAKHTIN DEFINES "CHRONOTOPE"

The last chapter explored Bakhtin's understanding of genres as embodying different human experiences, as "modes of thought," or "form-shaping ideologies." The chapter considered Bakhtin's concept of genre in order to observe the dynamics of genre dialogue (apocalyptic and prophetic and liturgical) in the book of Revelation. As a Christian apocalyptic work, the book of Revelation's genre is a form-shaping ideology remembered and re-formed. The book is an example of mutually engaged genres, or different modes of seeing reality, collaborating to create something new. Another way of considering these dynamics within a text is by noticing their different representations of the relationship between people and events to time and space. Such representations offer insights into the possibilities of human activity inherent in different genres.

The Representation of Time and Space

In his lengthy essay on the representation of time and space in literature, "Forms of Time and of the Chronotope in the Novel,"[22] Bakhtin coined the term "chronotope" in order to describe "the intrinsic connectedness of temporal and spatial relationships that are artistically expressed in literature."[23] Like Kant, Bakhtin believed that categories of time and space are necessary for cognition.[24] These categories were themselves interconnected. Chronotopes can be understood as timed-places (e.g., New York City on September 11, 2001), or placed-times (such as September 11 in front of the Pentagon). Wrote Bakhtin: "Time, as it were, thickens, takes on flesh, becomes artistically visible; likewise, space becomes

---

22. Bakhtin, "Forms of Time," 84–258.

23. Ibid., 84. Ladin, "Fleshing Out the Chronotope," 212, noted that "the chronotope gives the literary text the qualities of a world that can be imaginatively inhabited by readers."

24. Bakhtin, "Forms of Time," 258, wrote that for humans to experience meaning, the meaning must be chronotopic since "every entry into the sphere of meaning is accomplished only through the gates of the chronotope."

charged and responsive to the movements of time, plot and history."[25] Yet, the interconnectedness of time and space in Bakhtin's chronotope was more like Einstein's "space-time"[26] than Kant's transcendental categories. This was due to Bakhtin's conviction that time and space, while inseparable, vary, depending on the event's representation.[27] Different events demand different chronotopic considerations since it "is precisely the chronotope that provides the ground essential for the . . . representability of events."[28] Chronotopes were "the place where the knots of narrative are tied and untied."[29] This image referred not merely to the setting or background of a narrative plot, but to the very sense of time and space which made certain events and activities possible while eliminating the possibility of others.

After proposing the term "chronotope" as a way to analyze the representation of time and space in literature, Bakhtin evaluated how different genres go about doing this. A literary work represented time and space through the relationship between actions and contexts. In their discussion of Bakhtin's essay, Morson and Emerson provide helpful questions to ask a text when evaluating its chronotope,[30] starting with: "What is the relation of human action to its context? Is the context mere background, or does its activity shape events?"[31] Bakhtin observed that in the Greek romance,

---

25. Ibid., 84.

26. Ibid.

27. Morson and Emerson, *Creation*, 367. See also, Bakhtin, "Forms of Time," 85n2, which reads: "In his 'Transcendental Aesthetics' (one of the main sections of his *Critique of Pure Reason*) Kant defines space and time as indispensable forms of any cognition, beginning with elementary perceptions and representations. Here we employ the Kantian evaluation of the importance of these forms in the cognitive process, but differ from Kant in taking them not as 'transcendental' but as forms of the more immediate reality. We shall attempt to show the role these forms play in the process of concrete artistic cognition (artistic visualization) under conditions obtaining in the genre of the novel." On the relationship between Bakhtin and Kant, see Scholz, "Bakhtin's Concept of 'Chronotope,'" 141–72. In his essay, Scholz begins with Bakhtin's footnote quoted above. Scholz then suggests that the critical difference between Kant and Bakhtin is that Kant emphasized the *process* of cognition and the *internal* roles of space and time, while Bakhtin was concerned with the *historical evidence* of cognition (e.g., literature), and how time and space were represented in it *externally*.

28. Bakhtin, "Forms of Time," 250.

29. Ibid.

30. Morson and Emerson, *Creation*, 369–70.

31. Ibid., 369.

actions "leave no trace."[32] At the end of such a work, "nothing in its world is destroyed, remade, changed or created anew."[33] Thus, the relationship was extremely loose. This was in contrast to novels where events and their contexts were intimately connected, with actions leaving major traces along the way. Another consideration was the ordering of events within narratives. Morson and Emerson ask whether or not the order of events could be reversed without consequence. Unlike novels, the actions in Greek romances seemed to be unaffected by order. In considering the sense of time represented in narratives, Bakhtin noted that some genres—like epics, for example—placed greatest value on past time, while others—novels—emphasized the immediate future. In addition, some chronotopes depicted time as open, while for others the future was already decided.

The way time and space were represented in literature also affected a given work's portrayal of human characters. Some chronotopes allowed for active characters to be depicted as emerging or becoming, as in Goethe's works.[34] Other chronotopes contained passive characters, manipulated by endowed knowledge, and impotent to shape their own futures. Bakhtin's most valued genres were those whose chronotopes came closest to experienced reality, where context shaped actions and actions left lots of traces. In real life the order and duration of events made a difference, and people grew in experience and knowledge. The sense of time and space encountered in life allowed for the real possibility of creativity and ethical responsibility.

The chronotope concept was a way for Bakhtin to simultaneously address several of his on-going pursuits. First, it was a way to further explore genres as perspectives on human experience. Morson and Emerson suggest that a genre is a field of possible actions, and "to study the field is to study the chronotope."[35] Thus certain chronotopes provided the arena for the representation of certain actions and events in genres. In this way, particular chronotopes helped to shape particular genres. At the start of his essay Bakhtin wrote that chronotopes had "intrinsic generic significance."[36] In the "Concluding Remarks" section of his chronotope essay written in 1973, Bakhtin reaffirmed: "The chronotopes we have

32. Bakhtin, "Forms of Time," 94.
33. Ibid., 110.
34. Bakhtin, "*Bildungsroman* and Its Significance."
35. Morson and Emerson, *Creation*, 370.
36. Bakhtin, "Forms of Time," 84–85.

discussed provide the basis for distinguishing generic types."[37] Jay Ladin says that Bakhtin's "essay focuses almost exclusively on what he sees as genre-defining and historically significant chronotopes."[38]

Second, the study of the chronotope was a way to underscore the necessity of contextualization for actions, which was one of Bakhtin's earliest philosophical concerns.[39] Actions demanded context defined by time and space. The possibilities of true creativity and real responsibility required a sense of time and space that was open and responsive to human activity. Third, and related to the other two, the chronotope was another way to heighten the value of the novel genre as best representing real historical time and space. In his chronotope essay, Bakhtin favored the novel genre for its ability to capture the everyday, value-laden, decision-filled reality of human existence in its portrayal of time and space.

In contrast to his favorite genre, Bakhtin particularly disliked genres that incorporated the eschatology chronotope. Because of its portrayal of an absolute end (it did not matter which kind of end), Bakhtin concluded that eschatology denies openness and therefore the possibility of both creativity and responsibility. According to Bakhtin, eschatology "empties out the future, dissects and as it were bleeds it white."[40] In contrast to the novel's sense of time and space which heightened the value of the immediate future, Bakhtin said that the eschatology chronotope devalued the time between the present and the eschatological end.[41]

Given the nature of this present book and the introductory section of this chapter, it is important to note that Bakhtin was probably not a fan of the book of Revelation. However, Bakhtin's notion of the chronotope provides the language necessary for a more careful discussion of the book of Revelation's sense of eschatological time and space and its resulting ethics. Bakhtin helps readers see that it is inadequate to categorize the book of Revelation's eschatology simply as "apocalypse soon," with a devaluing of present time and moral responsibility.

37. Ibid., 250–51.

38. Ladin, "Fleshing Out the Chronotope," 212–13.

39. Bakhtin, *Toward a Philosophy of the Act*. Morson and Emerson, *Creation*, 367, state: "Actions are necessarily performed in a specific context; chronotopes differ by the ways in which they understand context and the relation of actions and events to it. All contexts are shaped fundamentally by the kind of time and space that operate within them."

40. Bakhtin, "Forms of Time," 148.

41. Ibid.

Pushing Bakhtin's Chronotope

While applauding Bakhtin's "chronotopic history of the novel,"[42] Jay Ladin raises questions concerning the helpfulness of the essay for analyzing texts. He calls Bakhtin's chronotope "a powerful but underdeveloped critical tool."[43] Ladin continues by stating that Bakhtin "never provides a systematic definition of the 'literary artistic chronotope,' nor does he present a clearly articulated protocol for identifying and analyzing chronotopes and the relations between them."[44] Thus in his essay, Ladin suggests ways to identify local chronotopes and to analyze the interaction between them, sometimes resulting in the description of major chronotopes.

As he begins a process for identifying what he labels "local" (what Morson and Emerson call "minor") chronotopes, Ladin suggests why such identification is not easy. He proposes that because of the tension between the centrifugal chronotopic implications of words and the centripetal forces pushing for coherent meanings, the real question is "how any chronotopes become perceptible and significant . . . given the semantic need to ignore them."[45] Ladin then takes as a starting point Bakhtin's discussion of chronotopes as "the organizing centers for the fundamental narrative events,"[46] and he determines that local chronotopes can be identified under the following conditions:[47] (1) when key events are given spatial and temporal qualities within the narrative; (2) when temporal and spatial language is used in the narrative; (3) when a particular time and space is distinct from others in the narrative; and (4) when space-time expressions carry abstract ideas in the narrative.

In order to take advantage of some of Ladin's points above, I will identify some of the local chronotopes found in the first five chapters of the book of Revelation. Revelation 1:4 suggests what I will call an epistolary chronotope, that is, the sense of time and space created when a writer is sending information to others through the written word. It begins: "John to the seven churches that are in Asia . . ." While readers are left wondering about John's specific situation (whether John is writing himself or using a scribe, how well he knows his readers), the

---

42. Ladin, "Fleshing Out the Chronotope," 213.
43. Ibid., 230.
44. Ibid., 213.
45. Ibid., 218.
46. Bakhtin, "Forms of Time," 250.
47. See the categories in Ladin, "Fleshing Out the Chronotope," 218–19.

narrative does locate the writer of this literary work in a time-space that is contemporary to people in seven churches. More importantly, the epistolary chronotope gives a *sense* of time-space: the narrative's pace (letter writing, letter reading), the events and human actions possible within this time-space (first-person descriptions of local settings, expressions of concern for recipients of the letter, greetings, encouragement, articulation of shared convictions), and the human characters possible within this time-space (readers or hearers connected to Christian congregations within the Roman Empire, those who embrace the letter, those who dismiss its contents, and other such matters).

John is barely beyond sending his initial greetings, when a new chronotope jars the narrative. Suddenly, in a description of Christian convictions concerning Jesus Christ "the faithful witness, the firstborn of the dead, . . . the one who loves us . . . " (1:5), the writer proclaims: "Look! He is coming with the clouds . . . " (1:7). A future, other-worldly chronotope is juxtaposed with the epistolary chronotope. Is John describing a first-hand account? Is he anticipating the later narrative? How does this exclamation fit within the epistolary chronotope? In just a few syllables, the sense of time and space changes completely. Just as quickly, and without explanation, the chronotope changes again. This time the voice of the LORD God declares: "I am the Alpha and the Omega" (1:8). Where is the voice coming from? What is its relationship to the parousia scene? What overarching time-space navigates between these local chronotopes? While the epistolary chronotope, as a first-person account of events, can logically hold other chronotopes (for example, later vision accounts), the brief description of the parousia and the declaration by God do not seem to fit at this point in the narrative.

Again without explanation, the chronotope changes. This time John identifies himself as a "brother" to the recipients of his literary work (1:9). He then locates himself spatially: "I . . . was on the island called Patmos" (1:9), and then spatially and temporally: "I was in the spirit on the LORD's day" (1:10). This chronotopic shift highlights the key moment, distinct from all others so far in the narrative, which provide the event for the letter.[48] Although narratively placed *after* the initial epistolary

---

48. There is much debate as to the authorship of the first three verses of the book, a debate that could also be entered from the perspective of chronotopic considerations. If added later in order to enhance the authority of the original author's work, the shifting time-space of this first chapter of Revelation becomes even more complex. The first three verses could also be a third-person introduction by the author in anticipation of

chronotope, the "in the spirit" chronotope helps to identify the key event in John's narrative, and it (at least claims to have) occurred historically (in real time and space) *before* his epistolary chronotope. Once "in the spirit," John experiences a new sense of time and space. John hears symbolic, mysterious words, and sees a strange, other-worldly figure, the "one like the son of man" (1:13–16). "In the spirit" John learns to interpret numbers and images in new ways (1:18–20). "In the spirit" John writes not one letter or literary work, but seven letters which remain one (2:1—3:22). The "in the spirit" chronotope maintains ties to the epistolary chronotope in fascinating ways as it intersects with the time-space of letter writing. The strange figure becomes the voice dictating the seven letters to the churches (2:1, 8, 12, 18; 3:1, 7, 14). The voice speaks as if he knows the earthly members of the seven churches better than John does (2:2, 9, 13, 19; 3:1b, 8, 15). Throughout the first three chapters, the "in the spirit" chronotope never really leaves earthly time and space. While the descriptions of the son of man figure are possible only in an other-worldly realm (he can hold seven stars in one hand, has a two-edged sword in his mouth, has feet made of bronze), his words are those of an earth-bound letter-writer like John, encouraging faithfulness, challenging immorality, and expressing hope for the future. In other words, the epistolary and "in the spirit" chronotopes seem to merge. At least initially, rather than John joining the other-worldly figure in the heavenly realm,[49] the other-worldly figure takes interest in, even becomes a co-writer to, the seven churches of Asia Minor, first by suggesting a book to all seven now named churches (1:11), and later by writing a brief letter to each church named individually (2:1, 8, 12, 18; 3:1, 7, 14).

At the end of the seven letters, a new chronotope emerges and dominates the narrative through most of the rest of the work. The narrator, presumably still John of Patmos, tells of being invited through a heavenly door into another realm. He is also told that he will see future things ("Come up here, and I will show you what must take place after this," 4:1b). Together, these spatial and temporal indicators distinguish this chronotope from the others before it, and also highlight this event as key within the narrative. For at least the next sixteen chapters, John will

---

1:9–11.

49. This type of activity is much more expected, since an apocalypticist could maintain the epistolary chronotope by telling his experience of the "beyond" (the "in the spirit" chronotope) within a first-person account. However, the narrative suggests another type of activity and spatial movement.

describe what he, as a character within the narrative, sees and experiences in this vision chronotope whose representation of time and space are closely associated with the apocalyptic genre. The vision chronotope, with its sense of future time and heavenly space, carries expectations of human behavior and possible events and activities that differ from other chronotopes. In the vision chronotope humans mostly look. Since they rarely actively enter into the realm of the vision, any actions would be irrelevant. Instead, seers are like tourists with an over-zealous tour guide. Pulled from city to city, museum to museum, historical monument to historical monument, the tourist's main job is to keep up. Quickly the cities and stories and monuments get jumbled, becoming more a mystery than information mastered. The tourist never has the chance to really enter the city, to even temporarily become part of it by eating its food, breathing its air, getting a sense of its history. Most seers remain distant observers looking at times and spaces that are never really experienced. Thus, readers acquainted with vision chronotopes and apocalyptic texts expect John to enter through this heavenly door and to begin describing a bizarre other-worldly journey with a strange being as his tour guide.

Instead, John immediately describes his experience as once again being "in the spirit" (4:2). Readers are reminded of his earlier experience "in the spirit" while on Patmos on the LORD's day, when a strange being joined him in writing letters to seven earthly churches. John seems to be simultaneously in the epistolary chronotope, the "in the spirit" chronotope, and the vision chronotope. It is almost as if the vision chronotope is kept from completely leaving the earthly realm behind. In addition, John then finds himself not touring the heavenly worlds through epochs of human history, but standing before a throne in heaven. Here John describes an array of amazing images and creatures and sounds. His first visual image after moving through the heavenly door is the throne room of the divine. As the throne room begins to be described, yet another sense of time and space is represented. The sense of time and space within the throne room exists prior to John's experience of it. The holiest of actions and characters exist within this chronotope. In the throne room time as linear is overshadowed by a sense of time as continuous action, particularly praise. However, divine actions of commissioning, warning, punishment, and pardon also issue forth from this chronotope. And human actions of petition and prayer can join the praise of other-worldly beings. The throne room chronotope carries a sense of time and space found in Hebrew prophetic literature as a prophet finds himself before the throne of God. While the prophet is suddenly present within God-space, the chronotopic sense is more of divinity moving into historical time and space, than the human transported to an other-worldly realm. God grants humans access into the divine dimension. Such an experience works to heighten the prophet's contemporary historical situation by calling for immediate and concrete actions of repentance, social justice, and proper worship. Thus, each of the chronotopes present in Revelation 1–5 (epistolary, "in the spirit," vision, and throne room) maintains a distinct field of activity. The chronotopes compete and collaborate, remaining unmerged and thus maintaining different space-time contexts, different senses of history, and different realms of possible human activity.[50]

The chronotopic complexity reaches its height during the first song of the book of Revelation: "Holy, holy, holy, the LORD God the Almighty, who was and is and is to come" (4:8b). This activity recalls divine winged creatures speaking similar words when the prophet Isaiah finds himself before God's throne (Isa 6:3). In Revelation 4, the singing is described within the throne room chronotope as performed by the four living creatures "day and night without ceasing" (4:8a). Within the throne room chronotope the singing is an ever-present (if not earthly) experience. As part of the vision chronotope, the song takes place in the heavenly future realm of an apocalyptic literary work. As the song is experienced by John (the character) who is aware that he is "in the spirit" (the narrator), this chronotopic level suggests some sort of relationship to John whose feet are on Patmos, and who remains connected to his "brothers and sisters" in the seven churches. And within the epistolary chronotope, John tells of the heavenly voices he heard after entering the heavenly realm and while "in the spirit" before God's throne.

As shown above, when identifying chronotopes in literature, one is simultaneously identifying the relationship between represented context (time and space) and the types of actions possible within that context.

---

50. It might be helpful to consider Bakhtin's discussion of the complexity inherent within the dream-vision chronotope. Bakhtin, "Forms of Time," 156–58, has far more appreciation for the sense of time and space within a dream vision than for the eschatology chronotope. The dream-vision embodies a complex vertical movement, while maintaining a horizontal historical axis. This brief discussion might actually be more helpful for discussing the book of Revelation than Bakhtin's quick dismissal of the simplistically defined eschatology chronotope. Like Dante's work, the book of Revelation moves simultaneously upward on a vertical axis while maintaining horizontal narrative movement. Likewise, the epistolary sections at the beginning and end of the book ground the narrative within an extremely horizontal historical framework.

The chronotope also creates a realm within which characters can be represented. Ladin argues that an additional distinction is crucial when doing chronotopic analysis of literary texts. That distinction is between a sense of time and space from the perspective of characters within the narrative (subjective or intrasubjective for a single consciousness, intersubjective for more than one consciousness), and a sense of time and space from the perspective of consciousnesses located outside of the narrative (transsubjective).[51] The transsubjective chronotope represents extradiegetic context, that is, time-space outside of the narrative, so that relationships between two or more chronotopes within the narrative can be examined. Transsubjective chronotopes make visible extradiegetic consciousnesses (consciousnesses outside of the narrative), like the author, narrator, and readers.

The chronotopes in the first five chapters of the book of Revelation are difficult to distinguish in this way. For the majority of the narrative, John, the narrator, describes what he is seeing and experiencing. Certainly the epistolary and "in the spirit" chronotopes are transsubjective; that is, they assume or create time-space that allows for consciousness outside of the narrative (author, readers). However, the vision chronotope seems unclear, perhaps unwilling to distinguish whether this chronotope is subjective or transsubjective; whether John is a character or a narrator. At first he seems to continue narrating since he mentions the door into heaven, describes himself as "in the spirit," and continues describing the heavenly throne room. But later John becomes part of the scene when one of the elders speaks to him (5:5). When the narrative moves into the hymns sung by the four living creatures, the chronotopic distinction between diegetic and extradiegetic contexts and consciousnesses becomes even less clear. Is John, as narrator, still describing the heavenly scene (extradiegetic chronotope), or has the chronotope of the living creatures (diegetic chronotope) taken over? In which chronotope do the hymns exist? Is this the time and space of John the narrator, or the time and space of perpetual praise before the throne? How might this chronotopic complexity be described and analyzed? Does this very complexity work to include readers of the book of Revelation?

Jay Ladin, quoting Barbara L. Pittman, challenges the idea that chronotopes can be studied on an individual basis as isolated units. Instead,

---

51. Ladin, "Fleshing Out the Chronotope," 224, states: "A chronotope cannot be identified without specifying the relation between the represented space-time and consciousness."

Ladin affirms Pittman's recognition that "'a novel is not finally reducible to a single chronotope but is a complex of major generic chronotopes and minor chronotopic motifs' that create 'a web of competing chronotopes in dialogue and a central chronotope that serves as a unifying ground.'"[52] Thus it quickly becomes crucial not only to *identify* local chronotopes, but to be able to analyze interactions between them. Wrote Bakhtin: "Chronotopes are mutually inclusive, they co-exist, they may be interwoven with, replace or oppose one another, contradict one another or find themselves in ever more complex interrelationships."[53] What might these "complex interrelationships" mean for the reading of a text like the book of Revelation? Chronotopes can change, argue with one another, and compete. In other words, "the relation of chronotopes to each other may be *dialogic*."[54] What does this dialogism sound like? These are questions for the next section.

Relationships between Chronotopes

After identifying chronotopes within a given text, further exploration must consider various relationships between the chronotopes, and any major chronotope which emerges from these relations.[55] In his essay, Ladin lists nine common relationships between chronotopes. I will briefly discuss those that are the most helpful in considering the relationships between local chronotopes found in the book of Revelation generally and Revelation 1–5 specifically.[56]

Ladin defines the "hierarchical" relationship among chronotopes as that where the "relations among chronotopes are determined by

---

52. Ladin, "Fleshing Out the Chronotope," 215, quoting Pittman, "Cross-Cultural Reading," 778.

53. Bakhtin, "Forms of Time," 252.

54. Morson and Emerson, *Creation*, 369.

55. Ladin, "Fleshing Out the Chronotope," 220.

56. In addition to those discussed below, the "paradoxical" relationship between chronotopes might be initially helpful in analyzing the abrupt "parousia" (1:7) and "declaration by God" (1:8) chronotopes found early in Revelation 1. Ladin describes the "paradoxical" relationship between chronotopes as unable to be resolved at any cognitive level. Ladin states: "Such paradoxes can create powerful, disturbing effects, for they interfere with the reader's ability to create a temporally and spatially coherent *fabula*. In most cases, these paradoxes are temporary interludes that are either resolved . . . or left behind as the narrative moves on" ("Fleshing Out the Chronotope," 225).

reference to a major chronotope, rather than by direct conflict or dialogization. This major chronotope thus 'interprets' the hierarchically related chronotopes."[57] Another relationship between chronotopes is described as "overlapping." In this case the chronotope's sense of time and space remains constant, but it is experienced at different diegetic levels, thus as different chronotopes. Such levels are further explained in a footnote: the subjective diegetic level refers to a character's perception; intersubjective to a socially shared time-space; and transsubjective to the narrator's, author's or reader's perception of disparate diegetic chronotopes.[58] This relationship highlights the different ways that a character and a narrator perceive a particular chronotope within the narrative. It is important to note that the transsubjective chronotopes are "chronotopes that extend to the reader a space-time in which the relations and contradictions between local chronotopes can be experienced and assessed."[59] The "simple dialogical" relationship between chronotopes occurs when local chronotopes are not so much in conflict as in dialogue with each other. "Each 'dialogized' chronotope is simultaneously read in itself and in relation to the other chronotopes with which it is in dialogue."[60] Together the chronotopes provide different but complimentary contexts for concepts that move beyond the realm of either isolated chronotope. The last relationship from Ladin's list to be considered here is called the "nested" relationship. It occurs when one chronotope contains other chronotopes within it. This is "extremely common in first-person narratives in which the narrator is a significant character."[61] The first five chapters of the book of Revelation will now be briefly considered in light of these different relationships between local chronotopes, since these relationships continue throughout the book of Revelation.

First, the "hierarchical" relationship is a helpful way to consider the relationship between the epistolary chronotope as the "major" chronotope among all other chronotopes identified in the narrative. Not only does the epistolary chronotope provide a frame for the entire work,[62] but, like other "major" chronotopes, it "enter[s] into dialogic relations with

57. Ibid., 227.
58. Ibid., 235n42
59. Ibid., 224.
60. Ibid., 226.
61. Ibid.
62. Barr, "Using Plot to Discern Structure," 25–26.

local chronotopes."⁶³ Because the book of Revelation begins as a message sent by its author to real recipients, all of the actions that take place within the local chronotopes must be finally understood within the context of the time-space of the writer of the text. Likewise, all characters represented in the local chronotopes are ultimately seen from the perspective of the epistolary chronotope. Major chronotopes "define and limit the ways in which human character can exist in the narrative."⁶⁴ The epistolary chronotope "thus 'interprets' the hierarchically related chronotopes."⁶⁵ In addition, the epistolary chronotope, as a major chronotope, becomes a transsubjective chronotope able to "'enter the worlds' of author, performer, and reader by requiring us to construct space-times . . . that can accommodate these complex relations; and . . . provide the ground for images of human possibility that also extend dynamically into the worlds of author, performer, and reader."⁶⁶ In other words, if the epistolary chronotope is truly a major chronotope in a hierarchical relationship with the other chronotopes, then to be aware of this relationship (as reader or performer) is to be both outside the narrative and a consciousness made visible by its transsubjective chronotope. Ladin states: "Transsubjective chronotopes are a primary means by which literature implicates readers and makes our responses (aesthetic, moral, or otherwise) part of the work."⁶⁷ The epistolary chronotope as Revelation's major chronotope will also be important when considering later parts of the narrative. The fact that this work begins and ends as a message to people living as John's contemporaries in major cities within the Roman Empire shapes all careful readings of the narrative.

The relationship between chronotopes described as "overlapping" is helpful when considering the relationship between the local chronotopes identified in Revelation 1–5. "Overlapping" chronotopes refer to the appearance of multiple chronotopes when a chronotope is shared by "different diegetic levels."⁶⁸ For example, within the throne room chronotope, the character John shares a sense of present time and space with the four living creatures. However, this same time-space is experienced

---

63. Ladin, "Fleshing Out the Chronotope," 224.
64. Ibid., 223.
65. Ibid., 227.
66. Ibid., 224.
67. Ibid.
68. Ibid., 226.

at least initially as the future (4:1b) time-space of the vision, and as past time-space recalled by the narrator within the time-space of writing. The presence of overlapping chronotopes suggests various diegetic levels, several of which create transsubjective chronotopes that expand time and space to include readers. As this present book focuses on the hymns found in Revelation, this idea of overlapping and transsubjective chronotopes will be critical to the analysis.

The relationship between chronotopes described as "simple dialogical" is a helpful way to understand the relationship between the vision chronotope and the throne room. "Simple dialogical" relationships are described as "local chronotopes . . . [that] are simultaneously present in the narrative and affect each other reciprocally."[69] As John narrates his entrance into the time-space beyond the heavenly door (4:1), he becomes a character within the vision time-space which is quickly confronted by the time-space of the throne room. The throne room chronotope is in a relationship to the vision chronotope; it is one of many possible scenes in a vision. But its unique sense of time and space make it not merely a backdrop for action. It is a distinct local chronotope whose sense of time and space provides new possibilities for action and character description.

The vision chronotope is certainly capable of containing throne room space, future time, and other-worldly creatures. However, this particular description of a throne room shifts from the sense of time and space possible in a vision chronotope, to the particular space where divinity and humanity meet. The vision chronotope and the throne room chronotope are in a dialogical relationship—with the one emphasizing the vast heavenly realm, the other the center of that realm. The vision chronotope considers the future, while the throne room remembers past encounters in similar space where present choices are critical. The vision chronotope highlights the human action of observing realms and epochs, the throne room chronotope highlights human participation in moral decisions of worship and petition and praise. The vast heavenly realm suddenly looks familiar—like the holy place of the temple permeated by divine presence. The creatures and activities of praise in the rest of Revelation 4–5 continue within the throne room and also within the vision. The chronotopes dance—a vision moment sees one dance partner twirl into the air as the narrator describes actions that are impossible within the earthly realm. Then the dance floor empties and the throne

---

69. Ibid.

room partner is left at center stage with feet firmly planted on the floor, refusing to remain merely an observer, and face-to-face with the One seated on the throne. Thus, the sense of time and space at the level of the vision maintains a dialogical relationship with the throne room chronotope. Chronotopes in dialogical tension create the possibility of actions and characters beyond the typical human figure within apocalyptic literature's vision chronotope. The observation of such tension means that, once again, readers are part of the text. Future discussions of the sense of time and space present in the hymns will be sensitive to such dialogical complexity and its ramifications for reading the book of Revelation.

The relationship between chronotopes described as "nested" can also aid this book's discussion of the local chronotopes in the book of Revelation. As already noted, the throne room chronotope is a complex chronotope in dialogical tension with the vision chronotope. It therefore maintains a sense of time as simultaneously past, present and future, and a sense of space as the earthly permeated by the divine. Underscoring this chronotopic complexity are the hymnic chronotopes nested within the throne room chronotope. In addition to all the other chronotopic relationships present in Revelation 4–5, careful readers sense further temporal and spatial ambiguity. The hymns could be taking place in Isaiah's time (throne room chronotope), during the continual experience of the four living creatures (vision chronotope), or during John's account of his experience in the throne room (epistolary or "in the spirit" chronotope). Therefore the nested hymnic chronotopes reinforce the throne room chronotope's complexity through their own ability to resist temporal or spatial finalization. In addition, awareness of this complexity and its possible readings suggests the presence of a transsubjective chronotope in which the consciousness of readers are included in the world of the text. Suddenly the experience of singing in the seven churches to which John writes adds to the time-space complexity of the throne room hymns.

Several summary statements should be made at this point. First, the hymns in the book of Revelation contain rich chronotopic activity as different contexts (times and spaces) and their different fields of human activity collide and collaborate. With careful attention to these different contexts, readers can identify the different ways literary characters exist within the chronotopes.

Second, the work of identifying chronotopes leads to considering how such chronotopes interact with each other. Close attention to such interactions in Revelation's hymns suggests that readers need more than one set of relations to account for the complex interactions of times and spaces.[70] In particular, the "hierarchical" relationship between chronotopes reminds readers of the dominance of the epistolary chronotope over all other chronotopes. Readers must consider the various contexts within the book of Revelation in relationship to the seer's experience, that is, his own location in time and space as he writes to Christians living in major cities of the Roman Empire at the end of the first century. The "simple dialogical" relationship between chronotopes highlights the mutually engaging throne room and vision chronotopes. Each of these two chronotopes can only be understood in relationship to the other. The "overlapping" relationship between the epistolary and vision chronotopes offers a way to distinguish John the narrator from John the character. As readers sense John's entry into the narrative's drama, the text's chronotope opens up to allow readers to enter as well. The "nested" relationship allows for further reflection on the hymnic chronotope's ability to resist temporal or spatial finalization.

Third, to highlight the relationships between chronotopes is to open up the texts to the inclusion of authors and readers who must maneuver these different contexts.[71] Readers make choices as their own contexts interact with the chronotopes in dialogic relationships within the book of Revelation.[72]

Finally for this chapter, the complex sense of time and space in Revelation's hymns allows the narrative to emphasize both the unusual actions of other-worldly beings outside historical time and space, and also the actions of human beings within historical time and space. Readers enter a text where heavenly figures act on behalf of humanity's redemption, and where people who see such activity respond in worship and in witness.

---

70. Ladin, "Fleshing Out the Chronotope," 234n38, states: "It is important to remember that any such list, no matter how extensively elaborated, will also be approximate rather than definitive, for there is no logical limit to the number of potential relations among chronotopes. It is also important to note that these relations are not mutually exclusive; a given chronotope can be simultaneously enmeshed in more than one kind of relationship with other chronotopes."

71. Ibid., 224, states: "Transsubjective chronotopes are a primary means by which literature implicates readers and makes our responses (aesthetic, moral, or otherwise) part of the work."

72. Bakhtin, "Forms of Time," 254, states: "The work and the world represented in it enter the real world and enrich it, and the real world enters the work and its world as part of the process of its creation, as well as part of its subsequent life, in a continual renewing of the work through the creative perception of listeners and readers."

HYMNS BEFORE THE COSMOS: REVELATION 7–16

At the start of Revelation 6, the activity within the throne room shifts from universal praise of the Lamb (5:13), to the Lamb's long-anticipated action (5:2–5) of removing the seven seals from the scroll (6:1). As each seal is broken, a sequence of events is unleashed (6:1—8:1). Although this section of the narrative never removes the Lamb from the throne room scene, the vision chronotope's sense of time and space dominates. The seals sequence narrates cosmic eschatological events that result in the earth's destruction. After the sixth seal is opened, the narrative describes the disruption of historical time and space. The people of the earth call for rocks to fall on them in order to hide them from God's wrath. They ask, "Who is able to stand?" (6:17).

The unsealing sequence begins a series of judgments upon the earth that grow in intensity until the city of Babylon is destroyed in chapter 18. Like the throne room scene of Revelation 4–5, the middle section of the book includes moments of worship and singing within the narrative. This section will show how the hymns in the book of Revelation not only reflect dialogic activity between ideologies, they also express dialogic activity between chronotopes. Such activity offers many choices and new interpretive possibilities for readers who enter into the narrative through these inviting textual moments.

The hymns in Revelation 7–16 reflect the complexity of Christian eschatology and ethics. In the hymns, the eschatological future is pulled into the narrative prior to the parousia at different and often unexpected moments. For the book of Revelation, Christian eschatology is complicated. Singers sense and celebrate a transformed earth prior to the end of the drama. Like Christians of Asia Minor and every era, worship proclaims the victory of the Lamb while acknowledging the call to witness before the wrath of the dragon.

This complex sense of time and space heightens both the activities of divinity and other-worldly beings, and also the responses of humans in acts of worship and witness. Rather than halting human activity, the eschatology of the book of Revelation expands the significance of such activity from the earthly realm into the cosmos. The witness of faithful martyrs spans time and space. The worship services of Christian house churches join celestial choirs.

The Multitude's Song (Rev 7:10b) and its Antiphon (Rev 7:12)

After the removal of the sixth seal but before the removal of the seventh, two back-to-back scenes are described (7:1–8, 9–17). The first scene begins with John's words, "After this I saw" (Μετὰ τοῦτο εἶδον) (7:1a), and continues as he describes angels who are preparing to destroy the earth. However, their preparations are delayed as another angel goes forth to seal the servants of God. Following the sealing, an activity John hears but does not actually observe, he introduces the second scene with a similar phrase: "After this I looked" (Μετὰ ταῦτα εἶδον) (7:9a). John then continues by describing a great multitude involved in actions of celebration and singing. The multitude's hymn of praise to God is followed by a doxological response by angels, elders, and creatures that fall before the throne (7:12).

Like the lengthy unsealing sequence (6:1–17), the first scene of chapter 7, that of sealing God's servants, seems to fall within the vision chronotope.[73] In it time is represented as future time, and space as other-worldly space. There are four angels at the four corners of the earth holding back the four winds of the earth. These are all images (including numbers), actions, and characters that typically exist within a vision chronotope, shaping the apocalyptic genre. They heighten a sense of separation from earth's daily activities. John, who earlier wept before the throne (5:4) and was addressed by an elder (5:5), is reduced to watching. Like his actions during the unsealing sequence, John watches as the angel prepares to seal the servants of God.

In the vision chronotope not only are the actions of other-worldly beings critical to the narrative (in contrast to human watching), they also operate outside of humanity's experience of time and space. The action of sealing does not take time or space. As soon as John hears that a sealing of God's servants will take place (7:3), he also hears that the sealing is already completed (7:4).[74] The seal is described as on the foreheads of the

---

73. Due to the book of Revelation's similar word usage, I am using "unsealing" to refer to the actions of the Lamb in opening up the sealed scroll (6:1–17), and "sealing" to refer to the actions performed by the angel upon the servants of God (7:1–8). The seventh seal is not yet broken (8:1). Because of this, most commentators call Revelation 7 an "interlude." While Revelation 7 does break up the unsealing sequence, "interlude" hardly seems appropriate given that the high chronotopic sense underscores, according to Bakhtin, "Forms of Time," 250, the place where the "knots of narrative are tied and untied."

74. The exact nature of the sealing (σφραγίσωμεν) is unclear in the narrative.

servants of God (7:3). Later in the narrative, the seal will be a protection from the fifth trumpet judgment (9:4), and will be further described as the name of the Lamb and the Father's name (14:1). Aune suggests that the sealing of God's servants is an eschatological action similar to Ezekiel 9:4–6.[75] In Ezekiel's narrative, as the people of Jerusalem begin to experience the end of the world as they know it, some are singled out. As an act of divine protection, God calls for a mark or sign (τὸ σημεῖον) (Ezek 9:4, LXX) to be placed on the foreheads (ἐπὶ τὰ μέτωπα τῶν ἀνδρῶν) (Ezek 9:4, LXX) of all residents of Jerusalem who "sigh and groan" at their city's sins. When judgment begins to fall upon the city, only people with the mark are spared. The sealed of Ezekiel 9 observe the sins of Jerusalem, sigh and groan for their city, and experience protection through the action of an other-worldly being. The people who are sealed in Revelation 7 are completely silent. They do not even sigh or groan. During the two verses that introduce the servants of God the passive participle of the verb "to seal" (σφραγίζω) is repeated three times (7:4–5). The passive form is used again as the very last word at the end of the first scene (7:8).

The scene continues as John hears a roll call of the sealed: 144,000 people total, with twelve thousand from each of the twelve tribes of Israel. Although this group of people is supposedly located on earth (the destruction of earth is delayed until God's servants are sealed), their location remains nebulous. The description of the servants of God as members of Israel's tribes also underscores the future temporal sense of the vision chronotope. The narrator knows that the twelve tribes of Israel existed only in the biblical past. A description of the people sealed as members of the twelve tribes suggests some type of future restored Israel.[76] Known historical realities move aside as the narrative depicts an ideal future. This is a "proleptic audition of a future eschatological event."[77] Yet the description suggests that the sealing takes place *prior to* destructive eschatological acts. How is Israel restored before the eschaton? Many

---

Perhaps this scene suggests an answer to the question that concludes chapter 6: who is able to stand the wrath of the one on the throne and the Lamb? (6:17). If so, it is unclear if such sealing also protects the servants of God from *human* wrath.

75. Aune, *Revelation 6–16*, 452.

76. Aune adds: It is the "eschatological restoration of the twelve-tribe nation of Israel" (ibid., 460). Aune also states: "That a particular number are selected from each of the twelve tribes presupposes that the eschatological restoration of the people of Israel as constituted by the twelve tribes has already taken place" (436).

77. Ibid., 461.

commentators wrestle with identifying the 144,000 without noticing these chronotopic issues.[78] If the identity of the 144,000 revolves around earthly realities, the time-space in which they find themselves certainly does not.

While the sequence of events seems to matter within this particular passage (winds are held back until the sealing of God's servants, 7:1–3), its placement within the larger narrative is far less clear. Chronologically, the sealing of God's servants should have taken place prior to the final eschatological events recorded in 6:12–17. The vision chronotope gives a particular sense of time and space where a reversal of order does not seem to affect the narrative. This is a strange eschatological, heavenly time-space that highlights the actions of other-worldly beings while humans are relegated to watching.[79]

The vision continues as John witnesses another[80] scene: a great multitude before the throne. While the narrative seems to remain within the vision chronotope, the throne room chronotope resurfaces creating temporal and spatial complexity. Some commentators suggest that the two back-to-back scenes describe different realities since the sealing scene is located on earth, and the great multitude scene portrays the crowd standing before a heavenly throne. However, given Bakhtin's understanding of chronotope, the two scenes of Revelation 7 can be further nuanced. Perhaps the sealing scene's vision chronotope is actually less earth-bound than the great multitude scene's throne room chronotope.

---

78. The most common interpretations of the 144,000 are: (1) the faithful remnant of Israel; (2) Jewish Christians; (3) Christian martyrs; (4) Christians generally including both Jews and Gentiles; and (5) primarily gentile Christians. Aune, *Revelation 6–16*, 459–65, includes a lengthy discussion of this topic.

79. Klijn, "2 (Syriac Apocalypse of) Baruch," 615–52, shows an apocalypse that contains a similar scene where four angels holding four torches stand at the four corners of Jerusalem (2 *Apoc. Bar.* 6:1–6). The angels are kept from lighting the city on fire until a fifth angel retrieves the sacred objects from the temple. Similar to the sacred objects, the 144,000 in Revelation 7 are protected from destruction. The 144,000 are the objects rather than the subjects of the action in the narrative.

80. Aune, *Revelation 6–16*, 439, calls these two scenes "a literary diptych in which both scenes present similar interpretive problems." Aune notes that "most scholars . . . [agree] that a single group is described from two different perspectives" (447), even as he argues that the scenes represent two different groups of faithful followers. I interpret the two groups as representing the same reality. However, they are differently described because of their locations in different chronotopes. Both scenes can be read as responses to the question posed in 6:17: Who is able to stand the wrath of the One on the throne and the Lamb?

While the sealing scene describes a numbering of people not unfamiliar to earthly military preparations,[81] its sense of time and space (a future other-worldly location where people are sealed prior to winds being unleashed) highlights the heavenly realm and realities beyond earthly experience. The sealing does not really take place on earth, but in some heavenly dimension where Israel's twelve tribes still (or will) exist, where events can be reversed, and where a seal of protection can be placed on one's forehead.[82] In contrast, the great multitude scene contains a sense of earthly time and space where events cannot be reversed, and where humans actively participate in ways that shape their contexts.

Instead of only passively being acted upon, the great multitude of human characters actively perform in various ways: they stand (7:9), they cry out (7:10), they sing (7:10), they wash their robes (7:14), they come out of the great ordeal (7:14), and they experience the presence of God (7:15). Unlike the 144,000 of the first scene, these victorious ones act in ways that affect the narrative's movement. They celebrate because they washed and overcame. The order of events is critical. Their actions are decisive. In addition, past experiences of the prophets are brought into this scene. The great multitude joins a host of humans from past eras who, standing in earthly temples, were granted access into the divine dimension. Such encounters called for loyalty of human heart and hand, of proper worship and moral action. The experience of the divine dimension always clarifies human activity in the earthly realm.

The great multitude scene is very similar to the throne room described earlier in Revelation 4–5. First, the growing concentric circles of beings surrounding the throne are similar: the four living creatures, the elders, the angels, the multitude (4:8, 11, 13; 7:11). There is also a similar mention of the Lamb and the One seated on the throne (5:13; 7:10). In both scenes created beings from across the universe burst forth in a seven-fold praise to the Lamb (5:12) and to God (7:12). And in both there is an elder who directly addresses John, and in so doing draws him into the scene (5:4–5; 7:13–14).

---

81. Bauckham, *Climax of Prophecy*, 210–37.

82. Aune, *Revelation 6–16*, 456–59, discusses the use of the word "seal" (σφραγίζ) at the end of the first century CE. Aune argues that the term had more in common with sealing with clay or wax than with tattoos or brands. The use of the word among Christians did not refer to a literal seal, but to having been sealed through baptism or by the Holy Spirit.

At the beginning of chapter 4, as John first entered the vision chronotope by going through the heavenly door (4:1), he found himself in the throne room. Immediately there was chronotopic complexity with the presence of both the vision chronotope and the throne room chronotope. That complexity returns here with the great multitude. Whether on earth or in the heavens, the sense of time and space in the throne room differs from that of the sealing scene.

The relationship between the two collaborating chronotopes is probably best described as a "simple dialogical" relationship with both scenes offering differing perspectives concerning the final events of earth's history. Aune suggests that the author is juxtaposing the two scenes, with the second one offering a Christian interpretation of the first.[83] Another way to read the two is as dialogized chronotopes with each presenting a different perspective of time and space that ask to be read in relation to the other. The sense of time and space for the 144,000 is being read in relation to the throne room chronotope. This chronotope suggests a sense of time and space where human actions, memories, and history are important. As in Revelation 4–5, the vision chronotope is again restrained from taking over the narrative's representation of time and space. Reciprocally the throne room chronotope is also enhanced, being read in relation to the vision chronotope. The great multitude scene's description of earth-bound people is taken into the heavenly realm where they stand before the throne which itself stands at the center of the universe. Unlike the 144,000, the great multitude cannot be counted or finalized.[84]

The two hymns in Revelation 7 heighten the chronotopic complexity of the great multitude scene. After the sealing scene, which contains a majority of aorist verbs,[85] the second scene presents a huge group of humans engaged in various activities in the present tense[86] culminating in their hymn to God to whom belongs the salvation of every age. This unusual choir sings:

---

83. Ibid., 434.

84. Ibid., 445–47, suggests that the promise to Abraham, Isaac, and Jacob (Gen 13:16; 15:5; 16:10; 22:17–18; 26:4; 28:14; 32:12) is fulfilled! The universal nature of this group will be repeated throughout the book of Revelation (5:9; 10:11; 11:19; 13:7; 14:6; 17:15).

85. Examples include: "saw" (εἶδον), and "called" (ἔκραξεν).

86. They are "standing" (ἑστῶτες), "clothed" (περιβεβλημένους), "calling out" (κράζουσιν), and "saying" (λέγοντες).

Salvation to our God [ἡ σωτηρία τῷ θεῷ ἡμῶν]
who is seated on the throne [τῷ καθημένῳ ἐπὶ τῷ θρόνῳ]
and to the Lamb [καὶ τῷ ἀρνίῳ].

The dative of possession used in referring to God's salvation (ἡ σωτηρία τῷ θεῷ ἡμῶν) suggests that the first line of the hymn better reads: "salvation *belongs* to our God." This hymn is connected to chapter 5. In the fifth and final hymn of the last throne room scene, "every creature in heaven and on earth and under the earth and in the sea, and all that is in them" (5:13a) sang "to the one seated on the throne and to the Lamb" (5:13b). States Aune: "The term σωτηρία, usually translated 'salvation,' is not exclusively a religious term but is closely associated with eschatological victory in Revelation and refers here to salvation in the sense of 'deliverance' or 'victory' over persecution."[87] This is a victory song. Like the songs of Moses (Exodus 15) and Miriam (Exodus 15) and Zechariah (Zechariah 9), the time of oppression and exile is over.

If earlier it was possible to decipher some of the local chronotopes in this chapter, now it seems an impossible task. All clues within this nested hymnic chronotope serve to enrich beyond our capacity to unwrap them. The eschatological deliverance, a future phenomenon, is celebrated as a present reality. Is the choir singing in the temporal future before a heavenly throne? Is the choir singing in the past as Isaiah listens? Is the choir singing in the present at earthly gatherings of the delivered? The hymnic chronotope is read in light of both the throne room chronotope and the vision chronotope. In this unique time-space, the future is pulled within reach of human experience as the present is simultaneously pushed into heavenly eternity. While the dialogical relationship between the sealing scene (vision chronotope) and the great multitude scene (throne room chronotope) somewhat prepared the reader for the chronotopic complexity of the hymns, still the hymns' openness, their refusal to be finalized, is breathtaking. The hymns demand readings where time and space are represented in a variety of ways. For the book of Revelation, Christian eschatology is complicated.

As a result of the multitude's hymn, other-worldly beings break into doxology. The scene is very similar to the elders in Revelation 5 who proclaim a new song in gratitude to the Lamb for having redeemed people from "every tribe and language and people and nation" (πάσης φυλῆς καὶ γλώσσης καὶ λαοῦ καὶ ἔθνους) (5:9). In response, angels, living creatures,

---

87. Aune, *Revelation 6–16*, 470.

and elders (5:11) sing a doxology that includes a seven-fold praise of the Lamb who is worthy to receive: "power and wealth and wisdom and might and honor and glory and blessing" (δύναμιν καὶ πλοῦτον καὶ σοφίαν καὶ ἰσχὺν καὶ τιμὴν καὶ δόξαν καὶ εὐλογίαν) (5:12). Revelation 7 describes the multitude with the same four-fold description used in chapter 5: "every nation, from all tribes and peoples and languages" (ἐκ παντὸς ἔθνους καὶ φυλῶν καὶ λαῶν καὶ γλωσσῶν) (7:9). The great multitude sings of the salvation which belongs to God and the Lamb. Immediately the angels, elders and living creatures (7:11) praise God with a doxology that includes a seven-fold praise (7:12):

> Amen [ἀμήν],
> Blessing [ἡ εὐλογία]
> and glory [καὶ ἡ δόξα]
> and wisdom [καὶ ἡ σοφία]
> and thanksgiving [καὶ ἡ εὐχαριστία]
> and honor [καὶ ἡ τιμὴ]
> and power [καὶ ἡ δύναμις]
> and might [καὶ ἡ ἰσχὺς]
> be to our God [τῷ θεῷ ἡμῶν]
> forever and ever [εἰς τοὺς αἰῶνας τῶν αἰώνων].
> Amen [ἀμήν].

The two throne room scenes are linked. The linguistic and descriptive similarities cannot be ignored. The throne room with the One seated on the throne and the Lamb has been re-entered this time by an entire multitude of people from all around the earth. The ceaseless praise of the four living creatures (4:8) is joined by voices that cannot be numbered. The dialogized chronotopes keep the narrative open to times and places in heaven and on earth. This chronotopic openness is affirmed by the second hymn. The other-worldly beings proclaim: "Amen! Blessing and glory and wisdom and thanksgiving and honor and power and might be to our God forever and ever! Amen" (7:12). The doxology contains no verb. It can be sung in any time or place. Readers sensing the chronotopic ambiguity become themselves part of the narrative. Their own singing of the doxology is yet another witness to the multiple possible contexts carried in this complex combination of chronotopes.

Following the doxology, one of the elders directly addresses John, pulling him into the narrative as a character. The elder asks John to identify the great multitude and John responds: "Sir, you are the one that knows" (7:14).[88] The elder then identifies the multitude first using past tense verbs: "they washed . . . they made them white." He then uses present tense verbs: "they are before the throne . . . they serve." And finally he uses future tense verbs which first describe the One seated on the throne: "who will live with them." Then he uses them to describe the multitude itself: "they will not hunger . . . they will not thirst . . . neither sun nor heat will fall on them." And lastly to describe the Lamb: "He will shepherd them . . . will guide them to water . . . will wipe away every tear from their eyes" (7:14–17).

John as a character within the narrative hears a temporally complex description of the redeemed. Completed actions result in present realities and future possibilities. If John stayed within the narrative he would, presumably, be a believer who had experienced and survived the tribulation (7:14), having washed his robe in the Lamb's blood (7:14). Like other members of the great multitude, he is before the throne of God in ceaseless worship (7:15). And he has the hope of a future experience where physical deprivations and sadness are no more (7:16–17). John as character has entered the throne room chronotope even as John the narrator continues reporting his visionary experience (7:13). These "overlapping" chronotopes, caused by different diegetic (world of narrated events) perspectives, are visible to the reader. At the moment of their visibility, the reader becomes a transsubjective consciousness within the narrative. This means that the moment John enters the narrative and experiences its time-space, readers are also pulled into its representation of time and space (after the tribulation, presently in continuous praise before God, and before the earth's final renewal).

Through this chronotopic complexity the narrative engages its readers. The subjective characters within the narrative go through being sealed, the great tribulation, and experiences of worship before the throne. The transsubjective characters sense the openness of time and space that welcomes the reader's social situation. The "overlapping" relationship gives a sense of time-space in flux: the present time-space of the throne room, the future time-space of a vision chronotope, and the past time being recalled by John the narrator. Such fluctuation provides an openness to the reader's time-space and to potential future readings.

---

88. This response recalls again the book of Ezekiel who responded similarly (and prudently) when asked if a collection of dry bones could live again. Ezekiel answered, "O LORD God, you know" (Ezek 37:3).

While the depiction of John the character being addressed by the elder (7:13) works to include readers in the work as transsubjective consciousnesses, John the narrator restrains textual meaning by reminding readers of the hierarchical relationship between chronotopes: the epistolary chronotope guides all other representations of time and space. John writes to contemporaries who hear allusions to Ezekiel and Isaiah in the future experiences of the great multitude (Ezek 34:11–31; Isa 49:10; Rev 7:16–17).[89] The book of Revelation was first read by those who believed that the great multitude embodied the ultimate end of exile brought about by the Good Shepherd, Jesus Christ.[90] John wrote to people living at a time and place where water was scarce, but where messiah would provide abundant water (Rev 7:17; 21:6; 22:1, 17).[91] The earthly temple was gone, but God and the Lamb were the only "temple" humanity would ever need (7:15; 21:22).

Many interpretations of these scenes in Revelation 7 support a New Testament eschatology of "apocalypse soon." They observe that otherworldly beings prepare for the earth's destruction while human beings are passive, waiting for the end. Time and space seem outside of human control. In such an interpretive scenario, the hymns are relegated to the future. Such an understanding of eschatology neglects ethics.

But the great multitude stands before the throne, a place that resounds with memories of prophetic encounters with divinity in the earthly realm. Before the throne human actions have consequences. Before the throne worship is the most effective act of all. Before the throne earthly experiences and actions affect the universe!

The hymns of Revelation 7 are best understood as supporting a New Testament eschatology of "apocalypse now *and* then." The representation of time and space is too complex to ignore either future-heavenly eschatology or present-earthly eschatology. These hymns contain chronotopes in dialogic relationship. The dialogic relationship means that each must be read in relation to the other. Heavenly future realities are pulled

---

89. The shepherd imagery also echoes Ezekiel, where the true shepherd is described as ending the exile by rescuing, bringing back, and feeding his sheep (Ezek 34:11–31). The last part of Revelation 7 recalls the words of Second Isaiah as God's people return to Zion from exile. Aune, *Revelation 6–16*, 477, says of Rev 7:16–17: "This is the longest allusion to an Old Testament passage found in Revelation, and it is clearly drawn from Isa 9:10 [sic]" (Aune means Isa 49:10).

90. This section of Revelation 7 anticipates Rev 14:1–5 when the Lamb is on Mt. Zion surrounded by those he has redeemed.

91. Aune, *Revelation 6–16*, 478.

towards the earthly and present human experience, as earthly present realities are given eternal universal significance. The sealing of the 144,000 and the great multitude scenes *require* multiple chronotopes in dialogic relationship with each other in order to represent the complexity of time and space that attempts to portray the redemption of humanity. This complexity is particularly evident in the hymns found in Revelation 7. On the heels of the sealing of the 144,000, the great multitude appears and sings of victory. The multitude is saved by the Lamb. For such a prophetic-apocalyptic text with Christian convictions, the sense of time and space *must* be complex; it must be represented as both present reality and future hope. The redeemed of the world stand before the throne, "yet it would be most unusual in Jewish apocalyptic to place the final consummation in heaven rather than on earth."[92] Because of the Lamb, time and space have become complex for Christian believers. The eschaton has arrived. The eschaton is still to come. Such dialogic relationships between chronotopes invite readers into a text that reflects the complexity of Christian eschatology and ethical response.

The Song of the Seventh Trumpet (Rev 11:15b) and its Antiphon (Rev 11:17–18)

Immediately following the elder's description to John of the great multitude, the narrative completes the unsealing sequence with the Lamb's removal of the seventh seal (8:1). After half an hour of silence (8:1), the trumpet sequence begins (8:2). Like the unsealing sequence, the relationship between events and their contexts reflects temporal and spatial realities within a vision chronotope. John says that *he saw* "the seven angels who stand before God and seven trumpets were given to them" (8:2). Later in the trumpets sequence the narrator says: "Then I looked, and I heard an eagle crying . . . " (8:13). John describes the act of looking, yet actually experiences an auditory event. Then John sees a star (9:1), describes the appearance of Apollyon's army (9:7–10), hears a voice (9:13) and a number of troops (9:16), then sees (9:17) and describes horses released to destroy a third of humanity (9:17–19). In this sequence John witnesses events from a perspective that is far from his earthly experience. He sees a falling torch (8:10), a bottomless pit (9:2), locusts with golden crowns and lions' teeth (9:7–8), and two hundred million fighters on horses with

---

92. Ibid., 439.

fire, smoke and sulfur coming out of their mouths (9:16-18). As John narrates these events he seems to maintain a neutral perspective, unaffected by the events. He witnesses actions that destroy much of the world (8:3—9:21) even as he himself is located apart from the world.

Like the unsealing sequence, after the events of the sixth trumpet blast there is a pause or "interlude" in the series (10:1—11:15). Also similar to the unsealing sequence, the pause between the sixth and seventh trumpets provides a change in chronotope as the sense of time and space shifts, with resulting changes in how human actions and characters are represented. An interesting difference between the unsealing sequence and the trumpet sequence involves the placement of hymns in the scenes. In the unsealing sequence the hymns are contained within the great multitude scene which is during the pause between the sixth and seventh in the series. However, in the trumpets sequence the hymns *follow* the seventh trumpet blast, after the pause has concluded.[93] Thus, in the first sequence, the two hymns take place during the pause. During the second, the two hymns take place after the seventh in the series. Due to this ordering, the intense chronotopic complexity seen earlier *between* the sixth and seventh unsealings is mostly reserved for the *end* of the trumpet sequence. The end of the sequence receives the most chronotopic activity.

The narrative's sense of time and space during the pause in the trumpet sequence suggests the "in the spirit" chronotope first portrayed in Revelation 1 as John was "in the spirit" while on Patmos (1:9f). Like the vision chronotope, John expresses events outside the realm of earthly experience. Yet, unlike the vision chronotope of the first six trumpets, John's perspective during the pause seems to be as someone located on earth (Patmos?). He describes seeing an angel coming *down* from heaven (10:1) who is able to place one foot on the sea and another on land (10:2). As John begins to write about the seven thunders, a voice *from* heaven tells him not to do so (10:4). While earlier it was the opposite command, this is the same kind of time-space that John experienced while "in the spirit" when told to write to seven churches (1:11). Two more times during this pause John will hear a voice *from* heaven (10:8; 11:12). Unlike the

---

93. During the unsealing sequence the narrator describes the events of the first six in the series (6:1-17), then the pause of the sequence (7:1-17) *which includes* hymns before the throne, followed by the seventh in the series (8:1). During the trumpet sequence the narrator describes the events of the first six in the series (8:6—9:21), then the pause of the sequence (10:1—11:14), then the seventh in the series (11:15), *followed by* hymns before the throne.

vision chronotope which takes John into the heavens, the "in the spirit" chronotope shows John amazing wonders while he remains on earth. At the end of the scene with the angel and the little scroll, John is commissioned to go to the people of the earth and to prophesy to them (10:11). The "in the spirit" chronotope allows John to be both participant and reporter of events within the narrative. While his feet are planted on the earth, he can see actions and characters that are not limited to the earthly realm. Like his apocalyptic experience as a whole, each "in the spirit" experience is for the benefit of those within the earthly realm (1:1–3, 9–11; 10:5–11).

During this pause between the sixth and seventh trumpets John does not merely witness extraordinary things from his unique perspective on earth, he also joins in. He starts to write, but is stopped (10:4). He eats the little scroll (10:8–10), experiencing its sweetness and bitterness. He is commissioned to prophesy (10:11). Then he is asked to measure the temple (11:1).

This last request made of John is perhaps the most earth-oriented action of all. John, like Ezekiel before him (Ezekiel 40), must measure the temple. This is a literally impossible act within his authorial world. Ezekiel was asked to measure the temple following its destruction by the Babylonians. John is asked to measure the temple decades after its destruction by the Romans. This is a powerful example of the strange time and space of the "in the spirit" chronotope. While deeply connected to earthly realities, an other-worldly sense also permeates the narrative. All prophets, including the two who will soon factor into the narrative (11:3–6), have authority over earthly realities (11:6), testify on the earth (11:6–7), experience persecution and even martyrdom at the hands of the people of the earth (11:7–8), and are rejected by the inhabitants of the earth even after death (11:10). During the "in the spirit" chronotope earthly realities are mingled with extraordinary events, including a bottomless pit (11:7), a beast (11:7), a breath-taking resurrection scene (11:11), and heavenly voices inviting the faithful to experience other-worldly realms (11:12). The resurrection scene is followed by earthly disasters (11:13) which are similar to the eschatological destruction after the sixth seal was opened (6:12–17).

After this pause in the narrative, a pause heightened by its change in chronotope, the seventh angel blows his trumpet. The narrator says that then "there were loud voices in heaven" (11:15), suggesting that the time-space is now other-worldly and that the narrator has gone again outside the earthly realm. Unlike the voices he had heard *from* heaven (ἐκ τοῦ οὐρανοῦ) during the pause (10:4, 8; 11:12), the voices *in* heaven (ἐν τῷ οὐρανῷ) hint that the vision chronotope has resumed even as the trumpet sequence has resumed. Since the events that follow the first six trumpets are so destructive to the earth, one might expect the same from the seventh trumpet blast. But, instead, loud voices sing a song of triumph:

> The kingdom of the world has become [ἐγένετο] the kingdom of our LORD
> and of his Messiah [καὶ τοῦ χριστοῦ αὐτοῦ],
> and he will reign forever and ever [καὶ βασιλεύσει εἰς τοὺς αἰῶνας τῶν αἰώνων].

The vision chronotope typically represents a future time and space outside of earthly experience. This chronotope therefore would place the hymn in an ideal future time when the kingdom of God and the kingdom of the world have merged into one. If each trumpet blast precedes eschatological events, the seventh and final trumpet blast must depict heavenly beings celebrating the end of judgment and the beginning of a renewed earth. The song begins with the verb "has become" (ἐγένετο), suggesting "the certainty of the final and complete eschatological rule of God."[94] Here is the hope of the world transformed into a new kingdom.

However, the narrative does not allow this song to be only relegated to the future. Other chronotopes are present during the singing, creating a temporally and spatially complex section of the narrative. For example, the seventh trumpet ushers in another throne room scene, where phrases from earlier encounters are repeated as the "LORD God Almighty" (4:8; 11:17) has "taken power" (4:11; 11:17). This becomes even clearer when the twenty-four elders respond to the first hymn by falling before God and singing their own song of thanksgiving:

> We give you thanks [εὐχαριστοῦμέν σοι],
> LORD God, Almighty [κύριε ὁ θεὸς ὁ παντοκράτωρ],
> Who is and who was [ὁ ὢν καὶ ὁ ἦν]
> for you have taken your great power [ὅτι εἴληφας τὴν δύναμίν σου τὴν μεγάλην]
> and begun to reign [καὶ ἐβασίλευσας].
> The nations raged [καὶ τὰ ἔθνη ὠργίσθησαν],
> but your wrath has come [καὶ ἦλθεν ἡ ὀργή σου],

---

94. Aune, *Revelation 6–16*, 638.

and the time for judging the dead [καὶ ὁ καιρὸς τῶν νεκρῶν κριθῆναι],
for rewarding your servants, the prophets [καὶ δοῦναι τὸν μισθὸν τοῖς δούλοις σου τοῖς προφήταις]
and saints [καὶ τοῖς ἁγίοις]
and all who fear your name [καὶ τοῖς φοβουμένοις τὸ ὄνομά σου]
both small and great [τοὺς μικροὺς καὶ τοὺς μεγάλους],
and for destroying those who destroy the earth [καὶ διαφθεῖραι τοὺς διαφθείροντας τὴν γῆν].

The elders are described almost exactly as they were in the very first throne room scene (4:10): "the twenty-four elders fall before the one who is seated on the throne and worship the one who lives forever and ever" (πεσοῦνται οἱ εἴκοσι τέσσαρες πρεσβύτεροι ἐνώπιον τοῦ καθημένου ἐπὶ τοῦ θρόνου καὶ προσκυνήσουσιν τῷ ζῶντι εἰς τοὺς αἰῶνας τῶν αἰώνων). In Revelation 11, "the twenty-four elders who sit on their thrones before God fell on their faces and worshiped God" (οἱ εἴκοσι τέσσαρες πρεσβύτεροι [οἱ] ἐνώπιον τοῦ θεοῦ καθήμενοι ἐπὶ τοὺς θρόνους αὐτῶν ἔπεσαν ἐπὶ τὰ πρόσωπα αὐτῶν καὶ προσεκύνησαν τῷ θεῷ) (11:16). This description now links the song of 11:15 with its antiphon of 11:17–18, as the earlier description of the elders links the song of 4:9 with its antiphon in 4:11.[95] The throne room scene is revisited, along with its sense of time and space. In the throne room God's reign is a constant reality. Here created beings continuously praise and honor the One seated on the throne. Time is always present time. And, as with the prophets of old, humans can enter this divine dimension. The elders sing as if the future has already broken into the present. Unlike earlier hymns of thanksgiving to the one "who is and was and is to come" (1:4, 8; 4:8), this time the hymn suggests a forever-present experience: "who is and was" (11:17). Indeed, not only "will he reign" (11:15), but he has "begun to reign" (11:17).

The second half of the antiphon seems to be in the wrong order. Logically it would seem that judgment and rewards would precede the hymn of victory and thanksgiving. But God's reign is also a present experience, not only a future one. The narrative expresses the ideological convictions of a re-formed genre. After Christ, eschatology is messy. After Messiah, times and spaces are in dialogical relationships with other times and spaces. Christian conviction claims that Messiah has already come.

---

95. In the great multitude scene, a similar linkage occurs with the description of elders, angels, and living creatures (7:11) connecting the multitude's hymn (7:10b) to its antiphon (7:12).

Like the two witnesses, Messiah has already witnessed through signs and wonders (11:6). He has already been crucified (11:7), been raised after three days (11:11), and has been called to heaven (11:12).

Thus these two hymns require careful reading of the relationships between chronotopes present in the text. First, the move from the vision chronotope to the "in the spirit" chronotope at the point of the pause (10:1—11:14) highlights the pause by placing it inside a different time-space where the narrator is located on earth, yet still able to see amazing wonders in the heavenly realm. When the trumpet sequence resumes, so does the vision chronotope. Yet, it is quickly disrupted again by the complex representation of time and space in the hymns.

As with the earlier scenes of singing, the relationship between the vision and throne room chronotopes is probably best understood through the "simple dialogical" relationship. Each chronotope must be read in relation to the other. This means that the moments in the vision time-space are brought down to earth through the throne room chronotope. Not only is the narrative futuristic and other-worldly (vision chronotope), it is a present experience too (throne room chronotope).[96] Messiah is come. The reigning God is present and praised. As with the prophets, divinity has met humanity before the throne. In that God-filled space within human history divinity calls humanity to proper worship and social justice; actions which are judged on earth, as they are in heaven.

Likewise, the throne room chronotope needs to be read in relation to the vision chronotope. Human actions of praise and justice have eternal significance. Acts of injustice, violence and destruction also result in eternal consequences. When humans worship in earthly spaces dedicated to the sacred, they join a host of other-worldly creatures already in continual praise to the God whose reign never begins nor ends.

The nested hymnic chronotopes highlight the dialogic relationship between the vision and throne room times and spaces. They are simultaneously the past experience of the seer who was "in the spirit" while on Patmos, the present experience of the narrator and reader who enter the throne room, and the future experience of all redeemed creatures who celebrate the beginning of Messiah's reign on earth. In the

---

96. Aune, *Revelation 6–16*, 647, states: "Just as prayers of thanksgiving frequently provide a retrospective narrative of that for which the worshiper is thankful, so in the second major part of this hymn (v 18) the anticipated eschatological activity of God is celebrated in past tenses, as if the events had already taken place."

hymns, time and space keep moving in a dialogic relationship. They are impossible to finalize.

The epistolary chronotope maintains the voice of John as narrator who is telling his experiences to the seven churches of Asia Minor. The epistolary sense of time and space recalls the temporal complexity of John's readers, Christians living both in the Caesar's kingdom and in the Kingdom of God. The epistolary chronotope maintains a hierarchical relationship with all other chronotopes, as it keeps moving the narrative forward from John's initial concerns for each church (Rev 2–3), to his inclusion of all readers into the apocalyptic text whose complex chronotopes provide many doorways.

As readers are aware of the different times and places in a given part of the narrative, the narrative expands to include them. For example, the final hymn in chapter 11 is the only time in the book of Revelation where the first person plural is used for the phrase "we give you thanks" (εὐχαριστοῦμέν σοι) (11:17). Readers who notice the shift in chronotope from the trumpet sequence to the pause, and who are aware of the dialogical relationship between the vision and throne room chronotopes during the hymns, and who recall that this narrative began as letters to local congregations, notice time and space represented in various ways. The narrative resists being simplified into one chronotope. The complex sense of time and space leaves open the possibility for their own contexts to dialogize with those of the narrative. Readers who sing hymns similar to those found in the work find their own experiences of worship couched in the language of throne room hymns and heavenly voices. Readers who notice the temporal and spatial shifts during the pause between the sixth and seventh trumpet blasts, find themselves confronted anew with the witness of the two prophets. Readers who act like prophets inside throne rooms are suddenly called to prophetic action and witness in the cities of the earth. The future reign of God is located in the present victory of the Messiah who will "reign forever and ever" (βασιλεύσει εἰς τοὺς αἰῶνας τῶν αἰώνων) (11:15). By the end of the narrative, the redeemed will join the One on the throne and they too will "reign forever and ever" (βασιλεύσουσιν εἰς τοὺς αἰῶνας τῶν αἰώνων) (22:5).

The Solo Song of Salvation (Rev 12:10b–12)

After the hymns of the seventh trumpet (11:15–18), the narrative declares that "the temple of God in heaven" (ὁ ναὸς τοῦ θεοῦ ὁ ἐν τῷ οὐρανῷ) is now open. This is the first reference in Revelation to a *heavenly* temple. Prior to the hymns of the seventh trumpet, John had been asked to measure "the temple of God" (τὸν ναὸν τοῦ θεοῦ). But it was not described as located in heaven (11:1–3). The chronotopic complexity of the seventh trumpet's hymns simplifies as the narrative moves unambiguously into the heavenly realm, into a divine temple holding the ark of God's covenant.

The narrative declares: "And the ark of his covenant appeared in his temple" (καὶ ὤφθη ἡ κιβωτὸς τῆς διαθήκης αὐτοῦ ἐν τῷ ναῷ αὐτοῦ) (11:19). In the entire book of Revelation, the verb "appeared" (ὤφθη) is only found in this and the next few verses. The ark appeared (11:19). Then "a great sign appeared in heaven" (12:1). Then "another sign appeared in heaven" (12:3). The first great sign is a pregnant woman. The second is a great red dragon. All three appearances are located in heaven. The repeated use of the verb "appeared" ties together the temple scene with the events to follow. This is a time and space where bizarre beings enter and exit contexts beyond human experience. The vision chronotope reigns supreme as John the narrator describes events that he is witnessing in other-worldly realms. John watches from outside the narrative. His is a neutral position, seemingly unaffected by the events he witnesses.

The appearance of the ark of the covenant is immediately followed by a series of events within nature that are frequently associated with the presence of God: flashes of lightning, rumblings, peals of thunder, an earthquake, and heavy hail (11:19). When a combination of these events is listed in the book of Revelation, emphasis is on the places and spaces that are filled with the presence of God. The first instance takes place before God's throne in Revelation's first throne room scene (4:5). The second instance begins the trumpet series as angels stand before the golden altar which is also before the throne of God (8:3–5). The third instance is the scene in God's heavenly temple (11:19). Thus far in the narrative, this is the only instance that does not include a reference to God's throne. Here emphasis is on the temple of God located in heaven. The final instance occurs during the last bowl plague (16:18–21). It begins when: "a loud voice came out of the temple, from the throne saying, 'It is done'" (16:17). This last instance connects the temple with God's throne. By comparing the four times when these events within nature associated with the presence of God are mentioned, it is possible to equate the temple of God in heaven with the throne of God mentioned throughout the book of Revelation. While additional concepts are being nuanced through the temple's description, the two heavenly locations are both associated with the presence of God.[97] The association made by the book of Revelation between the throne of God and the heavenly temple creates a complex sense of time and space within sections of the narrative that include the temple. Before God's throne/temple certain events can occur. Having introduced the throne room chronotope, the narrative suddenly returns to the vision chronotope and the entrance of two signs seen in the heavens.

Positioned far outside the realm of typical human experience, in an undisclosed location, John sees a pregnant woman clothed with the sun (12:1) who experiences the greedy gaze of a great red dragon hungry for her child (12:4). While neither in divine space, nor in earthly space, the woman and dragon "appear" in the heavens, almost awaiting their ultimate locations. Upon his birth, the child goes upward to God's throne (12:5) to a place that is safe from the dragon. The woman flees from the dragon by going into the wilderness (12:6), presumably within the earthly realm. This part of the narrative includes plentiful spatial movement, with the child moving upwards, the woman going downwards. For a time the location of the dragon is unclear. The perspective of the narrator underscores the vision chronotope at work during this part of the narrative: he can see all the different movements of these other-worldly characters.

Without a transition, or temporal clarity, the narrator describes another scene in the heavens. The scene is a war between Michael and the dragon. Each figure gathers other-worldly beings to fight against his foe. They are at war in space beyond human experience and in a time outside the human experience of time. Once again the narrative includes considerable spatial movement as it repeatedly declares that the dragon was defeated and "cast down" (ἐβλήθη), "he was cast down to the earth" (ἐβλήθη εἰς τὴν γῆν), he "and his angels with him were cast down" (καὶ

---

97. This last listing of events in nature also includes the same order as that found at the end of chapter 11. First there are flashes of lightning, rumblings, peals of thunder, then a "violent earthquake" (16:18), and a description of the fall of Babylon. Then there is a description of huge hailstones each weighing close to one hundred pounds (16:21). All the drama being introduced in 11:19 finds its completion during the final bowl plague, with its similar description before the temple/throne, as another loud voice proclaims: "It is finished" (16:17).

οἱ ἄγγελοι αὐτοῦ μετ' αὐτοῦ ἐβλήθησαν) (12:9).[98] Between the first two descriptions of being "cast down" the dragon is described with a variety of names (12:9). Aune suggests that the narrator is presenting him as a cosmic foe throughout all of human history.[99] Such a character fits perfectly within a vision chronotope and a typical apocalyptic narrative. This cosmic foe is "the one who deceives the whole inhabited earth." Throughout the book of Revelation, the deceiver (12:9; 20:3, 8, 10) has allies who join him in acts of deception. These include Jezebel (2:20), the beast from the land (13:14) who is also known as the false prophet (19:20), and Babylon (18:23).

While the narrative's scenes of the woman and the dragon and Michael and the dragon show a lot of spatial movement, the temporal sense is unclear. Is the dragon doomed because of the child's presence at the throne of God? Is the dragon present before the woman because of already being thrown down from heaven? If the dragon is confined to earth, how does he challenge a woman located in the heavens? The sense of time and space represented are those of a vision chronotope. Their temporal and spatial locations are of another realm. The order of events seems reversible. Humans can only watch.

After the description of his battle against Michael, it is clear where the dragon is located. He has been "cast down" to the earth. He is located in the same realm as the woman who fled into the wilderness (12:6). Rather than being thrown *out* of the earth, the dragon is thrown down *to* the earth.[100] Michael's victory over the dragon, and the dragon's removal from the heavenly realm is celebrated when a loud voice sings a solo song:

> Now has come the salvation [ἄρτι ἐγένετο ἡ σωτηρία]
> and power [καὶ ἡ δύναμις]
> and kingdom of our God [καὶ ἡ βασιλεία τοῦ θεοῦ ἡμῶν]
> and the authority of his Messiah [καὶ ἡ ἐξουσία τοῦ χριστοῦ αὐτοῦ],

---

98. The dragon's movement downwards will continue throughout the book of Revelation. After being banished to the earth, he will later be placed in the bottomless pit (20:1–3), then into the lake of fire (20:7–10), both places presumably "under" the earth. Aune, *Revelation 6–16*, 698, states: "In ancient mythologies, expulsions from heaven are much rarer than (attempted) ascents to heaven."

99. Ibid., 697. The narrative will give another list of the dragon's aliases in 20:1–3 when he is imprisoned.

100. That which is given eschatological meaning in the gospels (Luke 10:18; John 12:31) is made a primordial event here. See Aune, *Revelation 6–16*, 695.

for the accuser of our brothers has been thrown down [ὅτι ἐβλήθη ὁ κατήγωρ τῶν ἀδελφῶν ἡμῶν],

the one who accuses them before God day and night [ὁ κατηγορῶν αὐτοὺς ἐνώπιον τοῦ θεοῦ ἡμῶν ἡμέρας καὶ νυκτός].

But they have conquered him [καὶ αὐτοὶ ἐνίκησαν αὐτὸν]

by the blood of the lamb [διὰ τὸ αἷμα τοῦ ἀρνίου]

and by the word of their testimony [καὶ διὰ τὸν λόγον τῆς μαρτυρίας αὐτῶν]

and they did not love their lives unto death [καὶ οὐκ ἠγάπησαν τὴν ψυχὴν αὐτῶν ἄχρι θανάτου].

Therefore rejoice, you heavens [διὰ τοῦτο εὐφραίνεσθε, (οἱ) οὐρανοὶ]

and those who dwell in them [καὶ οἱ ἐν αὐτοῖς σκηνοῦντες];

woe to the earth and the sea [οὐαὶ τὴν γῆν καὶ τὴν θάλασσαν],

for the devil has come down to you with great wrath [ὅτι κατέβη ὁ διάβολος πρὸς ὑμᾶς ἔχων θυμὸν μέγαν],

because he knows that his time is short [εἰδὼς ὅτι ὀλίγον καιρὸν ἔχει].

The hymn begins with the temporal description: "now has occurred" (ἄρτι ἐγένετο), emphasizing the present reality of salvation, power, and the kingdom of God. Much of the same language was used in the hymns of the seventh trumpet: "The kingdom of the world has become the kingdom of our LORD" (ἐγένετο ἡ βασιλεία τοῦ κόσμου τοῦ κυρίου ἡμῶν) "and of his Messiah" (καὶ τοῦ χριστοῦ αὐτοῦ) (11:15). The same verb is found in both songs. In addition, both make reference to the Messiah. Here in 12:10, the solo voice sings of the "authority of his Messiah" (ἡ ἐξουσία τοῦ χριστοῦ αὐτοῦ). The Messiah's authority will soon be contrasted with the authority of the beast (13:2, 4), who receives his authority from the dragon (13:2). But in the solo song, salvation is a present experience precisely because the dragon/accuser "has been thrown down" (ἐβλήθη) (12:10), the same verb used three times earlier of Michael's victory over the dragon and his allies (12:9).[101]

Although there is much more dragon drama to come, the hymns of the seventh trumpet prior to the narrative entrance of the dragon, and the solo song immediately after his initial description both suggest that

101. Aune, *Revelation 6-16*, 712, says: "Between vv 7-9 and vv 13-17, the author has sandwiched a victory hymn, which both supplements and provides a commentary on the mythic narrative in vv 7-9 by explaining the significance for the history of salvation of Satan's expulsion from heaven (a protological event in Jewish tradition presented here as an eschatological event), by sketching Satan's role in heaven before his expulsion and by emphasizing the faithfulness of the Christian martyrs."

all his efforts ultimately fail. Before he starts, he is finished. Once again hymns allow for complex representations of time and space which are simultaneously present and future, heavenly and earthly. Like the narrative in which these hymns are found, the dragon both pursues and is defeated. The expulsion of the dragon from heaven is immediately followed by a hymn. States Aune: "Satan's expulsion means nothing less than the victory of God and his Messiah."[102]

In the middle of this vision chronotope, where heavenly "appearings" of other-worldly creatures and time-space beyond earthly existence suggest the apocalyptic ideology dominating the narrative, suddenly a voice declares present victory for all who worship the Lamb and witness unto death. This solo voice is not monologic. The voice's song suggests a collision of times and spaces and ideologies. The hymn from the heavens creates a focus upon the earth. The focus is not merely a voice reporting a scenic change. Instead, with the hymn comes a sense of time and space that is closer to human experience. It is more grounded, more this-worldly. It is more like the representation of time and space in a throne room chronotope, where prophets experience an encounter with the divine dimension and bow in praise to God. In the solo song there is rejoicing because of victory over evil and the present experience of the kingdom of God.

In the solo song both time and space are difficult to pin down; chronotopes collide and collaborate. The voice proclaims that God's kingdom is now (12:10), that the dragon has been defeated and that a new kingdom has begun. However, by the end of the song, he still has time (a little time) to show his wrath to those on the earth (12:12). There is a complex sense of time where a voice can simultaneously sing of victory against the dragon, and note the dragon's on-going destructive force. Similarly, the representation of space within the solo song is complex. The one who accuses the faithful has himself been thrown down in defeat. Yet, as the narrative around the hymn notes, it is down to the earth that the dragon has been thrown, to the realm where the woman and her children are located (12:6, 13–17). The spatial location of the soloist is fluid, having both a heavenly perspective, and a familial connection to believers located on earth. The dragon's spatial location is also complicated: he stands before God making accusations against believers in a ceaseless counter to the

---

102. Ibid., 699.

"day and night" praise by the four living creatures to God (4:8), all while the narrative repeatedly emphasizes his banishment to the earth.

The second stanza's account of the believing community's defeat of the dragon retains the complex sense of time and space. "They have conquered" (αὐτοὶ ἐνίκησαν) the dragon (12:11). The verb "to conquer" (νικᾶν) is used seventeen times in the book of Revelation. The majority of times it is used in reference to Christians who conquer through the sacrifice of the Christ, represented most often by the Lamb. The solo song suggests that people are victorious over the accusations of the dragon because of the Lamb's sacrifice. Rather than a future visionary time and space, the reference to the Lamb's sacrifice moves hearers back in time to Golgotha, to an experience in human time and space. Like "the word of their testimony" (12:11) and their willingness to face death (12:11), the Lamb's sacrifice took place within human time and space. The sense of time and space within the hymn allows for human actions with particular, ultimate consequences. Human characters testify, risk, and rejoice. Past and present earthly choices have future and cosmic ramifications.

The visionary chronotope highlights the cosmic significance of the Lamb's sacrifice, an event that took place within human history and earthly space. The sense of time and space that is closer to a throne room chronotope notices that the song is sung by a voice that associates itself with humans who know what it is like to put their lives on the line for speaking the truth. The earthly realities have cosmic ramifications. The heavenly proclamations maintain earthly consequences.

The song concludes with the soloist calling on the heavens to rejoice at the removal of the dragon. Yet, the earth and sea receive a "woe" because the dragon has been sent down to them, and he will remain a destructive force for a short time. This understanding of the universe as a three-tiered reality is a typical quality found in a vision chronotope and an apocalyptic text. Yet, the "woe" technique recalls prophetic forms and thus conveys a sense of time and space located amidst human history. The woe "conveys a prophetic gravity that calls to mind the great prophetic speeches of denunciation in the Old Testament, particularly in Isaiah and Jeremiah."[103] The two lower levels of the universe receive a "woe" because the great (μέγας) red dragon (12:3) has great (μέγαν) wrath (12:12) and has been sent and confined to their levels.

---

103. Ibid., 704.

The solo hymn's chronotopic complexity underscores the temporal and spatial movement of the narrative in which it is found. Movement in the heavens, the earth and the sea crisscross with movement forward and backward in time. The dragon sweeps stars down to the earth. A child is born to rule the earth who is taken to heaven. A war in the heavens results in angels being sent to the earth. A voice from heaven proclaims that God's kingdom has arrived. Yet the dragon still dwells on the earth. He follows after the woman as she flies through the wilderness. The vision chronotope remains in dialogic relationship with the throne room chronotope. The relationship keeps the narrative moving in complex ways.

The temporal and spatial movement, especially as it underscores various chronotopes, works to pull the reader into the narrative. As the reader is able to distinguish between the sense of time and space possible within a vision and that of hymn singing, the reader becomes a transsubjective character within the narrative. The reader is pulled into the work, along with the reader's own location in time and space. Suddenly the vision chronotope, the throne room chronotope, and the reader's chronotope are all in a dialogic relationship.

This relationship is complicated further when one recalls that the entire narrative is framed by an epistolary chronotope. The work was created to be read to local congregations in Asia Minor. Reading the solo song of salvation in light of the entire work suggests that the complex time and space of the song is similar to the location of the work's readers. The chronotopically complex hymn inserted between a defeated dragon and an angry active dragon suggests where believers are located in light of Christian eschatology—Christians live in the time and space between a victorious incarnation/ascension and an earth free of the dragon's wrath. When Christians sing along with the soloist, they declare victory over the dragon even at the moments of its most agonizing pursuits. The dialogic relationship between chronotopes which becomes most obvious in the solo song means that the other-worldly vision must be understood in relation to the earthly experience of singing before God's throne, and that the earthly experiences of singing and testifying and giving up one's life must be understood in relation to the child's victory over the dragon.

Within the vision's sense of time and space, Christians are "located" in the heavens (12:12). The vision chronotope proclaims a revealed reality: like the woman's first child, all her children are secure before God. They dwell in the heavens, even as their feet are firmly planted on earth. In their conquering and testifying and martyrdom, Christians are located on the earth. They know the wrath of the dragon. They exist within Roman society. When Christians sing, they affirm both realities. Because of Christian convictions concerning eschatology, the book of Revelation's narrative *must* be chronotopically complex. The solo song of Revelation 12 is another example of the representation of such complex time-space. The chronotopic complexity of the hymn is necessary to portray the dual temporal and spatial location of the believing community. The chronotopic ambiguity suggests that the song can be sung in various times and in different places. The victorious "brothers" are both those who know the wrath of the dragon, and those who "have conquered him by the blood of the lamb" (12:10–11). They are members of the seven churches in Asia Minor, and the churches of all times.

The Song of Moses and the Lamb (Rev 15:3b–4)

The figures first introduced in chapter 12 continue within the narrative. The woman who gave birth has more children who become the focus of the dragon's wrath (12:17). Then the dragon gathers allies by first calling a beast from the sea (13:1), and then another from the earth (13:11). Even as the dragon's allies seduce, deceive and persecute humanity (13:13–17), the Lamb secures the exact number of those who had been sealed earlier (7:1–8). The 144,000 stand on Mount Zion victorious against the dragon and his allies (14:1–5).

During the last half of chapter 14, John the narrator sees six different angels, divided by the appearance of "one like the son of man" (14:14). The first three angels participate in actions of warning directed to those living on the earth (14:6–11). The last three angels assist the one like the son of man in acts of judgment upon the earth (14:14–20). It is then that the narrator says: "Then I saw another sign in heaven" (15:1a).

The previous "sign" in the heavens was a great red dragon (12:3) filled with great wrath (12:12). Now the sign in the heavens is both "great and amazing" (μέγα καὶ θαυμαστόν), and it concerns the final plagues in which the wrath *of God* is complete (15:1). The vision language continues with "And I saw . . . a sea of glass . . . " (15:2). The narrator is located in a place beyond ordinary human experience where he can see great and wondrous things. The sense of time and space is that of a vision chronotope. The narrative seems to be concluding with the final events of human history enacted by divine and other-worldly beings. Aune states:

"In the NT the wrath or anger of God is primarily used in an eschatological sense of the final judgment of God."[104] Humans on earth are passive recipients of such actions. The narrator is a passive observer.

However, suddenly within the description of preparation for the final plagues there is a deluge of images from earlier parts of the narrative. Many of the images recall a throne room sense of time and space. For example, the "sea of glass" first mentioned in the first throne room scene (4:6) is mentioned twice in chapter 15. Also, the presence of harps before the throne is mentioned here (15:2) as earlier (5:8; 14:2). Those who have conquered (12:11) are again mentioned here (15:2). They are also similarly described as the great multitude that stands before the throne (7:9–12). The mention of the "song of the Lamb" is similar to the "new song" of 14:3 as the redeemed stand with the Lamb on Mount Zion singing. Additional descriptions recall the seven angels (8:2f; 15:1), the wrath of God mentioned earlier in the narrative (6:16–17; 11:18; 14:10, 19; 15:1), the beast (13:1; 15:2), the image of the beast (13:15; 15:2), and the beast's number (13:18; 15:2).

As the narrative prepares for another hymn, the temporal and spatial sense becomes more and more complex. As the narrator reports: "Then I saw what appeared to be a sea of glass" (15:2), both the vision and throne room chronotopes are present. The vision chronotope holds a sense of time and space where sight is crucial ("then I saw") and where comparative particles (here "as" or "what appeared to be") are frequent.[105] Yet, the sea of glass location also recalls the chronotopic complexity of the throne room scene and a sense of time and space where human actions are critical. As those who had conquered the beast prepare to sing before God, the narrative anticipates them singing "the song of Moses . . . and the song of the Lamb" (15:3). Once again, the vision and throne room chronotopes are both present within the narrative.[106] The victory song of Moses and Miriam took place beside a sea (Exod 15). The book of Revelation's reference to Moses' song recalls these prophetic figures from

---

104. Ibid., 870. See also Rev 14:10, 19; 15: 7; 16:1; 19:15.

105. The comparative particle "as" (ὡς) is used frequently in apocalyptic literature. See Aune, *Revelation 6–16*, 870. The counterpart of the sea of glass is the lake of fire (19:20; 20:10, 14, 15; 21:8).

106. Aune, *Revelation 6–16*, 872, and Schüssler Fiorenza, *Justice and Judgment*, 135, conclude that there is no literary relationship between Moses' song in Exodus 15 and the song here in Revelation 15. However, there is an important chronotopic relationship.

Israel's historical past. The Song of Moses and the Lamb remembers events in historical time and space that remain cherished. By recalling Moses' song in the midst of an other-worldly time-space with angels and beasts, chronotopes collide and complement. The "great and amazing" sign in the heavens (15:1) is partially described with earthly harps and human singing. Moses, the servant of God (15:3), is joined by all who have conquered the beast (15:2).[107]

The vision chronotope is restrained as the throne room chronotope enters the narrative. In the vision chronotope, the narrator waits for the actions of other-worldly beings in a strange, other-worldly time-space. In the throne room chronotope, humans conquer beasts, stand before God, and make music with harp and voice. In the throne room human actions affect narrative movement. They are active characters whose memories, history, and choices are important. The great and amazing actions of angels within a vision chronotope are temporarily halted, as the songs of human voices take center stage:

> Great and amazing are your works [μεγάλα καὶ θαυμαστὰ τὰ ἔργα σου], LORD God Almighty [κύριε ὁ θεὸς ὁ παντοκράτωρ].
> Just and true are your ways [δίκαιαι καὶ ἀληθιναὶ αἱ ὁδοί σου],
> King of the nations [ὁ βασιλεὺς τῶν ἐθνῶν].
> Who will not fear you, LORD, and glorify your name [τίς οὐ μὴ φοβηθῇ, κύριε, καὶ δοξάσει τὸ ὄνομά σου],
> for you alone are holy [ὅτι μόνος ὅσιος]?
> All nations will come and worship before you [ὅτι πάντα τὰ ἔθνη ἥξουσιν καὶ προσκυνήσουσιν ἐνώπιόν σου],
> for your judgments have been revealed [ὅτι τὰ δικαιώματά σου ἐφανερώθησαν].

Earlier in the description preceding the hymn, the heavenly sign is described (15:1) as "great and amazing" (μέγα καὶ θαυμαστόν). But what is this sign that the narrator sees? Is it the seven angels? The seven plagues? The wrath of God? The sea of glass? The presence of those who conquered the beast? The singing of the song of Moses and the Lamb? In the song itself the same description is used, and its subject is clear: "great and amazing are your works [τὰ ἔργα σου], LORD God the Almighty" (15:3).

---

107. Aune, *Revelation 6–16*, 873, refers to *Qoh. Rab.*1.9; *Mek.* Exod 15:1, and states: "There is a rabbinic tradition that just as Moses sang a song at the Sea of Reeds, so in the world to come he will sing a 'new song' of praise to God."

The phrase "LORD God, the Almighty" recalls earlier throne room scenes where divinity is addressed with this collection of holy names. In Revelation 4 the four living creatures ceaselessly sing these words to God giving honor to God's holiness (4:8). In Revelation 11 the twenty-four elders sing to God in gratitude for the new, eternal kingdom of God (11:17). Here in Revelation 15, all those who conquered the beast join in calling God the "LORD God the Almighty" (15:3). Future uses of this phrase include the solo song that follows the third plague (16:7), the song of celebration by the great multitude (19:6), and the proclamation by the narrator that in the New Jerusalem, the "LORD God the Almighty" *is* the temple (21:22). The presence of this phrase in the context of hymns heightens the chronotopic complexity of the hymns. In three of the six instances where this phrase is used, divinity is described as beyond a human sense of time and space. The LORD God the Almighty is the one who "was and is and is to come" (4:8). The LORD God the Almighty is the one who "is and who was" (11:16). The LORD God the Almighty is the "Holy One, who is and was" (16:4). While the vision chronotope underscores the heavenly location of these amazing signs, and while the throne room chronotope seeks to involve human actions and earthly activities, the description of divinity explodes all categories of time and space. The LORD God the Almighty exists in all times and spaces.

The next phrase in the hymn proclaims that God's ways are righteous (or just) and truthful, and that God is "king of the nations" (15:3). This last phrase, and the question that immediately follows ("LORD, who will not fear and glorify your name?"[108]) alludes to Jer 10:7 where the narrative reads: "Who would not fear you, O King of the nations?" (Jer 10:7a). On either side of Jeremiah's account of these phrases is the repeated proclamation: "There is none like you, O LORD" (Jer 10:6a, 7c). The "song of Moses and the Lamb" includes a similar concept when it proclaims: "For you alone are holy" (15:4b). This hymn will not only proclaim divinity "holy" (4:8), but will proclaim divinity unique in its holiness (ὅτι μόνος ὅσιος). The only two times this word for "holy" (ὅσιος) is used in the book of Revelation is in this hymn, and in the solo song found in the next chapter (16:5). This uniquely holy one is not only the "king of the nations," but is also the one to whom "all the nations will come" (15:4). This phrase is reminiscent of the description of the multitude before the throne "from every nation, from all tribes and peoples and

---

108. Aune, *Revelation 6–16*, 875, states that: "Rhetorical questions are characteristic in hymns."

languages" (7:9–10). It is also used throughout the book of Revelation as a description of the domain of wickedness (14:8; 18:3, 23). However, in Revelation's hymns, the phrase is consistently used to describe the just and righteous rule by divine beings (12:5; 15:4). The hymns recall the prophetic promise that all nations will come to worship God (Isa 2:2–4; 14:1–2; 45:14; 60:1–3; 66:18; Jer 16:19; Zech 8:20–23). The song of Moses and the Lamb is presented as the fulfillment of the earlier promises. Those who have conquered the beast through the Lamb (12:11) can now sing the song of Moses and the Lamb (15:3–4).

The hymn sung here by those who have conquered the beast holds and heightens the chronotopic tension of the description of this third sign in the heavens (15:1f). The plagues are going forth, yet the victory is won. Those who have conquered the beast sing, even before the final plagues have been administered by the seven angels. The vision and throne room chronotopes continue to be in a dialogic relationship within this hymn sung by the victorious ones. They sing before God's wrath has ended! They are victorious prior to a new heaven and a new earth!

As readers become aware of this chronotopic complexity, they become characters within the narrative. Heavenly realities are brought to earth by including victorious humans in the song of praise. Simultaneously, the praise before the throne takes on universal significance as historically located harps and voices sing to a uniquely holy God unlimited by time and space. The vision and throne room chronotopes maintain a dialogic relationship. As the narrator becomes one of the servants of God who has conquered the beast, readers can sense an overlapping relationship between chronotopes. This allows for readers to consider their own relationship to the song—as receiver of a literary work, as listener to a narrator, as listener to a participating character, as participant in the hymn to the LORD God the Almighty. This last possibility is underscored by the hierarchical relationship between chronotopes as seen in the epistolary chronotope which includes all others present within the narrative. The song in Revelation 15 is part of a larger visionary event experienced and expressed by John to the members of seven churches in Asia Minor during the end of the first century CE. All readings that take careful note of chronotopic considerations must keep in mind that this is an apocalyptic text within an epistolary framework.

Thus, at the location of this new song of Moses and the Lamb, time and space take on renewed complexity, a complexity that includes the times and spaces of readers. Here the narrative reflects the eschatological and ethical convictions of Christian readers who live in locations between the Lamb's "great and amazing deeds" and the time when all nations will worship before the LORD.

The Solo Song of Holy Justice (Rev 16:5b–7b)

The last line sung by those standing beside the sea of glass (15:2–3) anticipates the rest of the book of Revelation. Those who conquered the beast sing that all nations will worship the LORD because "your judgments have been revealed" (15:4c). After the hymn's last line, the narrator immediately sees the "temple of the tent of witness in heaven opened" (15:5). This is similar to the description following the seventh trumpet and its two songs (11:15–18) when "God's temple in heaven was opened" (11:19). This apocalyptic text itself includes scenes of opening up divine space and revealing divine activity. The opening of the temple introduces the bowl plagues as the seven angels receive seven offering bowls full of the wrath of God (15:7).[109] The stage is set for God's final judgments. As anticipated by the hymn in Revelation 15, this is the time that God's "judgments have been revealed" (15:4c).

The narrator then reports that he hears a loud voice from the temple commissioning the seven angels to begin pouring out the final plagues (16:1). Is the loud voice the voice of God? Although the book of Revelation contains many unidentified voices that are not necessarily divine (10:4, 8; 11:12; 12:10–12; 14:2, 13; 16:1, 7, 17; 18:4–8; 19:5; 21:3), this one from the temple seems to be divine in nature. Unlike most of the other unidentified voices, this one is not only from heaven, but *from the temple* in heaven. It is the same voice that will proclaim at the end of the bowls sequence: "It is finished" (16:17). Isaiah identifies such a voice from the temple as "the voice of the LORD, dealing retribution to his enemies" (Isa 66:6). The possible divine nature of this voice suggests that these last judgments issue forth from a place beyond the earthly realm. This is the time and space of divinity, where past and future, earthly and heavenly are effortlessly and simultaneously experienced.

The chronotopic sense encapsulated by this section of the narrative is of a location where the future can be seen. The narrative describes the final stages of earth's history. Earth as humanity knows it is coming to

---

109. Aune, *Revelation 6–16*, 879, argues that these bowls were for cultic use. For additional references to these bowls in the book of Revelation, see 5:8; 16:1, 2, 3, 4, 8, 10, 12, 17; 17:1; 21:9.

an end. In this future time and space it is the actions of other-worldly characters that are critical; their actions at the bidding of divinity cause the earth's demise. The role of human characters in the narrative is one of extreme passivity. John the narrator passively watches from an unclear neutral location. Those living on the earth experience a variety of horrible things thrust upon them including sores (16:2), bloody water to drink (16:3–7), burns (16:8–9), pain (16:10–11), and demonic spirits (16:13–14). It seems that the narrative's end is already determined. Human actions or conversations have no impact on the narrative. The whole sequence gives a sense of being finalized even before it has concluded. There is little chronotopic complexity in much of the bowls sequence. The vision chronotope's sense of time and space reigns supreme.

However, with the inclusion of a hymn comes some chronotopic complexity even within this final judgment sequence. Following the third bowl being poured out upon the earth's water sources, a solo song is sung by an other-worldly being described as the "angel of the waters" (16:5a). The angel's voice sings:

> You are just [δίκαιος εἶ],
>> the one who is and was [ὁ ὢν καὶ ὁ ἦν],
>> the Holy One [ὁ ὅσιος],
> for you have judged these things [ὅτι ταῦτα ἔκρινας].
> Because the blood of saints and prophets [ὅτι αἷμα ἁγίων καὶ προφητῶν]
>> they poured out [ἐξέχεαν],
>> you have given them blood to drink [καὶ αἷμα αὐτοῖς (δ)έδωκας πιεῖν],
> They are deserving (of it) [ἄξιοί εἰσιν].

This solo song is placed in an unusual location within the sequence. Rather than at the interlude or pause between the sixth and seventh in the series (like the unsealing sequence), and rather than after the seventh in the series (like the trumpet sequence), this song is placed after the third in the series. It contains similar elements to earlier hymns: discussion of God's justice (15:3; 16:5), reference to God as uniquely holy (15:4; 16:5), the temporal openness of the One who "is and who was" (4:8; 11:17; 16:5), and the sense of remembering what has happened in past time (4:11; 5:9, 12; 11:15; 12:10–11; 16:6). Here in the hymn one catches a glimpse of another chronotope, a time and space where prophets and saints have died rather than deny their LORD. The hymn's chronotope remembers that the blood of the Lamb gave people courage to testify even if it meant having their own blood poured out.

The song in the mouth of the angel of the waters is considered a "judgment doxology" containing an "eschatological vindication formula."[110] The similarities to the hymn in 11:17 are striking. Following the trumpets sequence the LORD God Almighty, who is and who was, receives honor because God has begun to reign. In the bowls sequence, following the third in the series, the Holy One who is and who was, receives honor because God has judged the earth. The hymns in the book of Revelation connect the reign of God and the judgment of God. The hymns celebrate both God's reign and judgment in temporal and spatial locations that are difficult to pin down. Like the placement of the solo song between the third and fourth plagues, those who embrace the angel's voice are located between the beginning of the end and its ultimate completion. During the most devastating events earth has ever experienced, the angel sings.

The angel of the waters sings that the punishment fits the crime. As the wicked of the earth thirsted for violence and so "poured out" (ἐξέχεαν) the blood of God's people (16:6), so the third angel "pours out" (ἐξέχεεν) the third bowl upon drinking water and it all becomes blood (16:4). The angel of the waters concludes the song with an ironic phrase stating that "they are worthy" (ἄξιοί εἰσιν) or "they deserve it" (16:6). This phrase is contrasted with the members of the church at Sardis who "are worthy" (ἄξιοί εἰσιν) to walk with the resurrected Christ (3:4).[111] The phrase also stands in contrast to the hymn sung to the worthy Lamb in celebration of his ability to take and open the scroll with seven seals (5:9).

The solo song by the angel of the waters proclaims that the judgments of God are just even before they have finished. And when the angel's voice ceases, there is a type of antiphon or verbal response from the altar (τοῦ θυσιαστηρίου), the place where sacrifices were made and blood was shed:

> And I heard from the altar saying [Καὶ ἤκουσα τοῦ θυσιαστηρίου λέγοντος]:
> Yes, O LORD God, the Almighty [ναὶ κύριε ὁ θεὸς ὁ παντοκράτωρ]
> your judgments are true and just [ἀληθιναὶ καὶ δίκαιαι αἱ κρίσεις σου].

---

110. von Rad, *Old Testament Theology*, 356–57. Aune, *Revelation 6–16*, 885–86, states: "In OT hymns the glorification of Yahweh as judge occurs more frequently than the celebration of Yahweh as creator or king." Aune also states: "The 'judgment doxology' is not really a literary genre; rather it is a theological motif used in a variety of hymnic and prayer contexts in the OT" (885).

111. Aune, *Revelation 6–16*, 888, makes this comparison.

The third in the bowls sequence recalls the fifth in the unsealings sequence, when souls under the altar cried out for God's just judgment upon the earth (6:9–10). These are they "who had been slaughtered for the word of God and for the testimony they had given" (6:9). This scenic change from earth's water supplies to the altar also heightens the complexity of time and space in this solo song and its unusual antiphon. Aune states: "The location under the *altar* symbolizes the nearness of these martyrs to God."[112] Those who had called for God's judgment early in the narrative, the people who had paid for their loyalty to God through their own blood, now respond as God acts in final judgment upon those who shed the blood of saints and prophets (16:6). The altar is a place within the temple in heaven. It is a location near the throne of God. Suddenly all that takes place before the throne of God—praise, testimony, sacrifice—supports a shift in the sense of time and space from a strict vision chronotope, to chronotopes in a dialogic relationship with each other.

In the vision chronotope the future is viewed from a distinct location. Other-worldly beings enact the wishes of divinity upon the earth. In the throne room/altar chronotope human characters shape their experience through their choices. Although the choices are limited within the apocalyptic genre—either one experiences one's own blood shed, or drinks blood—there is still a sense of human involvement in the shaping of the narrative. Those connected to the altar joined the prophetic community in worship and witness and can therefore join the angel of the waters in singing: "Yes, O LORD God, the Almighty, your judgments are true and just" (16:7).

Once again the chronotopic complexity invites readers into the narrative. Readers who sense the brief break in the vision chronotope sense a more earth-centered focus, with human characters who made choices within their own contexts and whose presence within the narrative invites readers to do the same. The solo song concludes in a multi-voiced chorus where readers of all ages can proclaim the justice and truth of the LORD God, the Almighty.

Summary: Hymns Celebrating the Presence of the Future

This section has illustrated that the hymns are locations within the book of Revelation when the vision chronotope is kept from dominating the

---

112. Ibid., 404. Italics in original.

sense of time and space and human activity by entering into a dialogic relationship with other chronotopes. The epistolary framework of the book, the reminders of throne room time-space, and the narrator's entrance into the drama all reveal the presence of different chronotopes. The presence and interactions of these competing and collaborating chronotopes welcome readers into the narrative at the scenes of hymn singing.

In addition, this reading of the hymns in Revelation 7–16 reflects the complexity of Christian eschatology and ethics. In the hymns, the eschatological future is pulled into the narrative prior to the parousia. The hymns reflect the presence of the future. While the earthly realm remains within reach of the dragon's wrath, those who join the choirs celebrate the victory of the Lamb while waiting for the time when all nations will come and worship before the Holy One (15:4).

During these moments of chronotopic complexity, human characters take a more active, rather than passive role. The activity revolving around other-worldly figures that typically moves the narrative pauses to describe human characters involved in acts of worship and witness before the throne and before the Lamb. These human actions possible in the time-space before earthly throne rooms do not remain located on earth. Acts of worship and witness expand across the vastness of the cosmos. Worshipers join celestial choirs in the presence of God.

The book of Revelation, as an apocalyptic text, is often considered a strange fore-telling of the conclusion of human history. The narrative seems to suggest an imminent eschaton that is essentially closed. Such a narrative provides, at best, an interim ethics for those awaiting the cosmic transformation of the heavens and the earth. However, as Bakhtin's concept of the chronotope helps careful readers to see, the representation of time and space in the book of Revelation is much more complex and open than might at first be perceived.

With the help of Bakhtin and essayist Jay Ladin the representations of time and space in the book of Revelation can be identified, along with the types of actions possible within different chronotopes. When a part of the narrative includes more than one time-space, possible interactions between the chronotopes can be explored. This chapter focuses on interactions described by Ladin as "hierarchical," "overlapping," "simple dialogical," and "nested." Identification of such relationships opens up the narrative to include transsubjective characters such as readers. This chapter observes that chronotopic activity (chronotopic dialogism), which is found throughout this complex narrative, occurs most intensely at the site of Revelation's hymns.

The temporal and spatial movement in the hymns keeps the narrative from settling down. Similar to the experience of Christians living in the Roman Empire, the hymns reflected the complex location of the believing community. For believers, the kingdom of God was eschatologically and ethically portrayed by a great multitude standing with washed robes, even while awaiting the end of all tears (7:9–17). The believing community celebrated the reign of God's kingdom while awaiting the final judgment (11:15–18). Christians lived between a defeated dragon, and the "little time" left for the dragon to vent his wrath (12:10–12). Believers stood on a sea of glass celebrating the amazing and completed deeds of the Lamb while anticipating all nations worshiping before God (15:1–4). The community of faith sang between the beginning of the end and its ultimate completion (16:5–7). In the hymns a sense of time and space typical of a vision kept colliding and collaborating with a sense of time and space typical of prophetic encounters with divinity before throne rooms. The future-heavenly realm maintained a dialogic relationship with the present-earthly realm. One chronotope had to be considered in relation to the other.

Thus the representations of time and space during the hymns yield potential for reconsidering the book of Revelation's eschatology and subsequent relevance for ethics. The chronotopic complexity of the hymns suggests that this work is not simply an apocalyptic work of imminent eschatology devoid of ethics. The dialogic relationships between chronotopes suggest a more nuanced portrayal of eschatological time and space, highlighting both the actions of other-worldly beings and the actions of human characters.

4

Hymns Responding in Worship and Witness
Answerability and the Book of Revelation

THUS FAR IN THIS study I have tried to demonstrate an approach that asks *how* the book of Revelation means by considering the book's hymns in conversation with Bakhtin's conviction that meaning, like language, is thoroughly relational. Bakhtin's dialogic imagination—specifically his understanding of genre and his concept of chronotope—provide helpful ways in which to consider the important choices available to readers who enter into this book and carefully attend to the hymns found throughout its narrative.

The hymns reflect dialogic relationships between ideologies that mutually engage each other and, in the process, create something new. In the book of Revelation's hymns, apocalyptic ideology recalls generic contacts with Hebrew prophetic literature and hymns are created that portray a God who both transcends all earthly limitations and who encounters humanity in earthly throne rooms. Also in the hymns, Christian convictions are reconceived as they are shaped by apocalyptic's strategy. The sacrifice of the Lamb takes on cosmic significance. Before such images of divinity, readers join the prophet Isaiah and all creatures of the cosmos in worship and in witness. The book of Revelation, as a Christian prophetic-apocalyptic text, reflects a new way of experiencing divinity's relationship to humanity.

The hymns also reflect dialogic relationships between chronotopes that mutually engage each other and, in the process, create a new way of considering Christian eschatology and ethics. In the book of Revelation's hymns, a vision time-space meets a throne room time-space. The actions of other-worldly beings move earthward as humanity's actions of worship and witness expand across the cosmos. Those who worship in small house churches join with the celestial choirs and experience the presence of the future even while knowing the suffering of a world not yet transformed.

These ideological and temporal-spatial movements or complexities within Revelation's hymns must inform the use of such texts in the Christian moral enterprise. If a dialogic approach to the book of Revelation shows *how* the text means, such an approach is critical when considering how texts function normatively for Christians in contemporary contexts.

The task of this chapter is to consider how readers can best engage the book of Revelation as a resource for the moral enterprise. The dialogic nature of language and meaning understands the book of Revelation as carrying potential for new contexts, unexpected voices, and unimagined situations. The dialogic nature of language and meaning also understands that different ideologies and their contexts mutually engage each other. Readers help to create meaning through their engagements with the book of Revelation. When such engagements consider the hymns of Revelation, readers quickly meet imaginative language located within liturgical moments.

This chapter will first consider this question within the larger discussion concerning the use of Scripture in Christian ethics. After briefly noting the absence of the New Testament Apocalypse in much of the discussion, the language of moral vision will be considered. Moral vision is a crucial aspect of the moral enterprise. It provides a framework for considering other ethical discourse. In addition, as scholars from a variety of disciplines will help to show, the language of moral vision and imagination capture key aspects of moral reasoning and the ability to appropriate Scripture in daily experience. Like the language of poetry, apocalyptic literature provides a vision of the world. However, unlike most poetry, apocalyptic moral vision extends across all time and space, giving the moral enterprise resources for challenging institutions, social norms, and global practices. In the book of Revelation, moral vision is also expressed as a liturgical experience. Once again, the hymns provide readers choices for articulating the book's moral vision within their own contexts. The work's moral vision involving a view of God and humanity reflected in a Christian prophetic-apocalyptic text, invites people to respond in acts of worship and witness which readers will contextualize.

The middle section of the chapter considers Bakhtin's understanding of answerability as a helpful reminder of the dialogic nature of all attempts to define the book of Revelation's moral vision. As demonstrated in earlier chapters, the book of Revelation's moral vision includes its new expression of God's relationship to humanity that is created by dialogizing ideologies. In addition, the book's moral vision includes its complex sense of time-space in Christian eschatology that is created by dialogizing chronotopes. Readers join this dialogic activity by entering into the book of Revelation's moral vision from their own contextualized points of view. Bakhtin gives readers additional language with which to consider this mutual engagement of readers and texts that creates meaning and invites people to answer with their lives.

The third section of the chapter considers the final hymns of the book of Revelation as liturgical moments when the apocalyptic moral vision of the book of Revelation invites readers to experience a dialogic engagement with its perspective on the world and for readers to answer with acts of worship and witness within their own lives and contexts.

THE USE OF THE BOOK OF REVELATION IN CHRISTIAN ETHICS

United States government agencies maintained a siege around the Mount Carmel center outside Waco, Texas, for fifty-one days. During the siege, as the media scrambled for information concerning the Mount Carmel community, many reports highlighted the influence of apocalyptic images on the community's theological convictions.[1] The community's bizarre practices were often credited to their interpretations of the book of Revelation and other apocalyptic writings. Many members of Mount Carmel saw the United States as a beast-like power threatening their community while they tried to follow God's inspired Word, as understood by their self-proclaimed prophet, David Koresh.

This section suggests how, especially in light of the tragedy at Waco, Christians might (re)consider the role of the book of Revelation in the

---

1. Beck, "Thy Kingdom Come," 52–55; Kantrowitz, "Messiah of Waco," 56–58, are two examples.

moral enterprise. As "Ranch Apocalypse" exemplified, using Revelation's imaginative language in moral discourse is potentially deadly. However, I suggest that such language also holds tremendous resources for good. As will be demonstrated, the New Testament Apocalypse contributes to the moral enterprise by embodying images that are vast in scope and so work with human imaginations to articulate moral visions that are normative for Christians, urging them to answer in ways that change society and the world. The hymns of the book of Revelation are filled with these apocalyptic images. As liturgical moments, the hymns reflect a medley of voices articulating different aspects of the images. Readings of the book of Revelation where one voice dominates misrepresent the work itself and an understanding of meaning as dialogic. Koresh, who had memorized the words of the book of Revelation, desperately needed to engage the work as a moral vision whose vast scope and medley of voices went far beyond the Mount Carmel compound. Koresh's apocalyptic vision was far too small.

Principles, Goals, Virtues, and the Use of Scripture in Ethics

In the interdisciplinary conversation concerning the use of Scripture in Christian ethics, the New Testament Apocalypse is frequently ignored.[2] Christian advocates of different common philosophical approaches to normative ethics each consider the role of Scripture within their chosen model. Those intent on using Scripture to support moral obligations find little in the book of Revelation that resonates with rules or principles for the moral enterprise. While careful attention is given to the Pentateuch,[3] wisdom literature,[4] the Sermon on the Mount,[5] and Pauline mandates for faithful communities,[6] the strange images and confusing movements in Revelation do not suggest clear and specific guidelines for moral behavior.

2. Although other sections of both the Hebrew Scriptures, or Old Testament, and the New Testament contain apocalyptic elements (Dan 7–12, Hag, Zech, Mark 13, Matt 24, Luke 21, 1 Thess), this project focuses on the book of Revelation. However, the same observation could be made concerning the absence of these other apocalyptic writings when wrestling with the use of Scripture in ethics. Spohn, *What Are They Saying*, explores various models for the use of Scripture by theologians.

3. Marshall, *Ten Commandments and Church Community*.
4. Wheeler, *Wisdom*.
5. Davies, *Sermon on the Mount*.
6. Furnish, *Moral Teaching of Paul*.

Christian theologians whose approach to ethics emphasizes the goals or consequences of moral behavior might consider some of the book of Revelation's imagery (a restored community in Rev 7; a New Jerusalem in Rev 21), but the majority of the vision is neglected. Instead, theologians typically turn to other places in the New Testament that emphasize the growth of the kingdom of God.[7]

Christian theologians who embrace the virtue ethics model gravitate to the character-shaping qualities of Scripture's narratives.[8] For these Christian theologians, it is the parables of Jesus,[9] and the invitations of the gospel narratives to discipleship[10] that move readers to become people of justice and faithfulness within their faith communities. However, the narrative of the book of Revelation is rarely included. Even when emphasis is placed on Scripture's liturgical moments as affecting moral dispositions, the many liturgical elements found in the book of Revelation are seldom part of the conversation.[11]

Perhaps Christians writing on ethics avoid a text that has been used to justify escape from involvement in the world.[12] However, scholarship during the last two decades places the book of Revelation within a social setting where its vivid portrait of life with the Lamb called its first hearers/readers to avoid accommodating with the evil Roman Empire by re-

---

7. Gutiérrez, *Theology of Liberation*; Perrin, *Kingdom of God*.

8. Hauerwas, *Community of Character*; McFague, *Speaking in Parables*; Birch and Rasmussen, *Bible & Ethics*. Birch and Rasmussen state: "The Bible can and ought to be a force in molding perspectives, dispositions, and intentions. It will always interact with many other forces, but that does not diminish the fact that Scripture can nurture a basic orientation and generate particular attitudes and intentions. In a word, the Bible can help form moral character" (*Bible & Ethics*, 191). Later they state: "In the shaping of moral agency the Bible has its greatest influence on the Christian moral life, and in the internal life of the gathered community many of the clearest opportunities for the development of moral agency occur" (197). Yet these theologians do not include the book of Revelation in their discussions. In graduate school, a professor of mine who has been teaching New Testament ethics for over thirty years admitted that he never uses the book of Revelation in his classes.

9. Donahue, *Gospel in Parable*.

10. Yoder, *Politics of Jesus*; Spohn, *Go and Do Likewise*.

11. Spohn, *What Are They Saying*, 114–16; Spohn, *Go and Do Likewise*, 120–25; Saliers, *Worship as Theology*. An exception is Peterson, *Reversed Thunder*.

12. Niebuhr, *Christ and Culture*, places millenarians and mystics into the "Christ against culture" category. Niebuhr notes that those who reformed their societies moved away from such exclusive perspectives to a more complex understanding of Christ and culture.

sisting even many of the social norms of daily life.[13] John's first audiences were challenged to embrace an alternative perspective on the world, a perspective which claimed to be the true reality "unveiled" when Rome's propagandist screen was pulled back. To embrace John's viewpoint placed a Christian substantially at odds with daily life in Roman cities.[14] Rather than encouraging escape from moral responsibility and social action, the book of Revelation's vision challenged some of the primary practices of Roman society.

Perhaps Christian theologians avoid the book of Revelation because it has far too often been used in support of horrendously *immoral* actions.[15] Given centuries of interpretations of Revelation that call various groups "beast" or "anti-christ" or "those having the mark," many decide it is best to leave these disturbing symbols alone. However, in ignoring the New Testament Apocalypse, Christian theologians and New Testament scholars concerned with ethics relinquish an important resource for the moral enterprise. This final book of the Christian canon provides a much needed moral vision. The book of Revelation, as a moral vision, contains the very resources needed to resist human systems which, like Rome, support evil actions against humanity. In addition, the book of Revelation contains the resources needed to counter visions that, like Koresh's, justify immoral behavior.[16]

13. Yarbro Collins, *Crisis and Catharsis*; Collins, *Apocalyptic Imagination*, 256–79; Schüssler Fiorenza, *Justice and Judgment*.

14. Wilder, *Theopoetic*, 28–29, agrees, observing that the early Christian movement challenged social norms: "It is true that if we look at the New Testament history in an anachronistic way we seem to see a movement devoted to soul-saving, indifferent to politics, slavery and other social patterns. But actually it was a guerilla operation which undermined social authority by profound persuasions. What no overt force could do it did by spiritual subversion at the level of the social imagination of the polis and the provinces of the empire. It was a case of liturgy against liturgy, of myth against myth. And these liturgies and myths had their institutional embodiments. . . . The ethical and social implications and goals of the movement are unmistakable."

15. In addition to Waco, the tragic loss of life at Jonestown in Guyana was motivated, at least in part, by proclaimed doomsday scenarios. More recently (March 2000), the loss of hundreds of lives in Kanungu, Uganda, was attributed to failed apocalyptic expectations. The leader of the Movement for the Restoration of the Ten Commandments of God, Joseph Kibwetere, allegedly ordered members set ablaze after the "end of the world he had long predicted failed to materialize" (*Newsweek*, June 2000). Eugen Weber has chronicled many similar responses to the violent images of apocalyptic literature in his work *Apocalypses*.

16. Branson, "Golden Crowns and Radiant Faces," explores the possible contributions of a tradition of apocalyptic imagination. Branson states: "Finally, the answer to

Perhaps another reason the book of Revelation is overlooked is that its symbols and images are not easily incorporated within the language of principles, goals, and virtues in different models of morality. The modes of moral discourse typically identified in Scripture do not seem fully to capture the language of the Apocalypse. John Howard Yoder, in his 1988 presidential address to the Annual Meeting of the Society of Christian Ethics, reports finding only one recent work within Christian ethics attempting to "retrieve apocalypse" for moral discourse.[17] While Scripture contains rules, principles, paradigms, and even symbolic worlds, Christian ethics also requires the language of moral visions. The moral enterprise needs general frameworks from which to assess different modes of moral discourse.

After demonstrating the important role of the language of moral vision for the use of Scripture in ethics, I will suggest that the book of Revelation's imaginative language works to expand moral vision to its widest possible scope. The language of moral vision also emphasizes the role of Scripture's liturgical and poetic elements within the moral enterprise. The book of Revelation's hymns reflect a dialogic relationship between the apocalyptic images which are vast in scope and the liturgical images of human experience. Human actions of worship and witness take on cosmic significance.

Moral Vision and the Use of Scripture in Ethics

The conversation concerning the use of the book of Revelation in Christian ethics falls within the larger issue of how to appropriate Scripture in Christian ethics. Several studies of this issue[18] build upon the different modes of ethical discourse James M. Gustafson located within

---

passion must be passion. The response to narrow loyalties must be grander, more inclusive visions. Or, as Lester Manning, the leader of the Reform Party in the Canadian Parliament said about confronting the Quebec separatists, 'When you're fighting a guy with a dream, you've got to have a dream of your own.'"

17. Yoder, "To Serve Our God," 129–30, states: "Apocalypse is only one of many modes of discourse in the believing community. We should not prefer it; we should use them all. Yet it is one of those with which we have the most trouble, and for that reason it may have more to teach us." Yoder continues by noting the many liturgical elements in the Apocalypse and, speaking to Christian ethicists, says, "doxology does not easily fit our grid. That is just one of the reasons we need it" (130).

18. Hays, *Moral Vision*.

Scripture.[19] In his major work on the topic, Richard B. Hays, also sees a relationship between the ethical discourse found in Scripture and the use of Scripture in ethics.[20] He begins his work by emphasizing the critical task of interpreting biblical texts by using the best available resources for exegesis and hermeneutics. In the process of interpreting texts, Hays calls for close attention to the various genres found within Scripture.[21] For example, parables and epistles contain different modes of moral discourse, and therefore contribute to Christian ethics in different ways. Hays cautions: "In our eagerness to discern ethical relevance, we must not force tone-deaf, literarily insensitive interpretations upon the texts. The New Testament is, after all, not a collection of general treatises on ethics."[22] After reviewing the moral discourse found throughout the New Testament, Hays argues for the need to synthesize his findings and suggests an overall moral vision of the New Testament. The synthesis must not impose a generalization upon the texts but must move from and reflect the texts. While acknowledging that the New Testament contains diverse voices, Hays proposes that it also provides a moral vision, or a general interpretive framework, that is crucial for the moral enterprise. Hays suggests that the moral vision of the New Testament can be more concretely articulated through three "focal images" or "root metaphors" shared by the great variety of texts: Community, Cross, and New Creation.[23]

To use the phrase "moral vision" is to suggest that a broad interpretive framework is crucial to the moral enterprise. This is the realm where focal images, root metaphors, even symbols and paradigms, work.

19. Gustafson, "Place of Scripture in Christian Ethics," 430–55.

20. Hays describes the four modes of ethical discourse in the following way: (1) rules, which are "direct commandments or prohibitions of specific behaviors"; (2) principles, defined as "general frameworks of moral consideration by which particular decisions about action are to be governed"; (3) paradigms, which are "stories or summary accounts of characters who model exemplary conduct"; and (4) a symbolic world which "creates the perceptual categories through which we interpret reality" (*Moral Vision*, 209). This last category includes the representation of the human condition and the character of God. Hays suggests that "the hermeneutical task is—in part—the task of rightly correlating our ethical norms with the modes of Scripture's speech" (ibid.). Hays says, "An ethic seeking to be responsive to the contours and emphases of the New Testament would seek to incorporate all of these modes appropriately within the church's ethical teaching. The first step toward doing that is to attend carefully to the mode in which the individual New Testament texts themselves speak" (294).

21. Ibid., 190–91.

22. Ibid., 190.

23. Ibid., 193–205.

If Hays were to expand the moral vision of the New Testament to include "focal images" from the Old Testament, he might use imaginative language such as Covenant, Exile, and Home Coming.[24] The language of moral vision includes the widest possible scope for articulating moral categories, and its images and metaphors "serve as *lenses* to focus our reading of the New Testament: when we reread the canonical documents through these images, our blurry multiple impressions of the texts come more sharply into focus."[25] As Hays describes various modes of moral discourse within Scripture (symbolic worlds, paradigms, principles, rules), the modes work in conjunction with the overall vision, becoming (as I have listed them) more and more specific. Thus, a story's paradigmatic value for normative ethics is set alongside the overall moral vision of the New Testament. Similarly, rules or principles for communal behavior are set alongside the moral vision of the New Testament as articulated in the images of community, cross and new creation.

Hays does not make moral vision a fourth category of common approaches to normative ethics,[26] nor does he subsume moral vision under one of the other three. Instead, he uses the language of Scripture's moral vision and its more concrete images as a way to express the crucial role of human imagination in the moral enterprise. When an imagination engages a moral vision, the moral enterprise takes on an expanded scope.[27] With the help of the imagination, moral vision works to shape human reason and to invite response.

Mark Johnson makes a major contribution to the discussion of the imaginative nature and structure of moral reasoning both in his joint project with George Lakoff on metaphors,[28] and in his own work on mor-

---

24. Hays, *Moral Vision*, 306–10, discusses a relationship between the proposed moral vision and its compatibility to the Old Testament's moral vision.

25. Ibid., 195.

26. Hays does not place moral vision alongside philosophical theories of normative ethics that center on obligations (duties), values (ends), or virtues (being). Frankena, *Ethics*, provides a very helpful analysis of duties and values. MacIntyre, *After Virtue*, explores the category of virtues.

27. Branson, "Virtues, Obligations, and the Prophetic Vision," 364, gives the following example: "An ethics of vision creates new understandings of the reality within which character is shaped and casuistry carried out. An ethics of virtue insists that the plantation owner should love the slave. An ethics of obligation argues that the legislature and the courts should acknowledge the rights of slaves in law. A visionary ethic dares to imagine a society without slavery at all."

28. Lakoff and Johnson, *Metaphors We Live By*.

al imagination.[29] Johnson argues that moral reasoning, like all reasoning, *is* imaginative in that the human mind understands through concepts that are metaphorical in nature.[30] The mind works metaphorically or analogically by "understanding and experiencing one kind of thing in terms of another."[31] Human beings reason on the basis of images, whether such images are described as metaphors (Johnson and Lakoff), as paradigmatic imagination (Garrett Green),[32] as symbols (Paul Ricoeur),[33] as "fancy" (Martha Nussbaum),[34] or as analogies (David Tracy).[35] Humans understand through the work of imagination, which, as Kant says, "is the faculty of representing an object even without its presence in intuition."[36] Human imagination takes one thing and sees it against another; the two are not the same, but there is a connection made possible by the imagination that enhances understanding.[37]

29. Johnson, *Moral Imagination*.

30. Lakoff and Johnson, *Metaphors We Live By*, 6, suggest that not only do metaphors fill language, but that even "human *thought processes* are largely metaphorical." Later, Lakoff and Johnson say that the metaphor "unites reason and imagination," making understanding possible (193). Niebuhr, *Christ and Culture*, uses broad metaphors to organize information about Christian communities and their relationship to the world. May, *Physician's Covenant*, uses various images to clarify the different roles of physicians within society.

31. Ibid., 5.

32. Green, *Imagining God*, 66, calls the paradigmatic imagination "the ability of human beings to recognize in accessible exemplars the constitutive organizing patterns of other, less accessible and more complex objects of cognition." Green continues, "Put most simply, the function of religious imagination is to tell us 'what the world is like' in its broadest and deepest sense" (79).

33. Ricoeur, *Interpretation Theory*, 53, states that "the concept 'symbol' brings together two dimensions, we might even say, two universes."

34. Nussbaum, *Poetic Justice*, 13–52, discusses "fancy" as the ability to see one thing for another; the ability to imagine nonexistent possibilities.

35. Tracy, *Analogical Imagination*. Spohn, *Go and Do Likewise*, 50–71, incorporates this concept of the analogical imagination into his discussion of ethics. For both Tracy and Spohn, imagination functions analogically as it considers how to act faithfully in a new situation.

36. Kant, *Critique of Pure Reason*, 88.

37. Niebuhr, *Meaning of Revelation*, 71, calls this discovery of a connection or pattern "revelation" or "right imagination." Niebuhr continues: "Reason does not dispense with imagination but seeks to employ apt images and patterns whereby an otherwise inscrutable sensation becomes a true symbol of a reality whose other aspects, as anticipated in the image, are available to common experience" (ibid.). Niebuhr concludes that, "reason is right imagination" (ibid.).

In order to even grasp moral concepts such as "duty" or "goodness" or "virtue," there must be an engagement of imagination. It is the imagination that recognizes images and patterns and can create metaphors, symbols, and paradigms.[38] The imagination is engaged when one recalls previous experiences, makes comparisons to other situations, even notices that a situation is morally charged. Through conceptual knowledge—that is, through imaginative thinking—humans identify, explore, compare, criticize and transform moral situations and ethical dilemmas. Imagination is critical for "all profound knowing and celebration; all remembering, realizing, and anticipating."[39] Ultimately, "it is at the level of the imagination that any full engagement with life takes place."[40]

Considering that moral reasoning involves creating imaginative constructs (visions, metaphors, images) that guide judgment in particular situations, one way that Scripture functions normatively is through its imaginative constructs which guide the moral judgment of those who embrace Scripture as authoritative. Imagination plays a critical role in discerning how the moral vision moves from its past contexts in Scripture to contemporary moral situations. Hays states: "The use of the New Testament in normative ethics requires *an integrative act of the imagination*, a discernment about how our lives, despite their historical dissimilarity to the lives narrated in the New Testament, might fitly answer to that narration and participate in the truth that it tells."[41] He goes on to say: "*Whenever we appeal to the authority of the New Testament, we are necessarily engaged in metaphor-making, placing our community's life imaginatively within the world articulated by the texts.*"[42] This is necessary because "timeless truths" cannot be wrenched from the "culturally conditioned" texts in which we find them. Hays concludes: "The fundamental task of New Testament ethics is to call us again and again to see our lives shattered and shaped anew by 'reading' them in metaphorical juxtaposition with this story."[43]

---

38. Spohn, *Go and Do Likewise*, 63–64, distinguishes these terms in a concise and clear way. My use of these terms, like Hays and Johnson, emphasizes the shared ability of images, metaphors, and symbols to engage imaginations.

39. Wilder, *Theopoetic*, 2.

40. Ibid.

41. Hays, *Moral Vision*, 298.

42. Ibid., 298–99.

43. Ibid., 302.

In a helpful chapter on the analogical imagination,[44] William C. Spohn speaks of the imagination as a "bridge" between the stories of Scripture and contemporary situations requiring moral discernment. For Spohn, Jesus' imperative in the gospel according to Luke, to "go and do likewise," continues to call Christians to moral action in a manner similar to the way of Jesus.[45] The imagination moves from the past context, to a new one, without neglecting the particulars of each. Spohn states that "Christians should be faithful to the story of Jesus yet creative in applying it to their context."[46] Through the analogical imagination, new realities are possible and therefore new actions are possible.[47] Spohn also calls the work of imagination "spotting the rhyme" between the stories of Jesus and the contemporary situation of the community of faith.[48] "Spotting the rhyme" is a more challenging task than merely "applying the rules." It takes careful attending to the past story and to the present situation. "Spotting the rhyme," is more like a dance, than a diagnosis. It is more like poetry than a proof. Or, as Nancey Murphy states: "Christian ethics is more like aesthetics than calculus."[49]

Because of the ability of the imagination to work analogically, one can move from Scripture's stories to the contemporary stories of believing communities. However, Hays argues that this work is done in conjunction with a general framework, a moral vision, which will "govern the interpretation of individual texts by placing them within a coherent narrative framework."[50] The crucial role of vision and its focal images must remain since "the unity and sense of Scripture can be grasped only through an act of metaphorical imagination that focuses the diverse contents of the texts in terms of a particular 'imaginative characterization.'"[51] Human imaginations need moral visions. Samuel Laeuchli shares this delightful observation: "No age can exist without poetry, without imagination creating the song, the dance, the poetic vision of life."[52] Garrett Green

44. Spohn, *Go and Do Likewise*, 50–71.
45. Ibid., 50–51.
46. Ibid., 4.
47. Spohn, *What Are They Saying*, 10.
48. Spohn, *Go and Do Likewise*, 54–56.
49. Murphy, preface to *Virtues and Practices*, xii.
50. Hays, *Moral Vision*, 195.
51. Ibid., 194. The phrase "imaginative characterization," is from Kelsey, *Uses of Scripture*. Hays prefers to use the phrase "focal images."
52. Laeuchli, "Christianity and the Death of Myth," 13.

defines imagination as the point of contact between divine revelation and human understanding. To do theology is to do the work of imagination; that is, to articulate patterns through an act of the imagination. Scripture aids this work of theology since Scripture, itself a work of imagination, provides the reader with a lens through which to see the world. Garrett Green concludes: "The Scriptures are not something we look *at* but rather look *through*, lenses that refocus what we see into an intelligible pattern."[53] For Hays, the "lens" Christians must use is best articulated as the New Testament's moral vision expressed through the "focal images" of Community, Cross, and New Creation.

Scripture's imaginative language shapes reason first by challenging the reader's perception of the world. Using images and metaphors, poetry and stories, Scripture provides a new framework in which to consider communal conflicts, decisions, and possibilities. States Hays: "Metaphors are incongruous conjunctions of two images—or two semantic fields—that turn out, upon reflection, to be like one another in ways not ordinarily recognized. They shock us into thought by positing unexpected analogies—analogies that could not be discerned within conventional categories of knowledge. Thus, metaphors reshape perception."[54] Since Scripture's imaginative language reshapes perception, it affects every other aspect of moral thinking.[55]

Iris Murdoch's works of fiction and metaphysics emphasize the importance of perception. Some things are noticed and some are ignored. She states: "I can only choose within the world I can *see*, in the moral sense of 'see' which implies that clear vision is a result of moral imagination and moral effort."[56] Perception determines which particularities are

---

53. Green, *Imagining God*, 107.

54. Hays, *Moral Vision*, 300. Hays discusses analogies and metaphors and concludes that "the difference, however, is one of degree, not of kind; both metaphors and analogies posit connections between disparate entities or fields" (311n8).

55. Blum, *Moral Perception and Particularity*, argues that moral perception is necessary even to grasp that a situation is morally loaded. Johnson, *Moral Imagination*, 210, credits the imagination with the ability to perceive or frame a situation: "Deciding how to act in a particular set of circumstances will depend on how we frame the situation." Hauerwas, *Vision and Virtue*, 36, acknowledges the vital role of vision: "The moral life, then, is more than thinking clearly and making rational choices. It is a way of seeing the world." Lorde, *Sister Outsider*, 36, agrees: "The quality of light by which we scrutinize our lives has direct bearing upon the product which we live, and upon the changes which we hope to bring about through those lives."

56. Murdoch, *Sovereignty of the Good*, 37.

noticed. Martha Ellen Stortz, commenting on Murdoch, observes: "What we see and how we see has the capacity to form, inform, transform, or deform who and how we are in the world; it has the capacity to shape or misshape what we do and how we do it."[57] When Christian ethicists consider Scripture's imaginative language, the ethical conversation includes perception and attention to particularities.

Scripture's imaginative language shapes reason by re-shaping perception. Scripture's imaginative language also invites response. Reflecting on what he calls the "religious imagination," Amos Wilder writes: "Our visions, stories, and utopias are not only aesthetic: they engage us."[58] Scripture's imaginative language engages the mind and the emotions, and so leads to active response. The human agent participates simultaneously in seeing and being and acting. In another work, Wilder states: "Now we know that a true metaphor or symbol is more than a sign, it is a bearer of the reality to which it refers. The hearer not only learns about that reality, he participates in it."[59] The language that articulates moral vision—the language of metaphor and symbol—works with human imagination to focus *and urge* moral action.

Metaphors and images enliven the imagination and launch its adherents into action. The prayers of Israel's worship created hope, resulting in actions on behalf of Israel's future.[60] The poetry of the prophets compelled people to action on behalf of society's poor.[61] The parables of Jesus "had the character, not of instruction and ideas, but of compelling imagination,"[62] that then acted on behalf of one's neighbor.

Scripture provides the imagination with normative moral visions expressed in a multitude of metaphors, images, symbols, and paradigmatic stories. To emphasize the importance of moral vision when considering the use of Scripture in ethics acknowledges the role of imagination

---

57. Stortz, "Vision and Choice," 16. Wilder, *Theopoetic*, 71, considers the imagination within the Christian tradition and states: "The 'theopoesis' or dramatic imagination of the New Testament writings arise out of hierophany and vision. Its more discursive aspects of teachings and ethic rest on these dynamics."

58. Wilder, *Theopoetic*, 79.

59. Wilder, "Scenarios of Life and Destiny," 83.

60. Westermann, *Praise of God in the Psalms*.

61. Brueggemann, *Prophetic Imagination*, considers the moral vision of the Hebrew prophets as an "alternative consciousness" that both criticized the status quo, and energized people to act in new ways.

62. Wilder, *Jesus' Parables*, 83.

in moral reasoning. Scripture's imaginative language enables readers to reconsider God and the world.[63] The stories, poetry and liturgy of Scripture recall and reshape images such as covenant, exile, journey, wilderness, home coming. Scripture takes symbols like tabernacles and lambs and explores their possible meanings in new situations. Images of hope—a land flowing with milk and honey, a new Jerusalem—create an alternative to stories of unfaithfulness and injustice. These images function normatively in Christian faith and practice.[64] Scripture's symbols, metaphors, and images help imaginations to catch Scripture's moral visions. When that happens, perceptions of the world are reshaped, and new actions are possible. Scripture's imaginative language carries moral visions which clarify perception and invite moral action.

Therefore, in addition to the language of moral discourse found in Scripture's rules, principles, and paradigms for character formation, Scripture also contains imaginative language that is concentrated in Scripture's liturgy, poetry, prophetic literature, and apocalyptic writings. This language is critical to Christian ethics as it moves readers to embrace a moral vision with which to consider themselves and the world.

Moral Vision as Apocalyptic Vision

In the conclusion of John J. Collins' book on the characteristics of apocalyptic writings, he states: "The apocalyptic revolution is a revolution in the imagination. It entails a challenge to view the world in a way that is radically different from the common perception. The revolutionary potential of such imagination should not be underestimated, as it can foster dissatisfaction with the present and generate visions of what might be."[65] The symbolic language of Revelation, the only book-length apocalyptic work included in the New Testament, creates just such a revolu-

---

63. Green, *Imagining God*, 109. Wilder, *Theopoetic*, 41, states: "Certainly man's deepest apprehensions of the world and the gods, or of God himself, have always been poetic in the sense of symbolic and metaphorical."

64. Green, *Imagining God*, 119. Niebuhr, *Meaning of Revelation*, 85, states: "Through Christ we become immigrants into the empire of God which extends over all the world and learn to remember the history of that empire, that is of men in all times and places, as our history. Such interpretation and apprehension of our past, such rationalization of all that has happened in our history is not an intellectual exercise but a moral event."

65. Collins, *Apocalyptic Imagination*, 283.

tion in the imaginations of its readers. To speak of its ability to merely awaken the imagination belittles the power of its pages. Rather, the book of Revelation inflames and excites, inspires and ignites. Its rich imagery works with the imagination to provide a moral vision or framework for seeing the whole world and beyond. Symbols and images in the book of Revelation include churches, candlesticks, and creatures in continuous praise. Readers meet a woman in white, another woman in red, a dragon, plagues, and rainbows. Beasts, banquets, bowls, and a baby flash across its pages.[66] There is movement in time—from the past to the present to the future and back again. And there is movement in space—from earth and sea to sky and heaven. If scholars are correct that literature opens up aspects of reality not previously imagined,[67] then the aspects of reality revealed through the images of the book of Revelation reach across the complete expanse of human history and fill the whole of space.

The images in scenes of conflict, judgment, and worship cover the sweep of time as readers remember past struggles (slavery, exile) and victories (freedom, resurrection) in light of the present. The locations of these scenes move between earth and heaven. The battle for earth is not confined to it. Beastly beings from sky, earth, and sea appear in order to battle angels and a cosmic rider on a white horse. Revelation launches the imaginations of readers on a fantastic journey that recalls creation, the exodus, and the exile. Believers remember Pentecost, and imagine the parousia, the depths of the grave, and the heights of heavenly splendor. The apocalyptic narrative moves from the chaos of pre-creation and post-fall, to the harmony of Eden renewed.

---

66. Barr, *Tales of the End*, 9, states: "A symbol does not so much *mean* something as it does *imply*, so deciphering symbols is less a rational act than an imaginative act. It is thus of the utmost importance that we read the Apocalypse with our imaginations engaged." Later Barr adds: "Literary texts especially invite a variety of readings, for they leave much to the imagination. We must imagine scenes, characters, connections; we must infer motives, values, character; we must reconstruct past events, relationships, sequence" (24). Schüssler Fiorenza, *Revelation*, 25, states: "Apocalyptic language functions not as predictive-descriptive language but rather as mythological-imaginative language. It is not like a cloak which can be stripped down to its theological essence or principle. It does not appeal to our logical faculties but to our imagination and emotions. It is mythological-fantastic language–stars fall from heaven; the world becomes as a palace with three stories: heaven, earth, and underworld; animals speak, dragons spit fire, a lion is a lamb, and angels or demons engage in warfare."

67. Hauerwas, *Character and the Christian Life*, 195–227; Nussbaum, *Poetic Justice*; McFague, *Literature and the Christian Life*.

The Apocalypse retells the stories of Scripture. Images from earlier traditions carry old meanings into new settings.[68] A larger-than-life son of man holds the keys to death and Hades (1:12-20). A slain Lamb stands amidst glorious heavenly praise (5:6-10). The twelve tribes of Israel are also a multitude that no one can count, which is made up of all the people of the world (7:1-12). Babylon is judged for arrogantly exploiting the poor in order to live in luxury (18:1-24). The New Jerusalem does not need a temple, for God and the Lamb are its temple (21:1-23).

This collection of symbols and images causes the imagination to work overtime as the book of Revelation proclaims a comprehensive vision. It claims to include and interpret all that has gone before. Bauckham observes: "John's vision creates a single symbolic universe in which its readers may live for the time it takes them to read (or hear) the book. . . . The power, the profusion and the consistency of the symbols have a literary-theological purpose. They create a symbolic world which readers can enter so fully that it affects them and changes their perception of the world."[69] Thus the book of Revelation is Scripture's best example of an all-encompassing moral vision, a framework from which to consider Scripture's various modes of moral discourse. The apocalyptic moral vision is a narrative that includes all of humanity past, present and future, and all of creation. When a community embraces the moral vision of the book of Revelation, it embraces a way of seeing the world across the sweep of time and the universe of space.[70]

Readers of this apocalypse certainly do experience an "unveiling" or "revelation." And the revelation does not remain with heavenly beings

---

68. Schüssler Fiorenza, *Vision of a Just World*, 31, states: "By working with associations and with allusions to divergent mythic and religious-political traditions, Revelation seeks to appeal to the imagination of people steeped in Jewish as well as Greco-Roman culture and religion. John achieves the rhetorical power of his work by taking traditional symbols and mythical images out of their original contexts and by placing them like mosaic stones into the new literary composition of his symbolic narrative movement."

69. Bauckham, *Theology of the Book of Revelation*, 10.

70. Wilder, *Jesus' Parables*, 153-68, makes some helpful statements concerning apocalyptic literature in his essay "Apocalyptic Rhetorics." Wilder states: "It [apocalyptic] pioneered the first universal view of history including all peoples and all times. It took history with utter seriousness, confronting the seemingly total disaster of the present and assigning meaning and hope to it in terms of the wider cosmic drama" (160). Schüssler Fiorenza, *Vision of a Just World*, 4, adds: "Biblical texts such as Revelation affect not only the perceptions, values, and imagination of Christians but also those of Western cultures and societies on the whole."

and distant worlds, but keeps unveiling the earthly realm and human society. States Barr: "The Apocalypse communicates not just John's vision of the other world, it communicates his vision of what is really happening in this world by allowing the reader to identify ordinary places with the extraordinary."[71] The moral vision of the book of Revelation was able to minimize the seat of Roman authority by describing the throne at the center of the universe. Instead of the earthly source of power, privilege, and persecution, the prevailing realities at the center of the universe are justice and joy.[72]

Spohn suggests that "moral perception gets sharpened when we start using our imaginations in new ways."[73] The all-encompassing moral vision of Revelation working with human imagination does just this. The moral vision urges its readers to sharpen their moral perception by using their imaginations in new ways. This makes possible new ways of acting. Barr agrees, saying: "Apocalyptic stories generally are designed to shape the imagination of the hearer, to allow one to view one's historical situation in a new way, and so allow one to act in a new way."[74] The moral vision becomes a new framework from which to consider the obligations, consequences, and virtues of Christian community. Schüssler Fiorenza

---

71. Barr, *Tales of the End*, 67. Rogers and Jeter state: "The images created by the wedding of the text with the imagination of the reader/hearer become what James Sanders called 'mirrors of identity rather than models of morality.' That, he maintains, is the proper hermeneutical approach to the Scriptures. All Scripture, like Revelation, is an unmasking of appearances, a revealing of ultimate truth behind present reality" (6).

72. Bauckham, *Theology of the Book of Revelation*, 159–60, states: "We have suggested that one of the functions of Revelation was to purge and to refurbish the Christian imagination. It tackles people's imaginative response to the world, which is at least as deep and influential as their intellectual convictions. It recognizes the way a dominant culture, with its images and ideals, constructs the world for us, so that we perceive and respond to the world in its terms. Moreover, it unmasks this dominant construction of the world as an ideology of the powerful which serves to maintain their power. In its place, Revelation offers a different way of perceiving the world which leads people to resist and to challenge the effects of the dominant ideology. Moreover, since this different way of perceiving the world is fundamentally to open it to transcendence it resists any absolutizing of power or structures or ideals within this world. This is the most fundamental way in which the church is called always to be counter-cultural. The necessary purging and refurbishing of the Christian imagination must, of course, always be as contextual as Revelation was in its original context, but Revelation can help to inform and to inspire it."

73. Spohn, *Go and Do Likewise*, 101.

74. Barr, *Tales of the End*, 178.

states: "The strength of Revelation's mythic symbolization and world of vision thus lies primarily in neither its theological reasoning nor its historical information but in the evocative, persuasive power of its symbolic language compelling imaginative participation."[75]

The book of Revelation's all-encompassing moral vision provides new ways of perceiving daily experiences. Ruling governments, religious convictions, and civic duties are understood in new ways. The Roman Empire's violence and greed stood condemned.[76] All who were able to "see" this true reality would experience a different relationship with the Empire. Rather than turn from engagement with the world, apocalyptic moral vision *infuses* the everyday with heightened meaning.[77] The imaginations of the first readers of Revelation ignited as the book's moral vision dialogued with their own experience of the world. For a follower of the Lamb, Rome was not protector, but beast. The Christian churches, relatively small communities on the margins of Roman society, made up the victorious multitude standing before the throne. The particular, daily experiences of life in the Roman Empire took on new meaning as the apocalyptic images and language of the book of Revelation sparked readers' imaginations. Temptations to accommodate with Rome meant compromising with the whore. Hays says: "In order to break Satan's power of illusion, Revelation must reimagine the world; and so it does. The book's imaginative power annihilates the plausibility structure on which the status quo rests and replaces it with the vision of a new world."[78]

---

75. Schüssler Fiorenza, *Vision of a Just World*, 31. For Schüssler Fiorenza, such imaginative participation meant political action that resisted Rome. She continues, saying: "Revelation provides the vision of an alternative world in order to motivate the audience and to strengthen their resistance in the face of Babylon/Rome's overwhelming threat to destroy their life and livelihood" (129). Peterson observes: "The Revelation is, in large part, a provisioning of the imagination to take seriously the dangers at the same time that it receives exuberantly the securities, and so to stand in the midst of and against evil" (*Reversed Thunder*, 111).

76. Bauckham, *Theology of the Book of Revelation*, 39, states: "Revelation takes a view from the 'underside of history,' from the perspective of the victims of Rome's power and glory. . . . For John and those who shared his prophetic insight, it was the Christian vision of the incomparable God, exalted above all worldly power, which relativized Roman power and exposed Rome's pretensions to divinity as a dangerous delusion."

77. Rahner, cited by Braaten, in *Christ and Counter-Christ*, 9, states: "To extrapolate from the present into the future is eschatology, to interpolate from the future into the present is apocalyptic."

78. Hays, *Moral Vision*, 183. Wilder, *Theopoetic*, 29–30, discussing the power of

Having noticed some of the imaginative language filling the pages of the Apocalypse, and considering the diverse morally-charged discourse in it, how could one synthesize its moral vision? What "focal images" are central to the work's moral vision? The moral vision of the book of Revelation could be articulated in a variety of ways. This study has emphasized the hymns in the book where the focal images of throne and Lamb are central. In the hymns, these images and the dialogic activity that surround them create a new expression of God's relationship to humanity: the God of the cosmos is present, and the Incarnate Redeemer is God of the cosmos. The complex context (time-space) within the hymns enhances these focal images by pulling the future into the present where the human actions of worship and faithful witness remain crucial. Readers help to further articulate the meaning of Revelation's moral vision through their own dialogic engagements between the text and their contexts.

The focal images of the throne and the Lamb are textually located within the book's liturgical scenes. The apocalyptic moral vision which expands across all time and space is expressed within the language of the human experience of worship. In worship, believers experience the presence of God and the presence of the future.

Moral Vision as Liturgical Experience

C. F. D. Moule makes the following statement: "The Christian Church was born within a context of Temple and synagogue."[79] The first Christians continued the worship forms that they had known within their Jewish communities. They "gathered together"[80] in order to hear Scripture, to praise God, to pray together, and to receive instruction.[81] As the Judeo-

---

Scripture's imaginative language to compel action, states: "It is related to this that the civil rights marches and demonstrations were reinforced by hymns and spiritual songs old and new as in the vigils of the early church. Bonhoeffer's harried congregations were sustained by newly eloquent apocalyptic imagery in hymn, sermons, liturgy, and letter. So in the early church there was much of what we would call subversive songs, guerilla theater, underground messages, and political graffiti. The empire did not know what to do with this clandestine movement whose dreams were more universal and contagious than those of the Sibyls and the oracles or of Vergil himself."

79. Moule, *Birth of the New Testament*, 15.
80. Ibid., 12, talks about the word "synagogue" as meaning "gathering together."
81. Martin, *Worship in the Early Church*, 39.

Christian tradition in worship emerges, the Hebrew worship elements are reinterpreted in light of Jesus Christ.[82] Moule observes that: "The Apocalypse certainly presents some splendid Christian enthronement Psalms (11:15; 19:6–8).... It is hard to doubt that they represent the kind of poetry which Christians actually used in corporate worship."[83] Thompson also emphasizes the corporate nature of Christian worship: "Hymns were not expressions of individualistic belief and religious experience; rather, they reflected the beliefs of the community as a whole."[84] Over and over again, the book of Revelation echoes the experience of the Christian communities at worship. The book is full of liturgical elements. Perrin observes that: "An important element in the visions of John of Patmos is their relationship to early Christian worship.... [John] constantly quotes what on form-critical grounds can be recognized as fragments of confessions, prayers, and hymns, which must come from the liturgy of his church or be modeled on it."[85] The liturgical elements in the book of Revelation suggest an echoing of worship experiences of the Christian communities. Barr suggests that the church members probably experienced a recitation or dramatic presentation of the Apocalypse itself, in which the community participated in imaginative engagement with the narrative.[86]

The liturgical elements in the book of Revelation, especially the hymns, enhance the work's ability to stir the imagination. As the readers/hearers are led into the many worship scenes, the moral vision proclaiming the presence of God becomes an experienced reality. Readers living in the present are able to enter holy space. Readers are really there, "praising, confessing, giving thanks, adoring, and interceding are modes of

---

82. Thompson, "Hymns in Early Christian Worship," 463, states: "Not only do early Christian hymns share stylistic and formal elements; they also draw upon the same themes and motifs. And, in almost every case, those themes and motifs are used to make a christological statement."

83. Moule, *Birth of the New Testament*, 23.

84. Thompson, "Hymns in Early Christian Worship," 465.

85. Perrin, "Apocalyptic Christianity," 142. Perrin goes on to include the sections from the book of Revelation that could be modeled on liturgical elements.

86. Barr, "Apocalypse of John," 252, says: "Most commentators posit a liturgical context for the performance of the Apocalypse. Indeed, it is hard to imagine any other occasion in which an audience would gather together to have such a work read to them, and it can be added that the portrayal of scenes of worship and the extensive liturgical language makes such a conclusion nearly inescapable."

being in the presence of God."[87] Such an experience changes the reader's perspective, and increases the possibility of active response.

The repeated use of worship scenes in a book full of imaginative language suggests a connection between worship and moral behavior. The moral vision of the book of Revelation involves both liturgy and ethics. Donald Miller agrees in the important connection between worship and morality. He states:

> Although worship is often isolated in time and space from life in the everyday world, to the extent that one applies the cognitive structure of the religious finite province of meaning to one's interpretation of everyday life it may significantly affect the moral judgments which one makes. For this to occur, it is necessary that one look at the world with split vision, on the one hand applying to the situation at hand the commonsense perspective of life in the everyday world, and on the other hand seeing the situation through the ideal perspective of the religious vision.[88]

Don Saliers believes that worship does this by reorienting the lives of participants.[89] For Yoder, hope itself emerges from the experience of the divine in worship.[90]

Hymns of praise and other moments of worship include a concentration of references to the "focal images" of throne and Lamb. During liturgical moments, readers must keep using their imaginations along with their senses to unpack the possible meanings held by these images. During the hymns, readers are constantly reminded of the importance of the images, and their place in the overall framework or moral vision of the book of Revelation. The hymns never rest from portraying the book's vision of how the world really is: God is ever present in the world. At the

---

87. Saliers, *Soul in Paraphrase*, 62.

88. Miller, "Worship and Moral Reflection," 319.

89. Saliers, *Worship as Theology*, 175, discusses the fundamental elements of worship: "What is required is an actual reorientation of life, a process of conversion of the heart and social imagination to the rule and reign of God that Jesus proclaims and embodies." Barr, "Transforming the Imagination," 8–9, considers the book of Revelation a story which, when used as a "ritual text" in worship, completely reorients its audience. Barr states: "The Apocalypse functions to transform its audience into a community embracing a shared vision of the struggle between Roman culture and Christian conviction; it engages them as participants in a cosmic struggle of good against evil; it transforms their identity and status" (9).

90. Yoder, "To Serve Our God," 138, says: "Hope is not a reflex rebounding from defeat but a reflection of theophany."

center of the universe is One seated on the throne and the Lamb. The worshiping community is eternally in the presence of the throne and the Lamb. Yoder describes the book of Revelation's use of the language of doxology as meaning that the primary role for the Christian churches was "to persevere in celebrating the Lamb's Lordship and in building the community shaped by that celebration. They were participating in God's rule over the cosmos."[91] Miller adds: "The perceived importance of collective worship is that it provides an occasion for the community on a grand scale to dramatize the important moments of the tradition's history and to make the members of the community to feel connected to the well-springs from which flow the spirit of the group."[92]

As explored in earlier chapters, the hymns are moments within the narrative when the book's genre and chronotope are particularly complex. Ideologies from past eras dialogue with present convictions, while time-space is in flux. Thus, in many ways, readers are pulled into the narrative, invited to experience the moral vision as insiders. In the hymnic sections, careful readers hear the presence of many other voices. Some of the voices recall prophetic texts, while others remember the earliest apocalypticists, and still others carry Christian convictions. The ideologies held by the hymns refuse to be silenced by one dominating perspective on human experience. They come from different timed-spaces and spaced-times, and this instability also works to draw readers into the narrative.

All of these aspects of the hymns in the book of Revelation make them key textual locations for exploring both the content and the compelling nature of Revelation's moral vision: the God of the cosmos is present, the Incarnate Redeemer is God of the cosmos. In the hymns readers focus upon a throne and a Lamb. Having experienced the presence of God and the future, having joined the cosmic choir, readers are invited to respond to the moral vision by considering ways it can change the world.

BAKHTIN AND ANSWERABILITY

Bakhtin's literary strategies give readers additional language with which to consider the mutual engagement of readers and texts. Readers join

---

91. Ibid., 130. Yoder continues: "They considered themselves to be participating in ruling the world primordially in the human practices of doxological celebration" (131).

92. Miller, "Worship and Moral Reflection," 319.

the dialogic activity already occurring in the hymns by entering into the book's moral vision from their own contextualized points of view.

While apocalyptic moral visions and liturgical moments engage the imaginations of readers, even potentially changing the perspectives of readers, Bakhtin's work on dialogism reminds readers that such experiences are not merely reenactments of the text. They are new creations. Such readings are not discoveries uncovered inside the text, but are creations through mutual engagements with it. Readers bring their own contexts (time-space) to each engagement. Bakhtin's work on the relational nature of meaning and language, and his understanding of answerability, are helpful reminders to New Testament scholars and Christian ethicists. In order to "spot the rhyme," or to make an analogy between a text and a reader's life, or to consider the vast scope of an apocalyptic moral vision, or to be moved in a liturgical experience, readers engage texts with imaginations that work dialogically. Such intentional engagements create meanings to which readers are answerable.

Since much of Mikhail Bakhtin's work considered the various relationships between ethics and aesthetics, he seems an appropriate conversation partner when considering the use of a particular text within the moral enterprise.[93] Some brief reflections on Bakhtin's consideration of ethics and aesthetics can help to clarify the relationship between the book of Revelation as a moral vision, and the dialogic nature of meaning and language.

For a reader to intentionally engage a text, like an intentional engagement with another person, the reader requires outsideness. Caryl Emerson calls Bakhtin's notion of "outsideness" an "enabling condition" for many of his insights into ethical and creative events.[94] Outsideness factored into Bakhtin's earliest essays on the self as separate from the other,[95] and on the author as distinct from the hero.[96] And the concept

---

93. Morson, "Bakhtin, Genre, and Temporality," 172–73, states: "Ethics and creativity were, in fact, the central concerns of his life. One could view his long career, and his many theories, as different ways of describing the sort of world in which ethics and creativity are *not* illusory."

94. Emerson, *First Hundred Years*, 208. A significant portion of her book (207–64) is devoted to "'Outsideness' as the Ethical Dimension of Art."

95. Bakhtin, *Toward a Philosophy of the Act*.

96. Bakhtin, "Art and Answerability." Bakhtin, "Author and Hero," 76, suggests that the hero's consciousness is "lovingly consummated" by the author's imagination. Later, Bakhtin, *Problem of Dostoevsky's Poetics*, will emphasize polyphonic heroes who cannot be consummated or finalized, but stand in relation to the author.

remained critical for Bakhtin through his very last essay, which suggested a methodology for the human sciences.[97]

In his early philosophical essays Bakhtin claimed that an ethical event required the epistemological position of outsideness. This did not connote aloofness or indifference. On the contrary, outsideness was a quality necessary for real engagement and participation; a description or quality of being both distinct from, and in relation to, something else. Outsideness was intentional, it did not just happen. Outsideness resisted apathy. And it resisted the temptation "toward reducing everything to a single consciousness, toward dissolving in it the other's consciousness."[98] Outsideness made it possible for a self to be challenged—even changed— by another's point of view.[99]

For Bakhtin, all viewpoints were located and therefore partial. One view needed others in order to fill in the blind spots. In other words, the two must make intentional use of a position of mutual outsideness. When an other was seen as truly separate from one's self, then the self was also able to see a "surplus" of additional aspects that surrounded the other. Such a "surplus" of viewpoint worked both ways. Consequently, when selves interacted with each other, if each retained its distinctiveness, then they both retained their surplus of view. Bakhtin wrote: "I empathize *actively* into an individuality and, consequently, I do not lose myself completely, nor my unique place outside it, even for a moment."[100]

Ethical choices and moral responsibility were not reducible to rules. Outsideness rendered abstract theories of generalized ethical norms invalid in real life situations. While theories were wrenched from life and the necessity of actions, "ethics depends on the assumption that what one

---

97. Bakhtin, "Toward a Methodology," 159–72.
98. Bakhtin, "From Notes Made in 1970–71," 141.
99. Ibid., 142.

100. Bakhtin, *Toward a Philosophy of the Act*, 15. Bakhtin, "Author and Hero," 26, elaborates further: "In any event my projection of myself into him [a suffering human being] must be followed by a *return* to myself, a *return* to my own place outside the suffering person, for only from this place can the material derived from my projecting myself into the other be rendered meaningful ethically, cognitively, or aesthetically. If this return into myself did not actually take place, the pathological phenomenon of experiencing another's suffering as one's own would result–an infection with another's suffering, and nothing more." Later, Bakhtin states: "Art gives me the possibility of experiencing not just one but several lives, and this enables me to enrich the accumulated experience of my own actual life" (80).

does at a particular moment truly *matters*."[101] Bakhtin wrote: "Integrity by means of response is infinitely more difficult to achieve than integrity through consistency of content or through a refusal to engage."[102]

Bakhtin's essays on literature suggested that an aesthetic event also required a position of outsideness. Similar to the ethical act, the work of art must be comprehended as an other which was distinct from self since, "for Bakhtin, art requires above all a second self who perceives the creation *as* art, that is, as a finalized object viewed from the outside."[103] Only then can art have an "evaluative position."[104]

For Bakhtin, people were "others" and so were artistic creations. Therefore, "aesthetic consciousness . . . is a consciousness of a consciousness."[105] Precisely because the reader and the art were different, precisely because of outsideness there could be interaction or "live entering"[106] between the two entities. Morson and Emerson state: "Bakhtin tends to stress the importance of boundaries and of unmerged horizons which provide the outsideness that ultimately makes all dialogue and all creativity possible."[107] The reader is not present in the text, but enters it.

Like outsideness in the ethical realm, aesthetic outsideness included a "surplus" of viewpoint. The reader could see the work as a whole, aesthetically finalized creation located in a "specific place in time, space, and culture."[108] Readers could choose to engage the text, entering into a dialogic relation with it in order to create meaning. Such an intentional offering of the self to a text was a willingness to respond to it, to be answerable to it with one's life. Bakhtin declared: "I have to answer with my own life for what I have experienced and understood in art, so that every-

---

101. Morson, "Bakhtin, Genres, and Temporality," 174.

102. Emerson, *First Hundred Years*, 219–20.

103. Ibid., 217.

104. Ibid., 210.

105. Bakhtin, "Author and Hero," 89.

106. Later, in *Problems of Dostoevsky's Poetics*, Bakhtin will explore the concept of "dialogue."

107. Morson and Emerson, *Creation*, 166. Bakhtin, "Author and Hero," 71–72, reflects: "If the author/contemplator were to lose his firm and active position outside each of the dramatis personae, if he were to merge with them, the artistic event and the artistic whole as such, i.e., the whole in which he, as a creatively independent person, is an indispensable constituent, would disintegrate."

108. Morson and Emerson, *Creation*, 230.

thing I have experienced and understood would not remain ineffectual in my life."[109]

State Morson and Emerson: "For Bakhtin, outsideness was the moral position necessary to co-experience a work of art, to finalize it, and then take responsibility for its content."[110] In a later essay, Bakhtin explored the idea of outsideness in the context of cultural studies. "In the realm of culture, outsideness is a most powerful factor in understanding. It is only in the eyes of *another* culture that foreign culture reveals itself fully and profoundly.... Such a dialogic encounter of two cultures does not result in merging or mixing. Each retains its own unity and *open* totality, but they are mutually enriched."[111] Morson and Emerson summarize Bakhtin's insight here by stating: "Outsideness creates the possibility of dialogue, and dialogue helps us understand a culture in a profound way."[112]

Outsideness is a way to understand a reader's engagement with the other "cultures" found in texts like the book of Revelation. Readers who offer themselves to the text encounter an (often strange) "other." To engage with integrity that other is to resist the temptation to fuse with it, and to resist the temptation to walk away. To really engage the book of Revelation is to be willing to answer with one's life.

THE MORAL VISION OF THE "HALLELUJAH" HYMNS: REVELATION 19

This section considers the final four hymns of the book of Revelation in light of the book as moral vision. In Revelation, the God of the cosmos is present and the Incarnate Redeemer is God of the cosmos. As a vision within an apocalyptic text, this expression concerning God's relationship to humanity is a vision vast in scope whose images of throne and Lamb work with human imaginations to reshape understanding. As a vision expressed within liturgical scenes, it interacts with the earthly experience of daily worship. Thus, Revelation's hymns reflect a dialogic relationship between apocalyptic images vast in scope and the liturgical images of daily human experience, both of which work to invite readers into the

109. Bakhtin, "Art and Answerability," 1.
110. Morson and Emerson, *Creation*, 82.
111. Bakhtin, "Response to a Question," 7.
112. Morson and Emerson, *Creation*, 55.

narrative. Human actions of worship and witness take on cosmic significance, even as the God of the cosmos is present in worship. Such a vision provides choices along the way for readers who intentionally engage this text. Readers are challenged to consider expressions of this apocalyptic moral vision within their own lives and worlds.

Hymns in Response to God's Judgment (Rev 19:1b–2, 3)

Revelation 19:1–8 "is the last and most complex hymnic section in Revelation and has been called the hymnic finale of the book."[113] The last hymn discussed at the end of chapter 3 was the solo song of holy justice (16:5b–7b). The solo song takes place after the third in the seven last plagues series (16:1–21). During the seventh plague, the judgment of the city of Babylon is proclaimed (16:19). This judgment is described in greater detail in Revelation 17–18. The city, described as a whore, is destroyed at the hands of her partners in sexual immorality (17:15–18). Her destruction is followed by a ritual lament,[114] as earth's people of power mourn Babylon's death, and mourn the loss of goods and services the city provided (18:1–24).

The final verse describing Babylon's wickedness reads: "and in her was found the blood of prophets and of saints, and all who have been slaughtered [ἐσφαγμένων] on earth" (18:24). This last description of the wicked city remembers the city's deadly violence against human beings. The phrase "the blood of prophets and saints" (αἷμα προφητῶν καὶ ἁγίων) recalls the solo song (16:6) as the angel of the waters proclaims that God is just in pouring out judgment on those who "poured out the blood of saints and prophets" (αἷμα ἁγίων καὶ προφητῶν ἐξέχεαν). The phrase at the end of Revelation 18 also recalls an earlier description of the whore (17:6), who was drunk "with the blood of the saints and the blood of witnesses to Jesus" (ἐκ τοῦ αἵματος τῶν ἁγίων καὶ ἐκ τοῦ αἵματος τῶν μαρτύρων Ἰησοῦ).

The use of the verb "slaughtered" referring to all those on earth who were victims of the whore/Babylon (18:24) recalls the references to the Lamb who was slaughtered (5:6, 12; 13:8), as well as to people who are slaughtered (6:4, 9–10). The judgment against the evil city remembers several attributes of the people under the altar (6:9–10) who cry out for

---

113. Aune, *Revelation 17–22*, 1039–40.
114. Ibid., 978.

God's judgment. First, they are described as those having been slaughtered (ἐσφαγμένων). Then they are described as killed for the testimony they had given (τὴν μαρτυρίαν ἣν εἶχον). Finally, they call upon God to avenge their blood (ἐκδικεῖς τὸ αἷμα ἡμῶν). In these ways, Revelation 18:24 remembers those who have been slaughtered, their prophetic witness, and their plea. Revelation 18:24 is divinity's ultimate response to their cry: "how long before you judge and avenge our blood on the inhabitants of the earth?" (6:10). A God who is present in the world hears and responds.

Following the laments of the earth's kings (18:9) and merchants (18:11), the laments of shipmasters and sailors (18:17), and the reminder of Babylon's deadly violence, the narrator shifts the scene to heaven where a great multitude bursts into song. As the narrative moves into the final scene of hymnic celebration, the narrator shifts the scene by stating: "After this I heard . . ." (Μετὰ ταῦτα ἤκουσα) (19:1a). It is the only time this phrase is used in the book of Revelation. Most transitions into new scenes use the phrase "after this I saw . . . (Μετὰ ταῦτα εἶδον) (4:1; 7:1, 9; 15:5; 18:1). However, the unique description here shows another relationship to the previous chapter. The laments cried out in response to Babylon's judgment in chapter 18 and the "Hallelujah" hymns sung in chapter 19 are auditory experiences. In chapter 19 the various voices are mentioned, followed by their different proclamations or laments (18:2–3, 4–8, 9–10, 11–14, 15–17a, 17b–20, 21–24). Aune calls 19:1–8 "an *intermezzo*, composed to connect two sections of the composition by concluding 17:1—18:24 and introducing 21:9—22:9."[115] He suggests that the hymnic material in Revelation 19:1–4 records the celebration at the conclusion of Babylon's judgment. Then Revelation 19:5–8 introduces hymnic material that calls people to respond in praise at the announcement of the Lamb's marriage. The presence of God in acts of both judgment and renewal call for cosmic rejoicing.

One additional observation concerning the placement of these hymns is the way that this scene (19:1–10) seems to conclude the larger narrative that began in Revelation 4:1. As the narrator begins his ascent through the open door into the heavens, he proclaims: "Behold a door in heaven opened" (ἰδοὺ θύρα ἠνεῳγμένη ἐν τῷ οὐρανῷ). This description introduces the narrative that follows (4:2—19:10), and is similar to the phrase that introduces the book's parousia narrative (19:11—22:7):

---

115. Ibid., 1021.

"Then I saw heaven opened" (Καὶ εἶδον τὸν οὐρανὸν ἠνεῳγμένον). Thus, these hymns seem to function in several ways: as the conclusion to the series of visions witnessed by the narrator through the open door into heaven, as praise to God for judging justly Babylon, as praise in response to God's reign, and in anticipation of the arrival of the Lamb's bride, the New Jerusalem (Rev 21). Given their placement, these final four hymns may also remind readers of the first hymns experienced by the narrator after going through the heavenly door at the start of his vision narrative in Revelation 4–5. The similar description of other-worldly characters present before the throne supports the relationship between the hymns that begin the narrative (4:1—5:14), and those that conclude it (19:1–8). Within the world of the narrative, the end of Babylon calls for celebration with hymns of praise. However, the many connections between these final hymns and the hymns earlier in the narrative highlight the invitation to worship a God who is present at each stage in the story. The images of throne and Lamb fill the first hymns as well as the final hymns. The hymns at the close of human history maintain complex time-space qualities as they remember the earlier hymnic contexts of the images: the act of creation (4:11), the Lamb's sacrifice (5:9), the great tribulation of God's servants (7:14), the reign of the Messiah (11:15), the victory through sacrifice (12:11), the just judgment by God against evil (15:3; 16:4), and the end of Babylon (19:1–10).

After hearing about Babylon's demise, the narrator hears what sounds like the "loud voice" (φωνὴν μεγάλην) of "a great multitude" (ὄχλου πολλοῦ) located "in heaven" (ἐν τῷ οὐρανῷ) saying,

> "Hallelujah [ἁλληλουϊά]!
> Salvation and glory and power to our God [ἡ σωτηρία καὶ ἡ δόξα καὶ ἡ δύναμις τοῦ θεοῦ ἡμῶν],
>> for his judgments are true and just [ὅτι ἀληθιναὶ καὶ δίκαιαι αἱ κρίσεις αὐτοῦ];
> he has judged the great whore [ὅτι ἔκρινεν τὴν πόρνην τὴν μεγάλην]
>> who corrupted the earth with her fornication [ἥτις ἔφθειρεν τὴν γῆν ἐν τῇ πορνείᾳ αὐτῆς],
> and he has avenged on her the blood of his servants [καὶ ἐξεδίκησεν τὸ αἷμα τῶν δούλων αὐτοῦ ἐκ χειρὸς αὐτῆς]."
> Once more they said [Καὶ δεύτερον εἴρηκαν],
> "Hallelujah [ἁλληλουϊά]!

The smoke goes up from her forever and ever [καὶ ὁ καπνὸς αὐτῆς ἀναβαίνει εἰς τοὺς αἰῶνας τῶν αἰώνων]."

And the twenty-four elders and the four living creatures fell and worshiped God who is seated on the throne, saying [καὶ ἔπεσαν οἱ πρεσβύτεροι οἱ εἴκοσι τέσσαρες καὶ τὰ τέσσαρα ζῷα καὶ προσεκύνησαν τῷ θεῷ τῷ καθημένῳ ἐπὶ τῷ θρόνῳ λέγοντες],

"Amen, Hallelujah [ἀμὴν ἁλληλουϊά]!"

"Hallelujah" (ἁλληλουϊά) is a word transliterated from a "Hebrew liturgical formula" meaning, "praise YHWH."[116] It is a call to praise that is only used in these final hymns of the book of Revelation. The invitation to "praise Yahweh" begins this judgment doxology that sounds so much like the solo song in Revelation 16:5–7.

The solo song and this first song of Revelation 19 surround the events of eschatological judgment. Between them are located the rest of the plagues sequence (16:8–21), the judgment of the whore (17:1–18), and the fall of Babylon (18:1–24). Both songs emphasize the justice of God's judgments (16:5, 7; 19:2). Both songs mention the shed blood of saints, prophets, and servants of God (16:6; 19:2b). And in both songs a brief pause in the song allows for a repetition or emphasis of an earlier part of the song (16:7; 19:3). In Revelation 16:7, the altar responds with a reaffirmation of God's justice: "your judgments are true and just" (ἀληθιναὶ καὶ δίκαιαι αἱ κρίσεις σου). In Revelation 19, the phrase concerning God's justice which is included earlier in the hymn (19:2) is not repeated. Instead, the pause (19:3) repeats the proclamation, "Hallelujah," and then emphasizes Babylon's destruction whose smoke "goes up forever and ever."[117] This same description anticipates Babylon's demise much earlier in the narrative (14:11), and is alluded to in the lament over Babylon (18:9, 18). As the hymns celebrate the "forever and ever" end of the city of bloodshed, the One who lives "forever and ever" (4:9, 10b; 5:13b; 7:12b; 11:15b) remains present and is praised.

The narrative then describes the twenty-four elders and the living creatures falling down in worship to God, "who is seated on the throne," and saying: "Amen. Hallelujah!" This description of the twenty-four elders and the living creatures reminds readers of the worship scenes throughout the narrative. For example, in 4:8–11, the four living creatures sing "holy,

---

116. Ibid., 1022.

117. Ibid., 1026, calls this phrase a hyperbole "emphasizing the finality and totality of the destruction."

holy, holy," and then the twenty-four elders fall down in worship before the one seated on the throne. In 5:8–13, when the Lamb takes the sealed book, the four living creatures and the twenty-four elders together fall before the Lamb in worship. Later, every creature sings to the One seated on the throne and to the Lamb, and the four living creatures respond with "amen," followed by the elders falling down in worship (5:13). In 11:16, the twenty-four elders (without the four living creatures) fall down before God in worship. The worship scene whose description comes the closest to 19:4, is the scene in 7:11-12. Except for the addition of angels (7:11a), the description is similar: "the twenty-four elders and the four living creatures fell before the throne on their faces and worshiped God saying, 'amen . . .'" In 19:4 the description reads: "the twenty-four elders and the four living creatures fell and worshiped God, the one seated on the throne, saying, 'Amen, Hallelujah.'"

The similarities give readers a hint as to the identity of the "great multitude" who is singing here at the conclusion of God's just judgments. If they are the same group, the great multitude before the throne who sang after being sealed, now sings because those responsible for the "great tribulation" (7:14) have been judged. In Revelation 7, the narrator is told that the great multitude stands in the very presence of God "day and night." They are so close to the One on the throne, that the One seated there "will shelter them." The multitude will never be hungry, or thirsty, or scorched by heat, but will be guided by the Lamb. Nurtured by "springs of the water of life," God will also "wipe every tear from their eyes." The great multitude in song recalls God's presence in the past and present (7:15–17), as well as God's promises for the future (21:3–6). The narrative remembers God's presence in tribulation and in triumph.

The images of throne and Lamb which depict a new expression of God's relationship to humanity and help to define Christian eschatology are present here in this final collection of hymns. Such images provide the moral vision, or the general framework within which to view human experience in the world. In this final hymnic section, the image of the throne initially dominates. Not only is it specifically mentioned (19:4), but the description of this scene of singing and worship recalls previous throne room celebrations.

The activities of this final scene of singing before the throne hold the images and its apocalyptic moral vision as a liturgical experience. The throne image which is held by the hymns, works with human imaginations to reshape understanding, to help people see in new ways, and therefore, to act in new ways. When a reader's perception of the world is shaped by the moral vision of the book of Revelation, she or he sees a world permeated by the presence of God and redeemed by the God of the cosmos. If a reader "joins" the great multitude, she or he lives "sheltered" by the One seated on the throne. In tribulation, she or he is sealed, waiting for the day when God will wipe away all tears. Even in death, she or he is near God, under the altar where pleas *are* heard and spilled blood (of the Lamb, of God's servants) is remembered.

The image of the throne gains meaning by considering its location in an apocalyptic work.[118] As already explored earlier, the form-shaping ideology of apocalyptic assumes a huge gap between earth-bound human experience and heavenly, transcendent realities. In apocalyptic literature, the present is overwhelmed by the sweep of the whole of human history, a drama between forces of good and forces of evil. Apocalyptic literature claims that humanity's best hope is divine intervention in history and the destruction of evil through an ending of human history. Because apocalypticists are given spatial or temporal journeys beyond human experience, they are able to see this unfolding of the end. Given this ideology, readers acquainted with the genre expect the liturgical elements in the book of Revelation to widen the gap between earthly and heavenly realities, carrying the apocalypticist into a realm where he can only watch the cosmic worship.

However, the hymns in the book of Revelation remember their generic contacts to Hebrew prophetic literature. In the form-shaping ideology of the prophets, humanity experienced divinity when earthly throne rooms suddenly filled with the splendor of God. Human acts of worship and social justice combine with the chorus celebrating the cosmic significance of God's true and just judgments. The throne room is in an other-worldly realm, far from human experience, *and* the throne room is where the true prophets of God encounter divinity on earth. In Revelation 19:1–4, the cosmic Creator who is just in judging Babylon avenges the death of servants who worship and witness in the spirit of the prophets (19:10).

Thus, in the book of Revelation, the hymns are the sites of ideological feasts. They reflect apocalyptic ideology with its emphasis on the realm beyond as humanity's best hope. Yet, instead of the expected exotic travels and flashes of historical epochs, the hymns remember the worship

---

118. The hymns exist only within the larger utterance of the book of Revelation, a "complex" genre.

of a cosmic Creator who is also present in the earthly realm. This immanent God occupies the throne at the center of the universe.

This ideological feast is further expressed through the representations of time and space in Revelation's hymns. In apocalyptic time-space human characters are merely observers of the drama unfolding, not participants. However, the time-space before earthly throne rooms expects humans to respond in actions of worship, repentance, justice, and praise. Here humans witness even in the face of death (12:11; 18:24; 19:2). Here worship is the greatest witness of all. These chronotopes—including the epistolary sense of time-space that frames the narrative—cause the hymns to maintain a complex sense of temporal and spatial location. The narrator continues to recall his vision that took place in other-worldly time-space. Yet, the vision keeps touching the earth in the time-space of throne rooms. In this way, the hymns reflect the complex sense of temporal and spatial location for Christians living between the sacrifice of the Lamb and the appearance of the New Jerusalem. The experience of divinity in a hymn before the throne reflects the experience of first-century Christians as they sensed the presence of God in worship.

The chronotopic movement of the liturgical elements pulls readers into the narrative. The temporally and spatially unsettling hymns draw readers into the choir. The invitation to "praise YHWH"—Hallelujah!—leaps from John's vision, to the author's audience in the first century and to contemporary readers. The great multitude's "loud voice" gains yet another voice and another.

The first hymn in the book of Revelation begins with "Holy, holy, holy" (4:8b). The last hymnic section contains four "hallelujahs" (19:1b, 3, 4b, 6b). Four times the narrative calls for those hearing to "praise YHWH." The call goes out to the four corners of the earth (7:1). The use of this word gives these final hymns "a greater liturgical solemnity."[119] This key liturgical element, a universal invitation to "praise YHWH," is in honor of a just God who is also holy.

The hymns in Revelation 19:1–4 also heighten the gap between text and reader. Readers moved by the moral vision should not expect nor desire the book of Revelation to merge completely with their own stories. The hymns remain strange, distant, and "other." For many

---

119. Aune, *Revelation 17–22*, 1023. Earlier, Aune stated: "Rev 19:1–10 does not reflect liturgical hymns or hymnic pieces used in churches but was expressly composed to fit its present literary context, even though some elements may have been drawn from Jewish and Christian liturgical tradition" (1022).

twenty-first-century individuals and communities, it is troubling when a group of people celebrates the destruction of their enemies. The female personification of Babylon is problematic for some readers. For some, the eternal visible reminder (smoke) of Babylon's destruction feels ghoulish. Located outside of the work, readers must wrestle with the possible relationships between the book of Revelation and contemporary communities of faith. The reader who resists fusing with the work is faced with a moral vision whose distinctive evaluative position on human experience always seeks new conversations with contemporary readers and their new contexts. Like the hymns found throughout the book of Revelation, the first two hymns in Revelation 19:1–10 help in shaping the moral vision of the book of Revelation *and* in compelling readers to respond to it.

Hymns in Response to God's Redemption (Rev 19:5, 6b–8)

After the elders and living creatures fall down saying, "Amen. Hallelujah," a mysterious voice from the throne summons to praise (19:5), but without using the word "hallelujah." The voice says:

> Praise our God,
> all you his servants,
> and all who fear him,
> small and great.

Three times in the book of Revelation an unidentified voice speaks from the throne.[120] The first instance occurs in Revelation 16:17 after the seventh bowl plague is poured out and a voice proclaims: "It is done!" Here (19:5) the voice summons to praise. In the third and final instance, as the New Jerusalem moves from heaven to earth (21:3), a voice from the throne proclaims that God is present and dwelling with God's people in a renewed world. All three instances follow divine actions of judgment and re-creation.

Those who respond to the unidentified voice are described in several interesting ways. First, theirs is the voice of a "great multitude" (ὄχλου πολλοῦ). This phrase is only found at the start of the earlier hymn of this section (19:1), and in describing the great multitude before the throne in Revelation 7:9. Aune suggests that the group mentioned in 19:6 is located on earth, whereas the group in Revelation 19:1 is located in

---

120. Ibid., 1027, says that this "indicates the divine authorization of the speaker."

the heavens.[121] However, there is much to suggest that the four hymns in Revelation 19 are sung by the same group, and that the great multitude of Revelation 7 is further described in these four final hymns.[122]

The "great multitude" in Revelation 7:9–17, Revelation 19:1, and Revelation 19:6 are all described as crying out in a "loud voice" (7:10; 19:1), or with the "voice of a great multitude" (19:6). The last description continues by emphasizing the sound as that "of many waters and the sound of mighty thunderpeals" (ὡς φωνὴν ὑδάτων πολλῶν καὶ ὡς φωνὴν βροντῶν ἰσχυρῶν). This series of phrases emphasizes loudness. The phrase is used earlier in the narrative to describe the voice of the one like the son of man (ὡς φωνὴ ὑδάτων πολλῶν) (1:15), and the voice of the 144,000 standing with the Lamb on Mount Zion (ὡς φωνὴν ὑδάτων πολλῶν) (14:2). This description increases the connection between the great multitude in 19:6 and the great multitude of 7:9, given their mutual associations with the 144,000. And, like the great multitude in 19:1, the voices of the 144,000 on Mount Zion are also heard as coming from heaven (14:2). If these observations are correct, those singing the final hymns are described in a reversed order from the images of the sealed/redeemed in Revelation 7. In Revelation 19:1–8, the scene first describes a great multitude singing (19:1–4), followed by the description of a group (19:6–8) earlier called the 144,000 (14:2). However, in Revelation 7, the first group mentioned is the 144,000 (7:1–8), followed by the great multitude that sings before the throne (7:9–17). The celebration scenes in Revelation 7 and Revelation 19 are the voices of redeemed humanity in praise to God for salvation. Both sets of hymns are followed by a verbal portrait of the presence of God with the redeemed. The portraits are dominated by future verbs (7:15–17; 21:3–4), even as the hymns carry a sense of the present (7:9–12; 19:1–8).

The descriptions of the great multitude in 19:6 and throughout the book suggest an intimate connection between the great multitude and divinity. The voice of the 144,000 and the great multitude sounds like the voice of incarnate God (1:15; 14:2; 19:6). Whether on earth or in the heavens, the great multitude is with God and the Lamb (7:1–8, 9–17; 14:1–5; 19:1–8). Even before the Lamb's marriage supper, the redeemed sing a new song in his presence (14:1–5). God seals, and saves, and robes

---

121. Ibid.

122. This is especially clear if one emphasizes the spatial complexity of Revelation's hymn scenes and if readers interpret the 144,000 and the great multitude as different ways of describing the same group of redeemed humanity.

the great multitude. The great multitude responds in worship (7:1–8, 13–14). The great multitude conquers through the blood of the Lamb (7:14; 12:11) and is willing to witness to Jesus even in the face of death (6:9–10; 12:11; 17:6; 18:24).

This last hymn in the final worship scene continues to emphasize the book's moral vision: the God of the cosmos is present and the Incarnate Redeemer is God of the cosmos. Having been summoned to praise, the great multitude calls out:

> Hallelujah [ἁλληλουϊά]!
> For the LORD our God reigns [ὅτι ἐβασίλευσεν κύριος ὁ θεὸς (ἡμῶν)]
> the Almighty [ὁ παντοκράτωρ].
> Let us rejoice and exult [χαίρωμεν καὶ ἀγαλλιῶμεν]
> and give him the glory [καὶ δώσωμεν τὴν δόξαν αὐτῷ]
> for the marriage of the Lamb has come [ὅτι ἦλθεν ὁ γάμος τοῦ ἀρνίου],
> and his bride has made herself ready [καὶ ἡ γυνὴ αὐτοῦ ἡτοίμασεν ἑαυτήν];
> to her it has been granted to be clothed [καὶ ἐδόθη αὐτῇ ἵνα περιβάληται]
> with fine linen, bright and pure [βύσσινον λαμπρὸν καθαρόν]
> for the fine linen is the righteous deeds of the saints [τὸ γὰρ βύσσινον τὰ δικαιώματα τῶν ἁγίων ἐστίν].

The earlier invitation to "praise our God" coming from the unidentified voice from the throne (19:1) is echoed here with the fourth and final "hallelujah!" The great multitude simultaneously responds and calls for more praise. This is a fitting final hymn for the book of Revelation as it perpetuates additional praise. All who can hear should "praise YHWH" because God reigns. The final hymn calls for perpetual singing. Readers can join a choir whose praise is without end.

This hymn "constitutes a *hymn of praise* that conforms to the OT genre of hymn frequently found in the Psalter."[123] Before introducing new concepts, the song resounds with the familiar: "LORD, God the Almighty" (4:8; 11:17; 15:3; 16:7; 21:22). Praise is appropriate because of God's reign, and because of the arrival of the marriage of the Lamb and the readiness of his bride. This reference to the wedding of the Lamb is only mentioned here and in 19:9. The bride or wife of the Lamb is mentioned here and also in 21:2, 9, and 22:17. The images and metaphors should not be too startling since the image of Christ as the Lamb

---

123. Aune, *Revelation 17–22*, 1028.

is established early in the narrative, and "the metaphor of Christ as the bridegroom and the people of God as the bride was quite widespread in early Christianity."[124] In contrast to the "fine linen" of those mourning the loss of Babylon (18:12, 16), the bride's "fine linen" is also "bright and pure," which, the narrator explains, "is the righteous deeds of the saints" (19:8).

This image of the Lamb works with the imaginations of readers to reshape understanding and to help readers see new possibilities for human response. Readers are invited to enter into the text, offering themselves to it, and forming a dialogic relation that creates meaning to which readers are answerable. Readers can enter a text whose vision is reflected in a new expression of God's relationship to humanity, and a new comprehension of the presence of the future. The image of the Lamb recalls the work's moral vision. For Christian readers the image of the Lamb contains the wonder of the incarnation, the sacrifice of Jesus, the resurrection of Christ, and the on-going presence of Christ's spirit among communities of faith. The Lamb is God, present throughout human history and the cosmos.

The image of the Lamb gains meaning by considering its location in an apocalyptic work. The Lamb is an earthly creature that takes on cosmic and transcendent meaning in this apocalyptic text. This is the Lamb who is God, worthy of worship. This is the character within this apocalyptic work whose actions are central to the movement of the narrative. The ideology of apocalyptic fills the reference to the Lamb's marriage with eschatological meaning. Revelation's liturgical hymns take the work and worship of the Lamb into the cosmos.

However, this final hymn also remembers generic contacts to Hebrew prophetic literature. The imaginative language of this final hymn remembers a much earlier song from Isa 61:10:

> I will greatly rejoice in the LORD,
> my whole being shall exult in my God;
> for he has clothed me with the garments of salvation,
> he has covered me with the robe of righteousness,
> as a bridegroom decks himself with a garland,
> and as a bride adorns herself with jewels.

---

124. Ibid., 1029.

The writer of Revelation's final hymn remembers an earlier voice that rejoiced and exulted in God whose salvation is described as clothing, and whose righteousness is a robe. This part of the prophetic tradition is recalled by the author of Revelation. He draws in Isaiah's imaginative language for salvation, and in so doing remembers the beginning of the Lamb's earthly ministry (Isa 61:1–2; Luke 4:18–19), God's love of justice and hatred of injustice (Isa 61:8), God's everlasting covenant (Isa 61:8b), and the global location of God's people (Isa 61:9). The final hymn in the book of Revelation is part of a larger utterance whose genre has a history in Hebrew prophet literature. The genre remembers its earlier contexts and the perspective of human experience present in the form-shaping ideology of the prophets.

Remembering requires re-forming. In continuity with the prophets, the final hymn in the book of Revelation exults in the God who supplies robes of salvation and wedding garments. At the same time, the imaginative language of the prophets takes on Christian convictions as *the Lamb* becomes the Bridegroom. This last hymn, like all the others, is a rich ideological feast. Christian ideology re-forms the apocalyptic genre. Divinity is a bridegroom. The cosmic marriage supper gathers God's people from all the nations. God is present and reigning in the Lamb, who is the agent of salvation and the supplier of robes of righteousness.

This ideological feast is further expressed through the representation of time and space in Revelation's final hymn. Visionary time-space collides with the time-space of throne rooms. The actions typically possible in apocalyptic vision chronotopes meet the actions of prophetic throne room encounters. The actions of the cosmic Lamb on behalf of humanity are closely related to the actions of humans who are both apocalyptic bride and prophetic witnesses to Jesus.

The conclusion of the final hymn scene in the book of Revelation is one of the most chronotopically complex places in the entire narrative. The continued use of the Lamb image, along with references to Jesus and the servants of God, work to enhance Revelation's moral vision concerning the presence of God in all places, including the world. At the conclusion of the hymns, an angel tells John to "write" (19:9). The sense of time and space becomes even more unstable as the angel's message refers back to the vision and gives a blessing to "those who are invited to the marriage supper of the Lamb" (19:9). The cosmic vision of the Lamb and his bride intersects with the members of earthly churches who will receive the narrator's writings. Overwhelmed by the collision of different times and spaces, the narrator falls down in worship before the angel.

The angel immediately resists this act. The narrator is *not* before the throne of God. He is a servant standing before another servant. The imperative is clear: "Worship God" (19:10). The narrator is a character inside this cosmic drama, a drama that remains intimately connected to earthly realities. The vision compels Christians to respond in worship and in witness *in the world*. All people who embrace the vision become witnesses, for those who have the testimony of Jesus have the "spirit of prophecy" (19:10). The phrase is only found here and can be understood as "the power that allows certain individuals to have visionary experiences and gives them revelatory insights not available to ordinary people."[125] But, according to the last phrase of Revelation's lengthy narrative (4:1— 19:10), this spirit is available to all who hold the testimony of Jesus.

The phrase "testimony of Jesus" is repeated throughout the book of Revelation and is usually associated with the "word of God" (1:2, 9; 6:9; 20:4). The entire work begins with John testifying to the word of God and the testimony of Jesus (1:2). The testimony of Jesus is also the reason for John and others being persecuted (1:9; 6:9; 12:17; 17:6; 20:4). Here at the end of the book, all readers who embrace its vision are embracing the testimony of Jesus (1:1a), and therefore join the prophetic tradition (19:10). This Christian apocalyptic work maintains its generic contacts to past form-shaping ideologies by claiming that the testimony of Jesus falls within the prophetic tradition. The compelling vision calls readers to respond in worship and witness; to become a people of prophets.

The moral vision of the book of Revelation invites readers to respond in actions of worship and witness. The imaginative language of the Lamb and his bride, located within the hymns, further invites readers to see themselves and the world from the perspective of Revelation's moral vision. The last "hallelujah" calls readers to praise God, for God reigns then and now and always. "Hallelujah," because the Lamb and the bride are one. "Praise YHWH," because the bride is covered in fine linen. "Hallelujah," because of the testimony of Jesus, which is the spirit of prophecy and the witness of the whole vision. It is the spirit of the prophets, and the witness of all who "worship God."

---

125. Aune, *Revelation 17–22*, 1039.

Summary: Hymns Responding in Worship and Witness

In the final four hymns of the book of Revelation, as in the earlier hymns, the focal images of throne and Lamb are central. In the hymns these images are surrounded by dialogic activity between genres and chronotopes. This activity or movement creates a new expression of God's relationship to humanity and a new way to understand Christian eschatology: the God of the cosmos is present and the Incarnate Redeemer is God of the cosmos. This moral vision with its vast apocalyptic scope is located within the book's liturgical scenes. The apocalyptic moral vision which expands across all time and space is expressed within the language of the human experience of worship. In worship, believers experience the presence of God and the presence of the future.

When readers engage the last hymns of Revelation, hymns that are in response to God's judgment and God's redemption, they meet choirs that, like the images of divinity, move in time and space. Readers are reminded that worship and witness have taken place at each stage of the story. God is present in tribulation and in triumph, and so are the witnesses of God's churches.

These final hymns embody what the book of Revelation itself is—a marriage between God and the church. The book of Revelation is a vision of God's presence in the experience of worship. This study suggests that such a vision expressed in the vast scope of apocalyptic language and within the daily experience of worship is an invaluable resource for Christian ethics.

The book of Revelation is often absent from discussions concerning the use of Scripture in ethics. This is probably due to many reasons, including its strange symbolism, and lack of typical modes of moral discourse. The language of moral vision and imagination provides a helpful way to consider the book of Revelation within the moral enterprise. The hymns contain key focal images, reflecting the imaginative language of the book. The hymns also provide a textual location for the dialogic activity between genres and chronotopes. Thus, careful attention to the hymns creates a new expression of God's relationship to humanity: the God of the cosmos is present and the Incarnate Redeemer is the God of the cosmos. Such a moral vision can guide reason in changing one's perspective of the world, resulting in new possibilities for moral response.

Moral philosophers, Christian ethicists, and New Testament scholars highlight the importance of imaginative language for all moral thinking. The book of Revelation's moral vision acts as a broad interpretive framework from which to consider the modes of moral discourse found throughout Scripture. The book of Revelation is an excellent example of how the literary imagination "can be a bridge both to a vision of justice and to the social enactment of that vision."[126] Its moral vision provides an all-encompassing perspective on the world. It is a perspective that shapes reason and compels response. As Schüssler Fiorenza expresses so well: "[Revelation's] rhetoric does not seek to evoke just an intellectual response but also wants to elicit emotional reactions and religious commitment."[127]

When readers offer themselves to this particular text, they experience an apocalyptic vision vast in scope. Here is a vision calling humanity to witness on a grand scale. When readers offer themselves to this particular text, they also experience a vision within the context of liturgical experience. The apocalyptic and liturgical elements together invite ever new expressions of Revelation's moral vision and ever new responses of worship and moral witness. In the presence of God, and in the presence of the future, those who embrace the book of Revelation's moral vision are called to transform the world.

---

126. Nussbaum, *Poetic Justice*, 12.
127. Schüssler Fiorenza, *Vision of a Just World*, 129.

5

The New Testament Psalter
The Book of Revelation as Moral Vision

THANKFULLY, CHRISTIAN READERS ARE not left with only monologic approaches to the book of Revelation. Dialogic approaches, which assume the relational nature of language and meaning, open up new possibilities for interpreting this final book of the New Testament. To engage the book of Revelation by considering *how* the text means, rather than by searching for *what* the text means, is to reposition the interpretive enterprise. Mikhail Bakhtin's convictions concerning dialogism, along with his insights into genre and chronotope, help readers identify the hymnic utterances in Revelation as textual locations bursting with dialogic activity. Such activity invites readers themselves to dialogically engage the book, thus creating new meanings to which readers are answerable.

Chapter 2 considered how the book of Revelation's first five hymns (found in Rev 4–5) reveal dialogic activity between genres, or "form-shaped ideologies." Awareness of this activity is critical for readers who are constantly making interpretive choices concerning meaning. The cosmic, other-worldly realm typically emphasized by earlier apocalyptic literature with its view of humanity as far removed from divinity, is unable to achieve complete dominance within the narrative. As illustrated above, generic contacts with Hebrew prophetic literature remain in a dialogic relationship with apocalyptic literature's ideology. Thus the "form-shaping ideology" of prophetic literature helps to shape the work's strategy. As these ideologies meet in the hymns, readers can glimpse a

God who not only exists in the realm beyond human history, but a God who is also present. This God meets humans in earthly throne rooms. Instead of exclusively depicting a realm devoid of human responses and actions, Revelation's hymns recall human encounters with the Divine where humans respond in worship and in faithful witness to a God of social justice.

The book of Revelation's hymnic utterances also resonate with Christian convictions. The presence of these elements within this apocalyptic work reveals dialogic activity shaping the work's strategy in new ways. The work of the Lamb, which is partially articulated within the prophetic tradition, is then expanded by apocalyptic ideology to all living beings on earth and in the heavens. The work of the Lamb on earth extends into the universe. The Lamb's victory invites cosmic celebration. The dialogic activity between generic ideologies reveals a God whose presence in history calls for proper worship and faithful witness, and whose cosmic existence invites universal praise. This particular work reflects apocalyptic, prophetic, and Christian ways of thinking that together create a new genre. The new genre, a Christian prophetic-apocalyptic text, reflects the book of Revelation's unique perspective on divinity and humanity.

Chapter 3 explored how the book of Revelation's middle seven hymns (found in Rev 7–16) reveal dialogic activity between chronotopes, or "time-spaces," in the text which conflict with and complement each other. The book of Revelation's eschatology, or sense of the end, is messy and moving. It is temporally and spatially complex, leaving open important choices for readers. Sometimes the book's representation of future, other-worldly space seems to conflict with its representation of present, earthly space. The scenes seem temporally and spatially unstable. But this very chronotopic richness and dialogic activity reflects meaning. Emphasis of one type of time-space to the exclusion of others misses the interpretive possibilities of chronotopes that are in dialogic relationships. For example, readers are invited to consider ways the chronotopic activity within the text might reflect the location of Revelation's first Christian readers, as well as Christians of later eras. Similar to those who believe that they live between the Resurrection and the parousia, readers must negotiate between heavenly and earthly realms, and between present and future times.

In addition, each chronotope provides an arena of possible events and activities within the literary work. The hymns move between an arena where other-worldly beings act while human characters (usually seers or apocalypticists) watch from detached locations, to an arena where human characters join in the scene, participating in actions of worship and faithful witness. This chronotopic complexity reflects an eschatology which heightens, rather than negates, the moral actions of human beings. The actions of other-worldly beings affect the earth. And the human activities of worship and witness take on cosmic significance. Also, the temporal and spatial complexity of the hymnic utterances increases the reader's sense of being pulled into the narrative. Thus, the chronotopic complexity expands further as readers bring their own chronotopes into the text.

Chapter 4 considered how the book of Revelation's final four hymns (found in Rev 19) reveal the dialogic activity between the text and readers, especially given the book's intensely imaginative language. The book of Revelation contains symbols, images, and metaphors that spark the human imaginations which engage the work. Such imaginative language helps to expand a reader's perspective as the reader begins to see the moral vision of the book of Revelation as an experience of the presence of God. This moral vision invites readers who engage it to answer or respond with their lives. In this way the New Testament Apocalypse makes a critical contribution to the moral enterprise. The language of the book is so deeply imaginative that scenes of worship and the call to witness cannot ultimately be separated. In this Apocalypse, liturgy cannot be separated from moral action. The book of Revelation's moral vision invites people of all nations to worship in song and to witness through their lives. Readers who engage the hymnic utterances are invited to worship and witness in times and spaces where worship can be the greatest witness of all. The moral vision includes a God of earth and cosmos. Divinity is revealed as both in history and beyond history. Eschatology and ethics come together in these moments of liturgy as hymns herald the presence of the future, as well as the future implications of the present.

Readers make choices all along the way. Different readers emphasize different aspects of divinity, different chronotopes, and consequently different possibilities for human response. Different readers contextualize the invitation to worship and witness in a variety of ways. But to deny the dialogism of the hymns is to miss the book's internal dialogism which is inseparable from its moral vision.

The images of throne and Lamb found so often in the hymn scenes reinforce the book's moral vision.¹ Engagement with such a text invites, even compels, an answer. Readers are invited to answer with their lives. Multivoiced songs celebrating God's judgment and redemption spark the imaginations of readers to join the choir and in doing so to embrace the song's vision by answering with their lives.

A dialogic approach to the book of Revelation notices ways that the hymns function similarly to the book as a whole. For example, within the hymns and with the entire book, the throne of God and the life of the church come together. The location of the believing community becomes the dwelling place of God. Likewise, both in singing and in the experience of the entire narrative, earth and heaven meet. The future is present. Worship and witness celebrate the sacrament of God's presence.

Dialogic readings open up tremendous possibilities for the use of Scripture in the moral enterprise. The book of Revelation's imaginative language welcomes new interpretive possibilities. The book of Revelation's liturgical language provides places for readers to enter the narrative, joining their contextualized voices to the voices of others in the choir. The book of Revelation offers a moral vision of worship and witness before the presence of God. Readers are invited to respond to the vision with their lives. The following is a brief account of such a response.

NATIONS IN SONG

On September 23, 1995, the Sligo Seventh-day Adventist church, located in Takoma Park, Maryland, ordained three women pastors to gospel ministry.² This was the first ordination service to take place in the de-

---

1. Hays, *Moral Vision*, 184, says: "The ethical staying power of the Apocalypse is a product of its imaginative richness. The text throbs with theopoetic energy, expressed in its numerous songs of praise and worship."

2. Most men in Seventh-day Adventist pastoral ministry receive ordination after working for the denomination full-time for approximately four years and following a review by one or more ordained ministers. Ordination typically occurs during a worship service before the congregation where the ordinand (pastor to be ordained) serves. The service must be conducted by an ordained minister. The ordinand and ordained minister kneel before the church, and the ordained minister places his hands upon the ordinand during a prayer of dedication. In recent years, the ordinand's family and members of the congregation may join him on the platform. This better reflects the SDA understanding of the service as an affirmation of the gifts of pastoral ministry as witnessed by the church, rather than a bestowing of special powers upon the

nomination's one hundred and fifty-one year history, which openly acted outside of church policy and ordained women.[3]

Two months earlier, on July 5, the denomination's delegates to the 56th General Conference Session[4] in Utrecht, the Netherlands, considered a proposal presented by the North American Division to allow each of the denomination's then twelve divisions to decide for themselves concerning the ordination of women issue. The delegates voted the proposal down 1,481 to 673. The denomination's policy against the ordination of women was upheld. No area within the entire Seventh-day Adventist denomination was allowed to ordain women pastors.

Ten days after the July 5 vote, approximately fifty Sligo church members began a grass roots movement to ordain qualified women pastors at the local church level. The concerned church members asked that the topic of the Utrecht vote and its possible consequences for Sligo be an agenda item for the regularly scheduled board meeting on July 18. Sligo church had employed women ministers since the early 1970s. The pastoral staff and local laity, along with members of other North American congregations with women pastors, had tried to work with the denomination's leadership for decades. After the Utrecht vote, many members

---

ordinand. After the service, the ordained minister receives credentials that qualify him to conduct his duties as a minister in Seventh-day Adventist churches throughout the world. Unordained men and women pastoral ministers serve their local communities only, and must be granted permission when performing weddings, funerals, and baptisms outside of their local communities. Only ordained ministers can found congregations, ordain other ministers, and hold key leadership positions within the church's hierarchy.

3. The policy had been reaffirmed five years earlier on July 11, 1990, when the delegates to the 55th General Conference Session, received the following recommendation from the Role of Women Commission: "(1) While the commission does not have a consensus as to whether or not the Scriptures and the writings of [major denominational founder] Ellen G. White explicitly advocate or deny the ordination of women to pastoral ministry, it concludes unanimously that these sources affirm a significant, wide-ranging, and continuing ministry for women, which is being expressed and will be evidenced in the varied and expanding gifts according to the infilling of the Holy Spirit. (2) Further, in view of the widespread lack of support for the ordination of women to the gospel ministry in the world church and in view of the possible risk of disunity, dissension, and diversion from the mission of the church, we do not approve ordination of women to the gospel ministry." The delegation voted 1,173 to 377 in favor of the recommendation. See "Ordination of Women to the Gospel Ministry," 15.

4. This worldwide meeting of Seventh-day Adventists takes place every five years. Delegates from each of the denomination's divisions (one of which is the North American Division) include elected church officials holding a variety of positions, and a number of lay members correlating to its church membership population.

expressed that their spiritual and moral convictions called them to take action, even if that meant acting at the local level against denominational policy.[5] At the board meeting, an *ad hoc* committee was appointed to draft a statement that articulated Sligo's convictions concerning the issue of the ordination of women. Senior pastor Arthur R. Torres suggested that the statement be presented at a Sligo church business session on August 1. Since business sessions are open to the entire congregation, everyone interested could attend and respond to the statement. Discussion on August 1 was candid and respectful.[6] After an hour and a half of speeches expressed within an agreed-upon three-minute time limit, the church in business session voted by over 86 percent to adopt the statement, which included conducting an ordination service on September 23 of qualified women who were willing to participate. The church's senior pastor and other ordained Seventh-day Adventist clergy would officiate at the service.

In the weeks between the business session and the service, as at least one of the men scheduled to officiate was told that his participation would cost him his job as president of a Seventh-day Adventist college, and as all three women planning to participate received numerous phone calls from church leaders discouraging their involvement in the service, those planning the event kept finding themselves drawn to the book of Revelation.[7] Several artists within Sligo's congregation created seven banners for the event. Each banner depicted one of the seven churches of

---

5. At least one other Seventh-day Adventist congregation made a similar resolution. The La Sierra University Church, in Riverside, California, voted a request that the denominational leadership of the Southeastern California Conference authorize a pastoral ordination for qualified women by November 1, 1995. When their request was not met, the La Sierra University Church and the Victoria Church in Loma Linda, California, conducted ordination services for their women pastors on December 2. The three women who had been ordained at Sligo were present for the services. A litany created for the two services repeated the familiar phrase from the book of Revelation: "Hear, you who have ears to hear, what the Spirit says to the churches!"

6. Branson devoted almost the entire fall issue of the journal *Spectrum* to the events that took place "From Utrecht to Sligo." The issue includes, "Sligo's Action: The Documents," 37–44, a partial transcript documenting excerpts from the business meeting on August 1, 1995.

7. During this time, the level of church administration directly above Sligo, the Potomac Conference Executive Committee, voted 11 to 8 against granting women ordained ministers' licenses. This meant that any action by Sligo church on September 23 would not include any official support by the local conference of SDA churches.

Asia Minor mentioned in the book of Revelation.[8] Another set of banners was created for the area above the choir loft. These banners contained images from the final scenes of the book of Revelation (Rev 21–22). The Sligo church choir practiced the processional hymn "Joyful, Joyful, We Adore Thee," which alludes to scenes of singing before God's throne. The senior pastor wrote his homily, echoing Revelation's temporally complex language with his theme and title: "Let the Future Begin."[9]

More than eleven hundred people from across the United States and around the globe attended the service on September 23.[10] The event received some notice by local and national news organizations,[11] and, of course, mixed reactions from Seventh-day Adventists. Many of those in attendance felt that Penny Shell, one of the three women ordained that day, expressed their own feelings when, in her "response" after the prayer of ordination, she made the following statement: "I think only those who are women in ministry without ordination have any idea what is involved in that, when you are in a public ministry where ordination is expected. I'm not going to detail that before you, but I'll tell you, even more difficult than not being ordained when it's expected is to belong to a church that will not ordain women. I no longer belong to such a church, and it's a great joy."[12]

THE NEW TESTAMENT PSALTER

The ordination service at Sligo on September 23, 1995, was, I believe, an example of a dialogic approach to the book of Revelation. The people who planned and participated in the service experienced, in most cases unconsciously, both the internal dialogism of the book of Revelation and the dialogic relationship between the book and its readers.

---

8. The banner of the church at Pergamum (Rev 2:12–17), which was placed at the center of the ordination platform, included the initials of all the women who had served on Sligo's pastoral staff throughout the church's history. Rosemary Peterson designed the banners. Barbara Djordjevic created them in fabric.

9. A transcript of Torres' homily is available in *Spectrum*, 56–58.

10. A video of the service was prepared by TEAM. See *Ordination to the Gospel Ministry*.

11. Gustav Niebuhr, "Adventists Break Ranks"; Witham, "Sligo Rebels"; Wilgoren, "Three Women's Act"; and a brief mention in the Religion section of the Twentieth Anniversary Collector's Issue, "350 Women Who Changed the World 1976–1996," in *Working Woman* (November-December 1996), 76, which included some inaccurate information.

12. Shell, "Women Pastors Respond," 59.

The ordination service reflected a dialogic relationship between genres in Scripture. Arthur Torres considered the vision of the Hebrew prophet Joel next to the story of Pentecost found in Acts 2. The congregation was challenged to consider possible relationships between the two. Luke's narrative depiction of convictions concerning the risen Christ took on new meaning when placed in a dialogic relation with Joel's prophetic vision of the "Day of the LORD." Joel's vision of divine activity that brings about an earthly society where all people are valued (Joel 2:28–29), was juxtaposed with the narrative account of the arrival of the Holy Spirit at Pentecost. Both the vision and the story were then juxtaposed with the present work of the Spirit through the witness of women ministers at Sligo and throughout the SDA church.

Torres brought Luke's and Sligo's "surplus of seeing" to the book of Joel and the congregation experienced a dialogic engagement with the book. This approach reflected the dialogic nature of the passages themselves. The transcendent God of history-changing visions stands in dialogic relation to the immanent God of the Holy Spirit. God is holy Creator incarnate. God is worthy Redeemer of the cosmos. Other moments in the ordination service also invoked the imaginative language of the Hebrew prophets. It was as if the social ramifications of the Lamb's life and work were, in light of Sligo's particular moment, best articulated through the poetry of the prophets.[13]

The ordination service also reflected a dialogic relationship between many different chronotopes. Times and spaces kept colliding during the service. The chronotope of Joel's context, with its all-male priesthood and its swarming locusts, met the chronotope of first-century Jerusalem where the first Christians met together, and then Sligo's chronotope, a group of people from many nations who embraced the leadership of men and women in society and in their local church.

Joel's vision and Luke's narrative reflected temporal and spatial tension as their sense of present and future mingled. Torres said that prophets take the present very seriously, but do not allow it to define the future.[14]

---

13. As one of the three women ordained that day at Sligo, I prepared a "response" that reflected upon Amos 5:24 and Rev 21:1–3. Although I would not be introduced to Bakhtin's "dialogism" and his understanding of genre as "form-shaping ideology" for several more years, my response was an attempt to consider the ways these passages in Scripture related to the contemporary moral issues facing the members of Sligo church, and how such passages invited us to respond with our lives.

14. Torres, "Future Is Now," 56.

Prophets can imagine a better world.[15] "Prophets," he said, "live in the present, but they see a glorious future."[16] Suddenly the eleven hundred people present in the Sligo sanctuary were living within the prophetic tradition. They, too, had engaged a glorious future, a moral vision not yet realized. And, having engaged the moral vision, they had responded in worship and in witness.

The book of Revelation stands within the prophetic tradition. The book's ideology, its sense of time and space, its realm of human activity, all keep working to bring Revelation's hymns in the heavens down to earth. Simultaneously, the strategy of apocalyptic takes earthly worship experiences and floods them with the presence of a cosmic God. Such a moral vision, expressed especially by Revelation's hymns, holds together eschatology and ethics, worship and social action, the future and the present. Revelation, as a collection of hymns, a sort of New Testament Psalter, exposes the folly of approaching the book monologically. Like the poetry of the Psalms, Revelation's hymns invite ever new engagements with its imaginative and dialogic language.

The ordination service concluded with the entire congregation singing a hymn while surrounded by the colorful banners depicting images from the book of Revelation. The hymn's words recalled an earlier Scripture reading taken from Revelation 1:

> To Him who loves us
> and freed us from our sins by His blood,
> and made us to be a kingdom of ministers
> serving our God and Father,
> to God be glory and dominion forever and ever. Amen.

Even more than the words, the experience of singing the hymn together recalled the book of Revelation. The Sligo congregation had seen a moral vision where all members of society stand valued before the One seated on the throne and before the Lamb. The members of Sligo's congregation had seen the vision and had responded with their lives.

---

15. Bauckham and Hart, *Hope against Hope*, 53, make the following similar statement: "Possession of a future tense is the preserve of those who are able to imagine otherwise, to envisage the possibility of change; to hope." They continue: "Hope is that which insists on expanding our perceived horizons of possibility, broadening the landscape of reality in such a way as to set our present circumstance in a wider perspective and thereby to rob it of its absoluteness" (54).

16. Torres, "Future Is Now," 56.

Bibliography

Aune, David E. *The New Testament in Its Literary Environment*. Library of Early Christianity 8. Philadelphia: Westminster, 1987.
———. *Prophecy in Early Christianity and the Ancient Mediterranean World*. Grand Rapids: Eerdmans, 1983.
———. *Revelation 1–5*. Word Biblical Commentary 52a. Dallas: Word, 1997.
———. *Revelation 6–16*. Word Biblical Commentary 52b. Dallas: Word, 1998.
———. *Revelation 17–22*. Word Biblical Commentary 52c. Nashville: Nelson, 1998.
Bakhtin, M. M. "Art and Answerability." In Holquist and Liapunov, *Art and Answerability*, 1–3.
———. "Author and Hero in Aesthetic Activity." In Holquist and Liapunov, *Art and Answerability*, 4–256.
———. "The *Bildungsroman* and Its Significance in the History of Realism (Toward a Historical Typology of the Novel)." In Emerson and Holquist, *Speech Genres*, 10–59.
———. "Discourse in the Novel." In Holquist, *Dialogic Imagination*, 259–422.
———. "Epic and Novel." In Holquist, *Dialogic Imagination*, 3–40.
———. "Forms of Time and of the Chronotope in the Novel." In Holquist, *Dialogic Imagination*, 84–258.
———. "From Notes Made in 1970–71." In Emerson and Holquist, *Speech Genres*, 132–58.
———. "From the Prehistory of Novelistic Discourse." In Holquist, *Dialogic Imagination*, 41–83.
———. "The Problem of Speech Genres." In Emerson and Holquist, *Speech Genres*, 60–102.
———. *Problems of Dostoevsky's Poetics*. Edited and translated by Caryl Emerson. Theory and History of Literature 8. Minneapolis: University of Minnesota Press, 1984.
———. "Response to a Question from the *Novy Mir* Editorial Staff." In Emerson and Holquist, *Speech Genres*, 1–9.
———. "Toward a Methodology for the Human Sciences." In Emerson and Holquist, *Speech Genres*, 159–72.
———. *Toward a Philosophy of the Act*. Edited by Vadim Liapunov and Michael Holquist. Translated by Vadim Liapunov. Austin: University of Texas Press, 1993.

———. "Toward a Reworking of the Dostoevsky Book." In *Problems of Dostoevsky's Poetics*, 283–302.

Bakhtin, M. M./P. N. Medvedev. *The Formal Method in Literary Scholarship: A Critical Introduction to Sociological Poetics*. Translated by Albert J. Wehrle. Baltimore: Johns Hopkins University Press, 1978.

Barr, David L. "The Apocalypse of John as Oral Enactment." *Interpretation* 40 (1986) 243–56.

———. *Tales of the End: A Narrative Commentary on the Book of Revelation*. Santa Rosa, CA: Polebridge, 1998.

———. "Transforming the Imagination: John's Apocalypse as Story." Lecture presented at Wright State University, January 28, 2000.

———. "Using Plot to Discern Structure in John's Apocalypse." *Proceedings of the Eastern Great Lakes and Mid-West Biblical Societies* 15 (1995) 23–33.

Bauckham, Richard. *The Climax of Prophecy: Studies on the Book of Revelation*. Edinburgh: T. & T. Clark, 1993.

———. "The Lord's Day." In *From Sabbath to Lord's Day: A Biblical, Historical, and Theological Investigation*, edited by D. A. Carson, 221–50. Eugene, OR: Wipf & Stock, 1999.

———. *The Theology of the Book of Revelation*. New Testament Theology. Cambridge: Cambridge University Press, 1993.

Bauckham, Richard, and Trevor Hart. *Hope against Hope: Christian Eschatology at the Turn of the Millennium*. Grand Rapids: Eerdmans, 1999.

Bauer, Walter. *A Greek English Lexicon of the New Testament and Other Early Christian Literature*. 2nd ed. Translated by William F. Arndt and F. Wilbur Gingrich. Chicago: University of Chicago Press, 1979.

Beale, G. K. *The Book of Revelation: A Commentary on the Greek Text*. New International Greek Testament Commentary. Grand Rapids: Eerdmans, 1999.

Beasley-Murray, G. R. *Jesus and the Kingdom of God*. Grand Rapids: Eerdmans, 1986.

Beck, Melinda. "Thy Kingdom Come: Secrets of the Cult." *Newsweek*, March 15, 1993.

Birch, Bruce C., and Larry L. Rasmussen. *Bible & Ethics in the Christian Life*. Rev. ed. Minneapolis: Augsburg, 1989.

Blum, Lawrence. *Moral Perception and Particularity*. Cambridge: Cambridge University Press, 1994.

Booth, Wayne C. Introduction to *Problems of Dostoevsky's Poetics*, edited and translated by Caryl Emerson, xiii–xxvii. Minneapolis: University of Minnesota Press, 1984.

Borg, Marcus. "The Historical Jesus and Contemporary Faith" and "Jesus Was Not an Apocalyptic Prophet." In *The Apocalyptic Jesus: A Debate*, edited by Robert J. Miller, 31–48 and 152–57. Santa Rosa, CA: Polebridge, 2001.

Braaten, Carl E. *Eschatology and Ethics: Essays on the Theology and Ethics of the Kingdom of God*. Minneapolis: Augsburg, 1974.

———. *The Future of God: The Revolutionary Dynamics of Hope*. New York: Harper & Row, 1969.

Branson, Roy. "Golden Crowns and Radiant Faces: Adventism's Passionate Imagination." Presidential address presented at the annual meeting of the Adventist Society for Religious Studies, November 1995.

———, ed. "Sligo's Action: The Documents." *Spectrum* 25 (1995) 37–44.

———. "Virtues, Obligations, and the Prophetic Vision." *Kennedy Institute of Ethics Journal* 6 (1996) 361–66.

Brueggemann, Walter. *The Prophetic Imagination*. Philadelphia: Fortress, 1978.
Bultmann, Rudolf. *The History of the Synoptic Tradition*. Rev. ed. Translated by John Marsh. Oxford: Blackwell, 1963; reprint, Peabody, MA: Hendrickson, 1994.
Bursey, Ernest. "In a Wild Moment, I Imagine . . ." *Spectrum* 23 (1993) 50–52.
Caird, G. B. *The Revelation of Saint John*. Black's New Testament Commentary. Peabody, MA: Hendrickson, 1966.
Charles, R. H. *A Critical and Exegetical Commentary on the Revelation of St. John*. 2 vols. International Critical Commentary. Edinburgh: T. & T. Clark, 1985–89.
Charlesworth, James H. "Jewish Hymns, Odes, and Prayers (ca. 167 BCE–135 CE)." In *Early Judaism and Its Modern Interpreters*, edited by Robert A. Kraft and George W. E. Nickelsburg, 411–36. Atlanta: Scholars / SBL, 1986.
———, ed. *The Old Testament Pseudepigrapha*. Vol. 1. Garden City: Doubleday, 1983.
Clark, Katerina, and Michael Holquist. *Mikhail Bakhtin*. Cambridge: Belknap of Harvard University Press, 1984.
Cohn, Norman. *Cosmos, Chaos, and the World to Come: The Ancient Roots of Apocalyptic Faith*. New Haven: Yale University Press, 1993.
Collins, John J. "Apocalyptic Eschatology as the Transcendence of Death." In *Visionaries and Their Apocalypses*, edited by Paul D. Hanson, 61–84. Philadelphia: Fortress, 1983.
———. *The Apocalyptic Imagination: An Introduction to Jewish Apocalyptic Literature*, 2nd ed. Grand Rapids: Eerdmans, 1998.
———. "From Prophecy to Apocalypticism: The Expectation of the End." In *The Encyclopedia of Apocalypticism*, vol. 1, edited by John J. Collins, 129–61. New York: Continuum, 2000.
———. Preface to *Semeia* 14 (1979) iii–iv.
———. "Towards the Morphology of a Genre." *Semeia* 14 (1979) 1–20.
Cook, Stephen L. *Prophecy & Apocalypticism: The Postexilic Social Setting*. Minneapolis: Fortress, 1995.
Cooper, Douglas. "Did David Die for Our Sins?" *Spectrum* 23 (1993) 47–48.
Crossan, John Dominic. *The Birth of Christianity: Discovering What Happened in the Years Immediately after the Execution of Jesus*. San Francisco: HarperCollins, 1998.
Cullmann, Oscar. *Christ and Time: The Primitive Christian Conception of Time and History*. Rev. ed. Translated by Floyd V. Filson. London: SCM, 1962.
Davies, W. D. *The Sermon on the Mount*. Cambridge: Cambridge University Press, 1966.
Dodd, C. H. *The Parables of the Kingdom*. Rev. ed. New York: Scribner, 1961.
Donahue, John R. *The Gospel in Parable: Metaphor, Narrative, and Theology in the Synoptic Gospels*. Philadelphia: Fortress, 1990.
Emerson, Caryl. *The First Hundred Years of Mikhail Bakhtin*. Princeton: Princeton University Press, 1997.
Emerson, Caryl, and Michael Holquist, eds. *Speech Genres & Other Late Essays*. Translated by Vern W. McGee. University of Texas Press Slavic Series 8. Austin: University of Texas Press, 1986.
Farmer, Ron. "The Kingdom of God in the Gospel of Matthew." In *The Kingdom of God in 20th-Century Interpretation*, edited by Wendell Willis, 119–30. Peabody, MA: Hendrickson, 1987.
Felch, Susan M., and Paul J. Contino. "A Feeling for Faith." In *Bakhtin and Religion: A Feeling for Faith*, edited by Susan M. Felch and Paul J. Contino, 1–24. Evanston, IL: Northwestern University Press, 2001.

Ford, J. Massyngberde. *Revelation*. Anchor Bible 38. Garden City: Doubleday, 1975.
Frankena, William *Ethics*. 2nd ed. Foundations of Philosophy. Englewood Cliffs, NJ: Prentice Hall, 1973.
Furnish, Victor Paul. *The Moral Teaching of Paul: Selected Issues*. Rev. ed. Nashville: Abingdon, 1985.
Green, Barbara. *Mikhail Bakhtin and Biblical Scholarship: An Introduction*. Semeia 38. Atlanta: SBL, 2000.
Green, Garrett. *Imagining God: Theology and the Religious Imagination*. Grand Rapids: Eerdmans, 1989.
Gustafson, James M. "The Place of Scripture in Christian Ethics: A Methodological Study." *Interpretation* 24 (1970) 430–55.
Gutiérrez, Gustavo. *A Theology of Liberation: History, Politics, and Salvation*. Rev. ed. Translated and edited by Caridad Inda and John Eagleson. Maryknoll: Orbis, 1988.
Haloviak, Kendra. "One of David's Mighty Men." *Spectrum* 23 (1993) 39–42.
Hanson, Paul D. "Biblical Apocalypticism: The Theological Dimension." *Horizons in Biblical Theology* 7 (1985) 1–20.
———. *The Dawn of Apocalyptic: The Historical and Sociological Roots of Jewish Apocalyptic Eschatology*. Rev. ed. Philadelphia: Fortress, 1979.
———. "Old Testament Apocalyptic Reexamined." In *Visionaries and Their Apocalypses*, edited by Paul D. Hanson, 37–60. Philadelphia: Fortress, 1983.
Harris, Michael A. "The Literary Function of Hymns in the Apocalypse of John." PhD diss., Southern Baptist Theological Seminary, 1989.
Hauerwas, Stanley. *Character and the Christian Life: A Study in Theological Ethics*. Rev. ed. Notre Dame: University of Notre Dame Press, 1985.
———. *A Community of Character: Toward a Constructive Christian Social Ethic*. Notre Dame: University of Notre Dame Press, 1981.
———. *Vision and Virtue: Essays in Christian Ethical Reflection*. Notre Dame: Fides, 1974.
Hays, Richard B. *The Moral Vision of the New Testament: A Contemporary Introduction to New Testament Ethics*. San Francisco: HarperCollins, 1996.
Hellholm, David. "The Problem of Apocalyptic Genre and the Apocalypse of John." *Semeia* 36 (1986) 13–64.
Holbrook, Frank B., ed. *Symposium on Revelation*. 2 vols. Daniel and Revelation Committee Series 6–7. Silver Spring, MD: Biblical Research Institute, 1992.
Holquist, Michael, ed. *The Dialogic Imagination: Four Essays by M. M. Bakhtin*. Translated by Caryl Emerson and Michael Holquist. University of Texas Press Slavic Series 1. Austin: University of Texas Press, 1981.
———. *Dialogism: Bakhtin and His World*. London: Routledge, 1990.
Holquist, Michael, and Vadim Liapunov, eds. *Art and Answerability: Early Philosophical Essays by M. M. Bakhtin*. Translated by Vadim Liapunov. University of Texas Press Slavic Series 9. Austin: University of Texas Press, 1990.
Hudson, Winthrop S. *Religion in America*. 4th ed. New York: Macmillan, 1987.
Isaac, E. "1 (Ethiopic Apocalypse of) Enoch." In Charlesworth, *Old Testament Pseudepigrapha*, 1:5–89.
Jackson, Robert Louis. *Dialogues with Dostoevsky: The Overwhelming Questions*. Stanford: Stanford University Press, 1993.

Johnson, Mark. *Moral Imagination: Implications of Cognitive Science for Ethics.* Chicago: University of Chicago Press, 1993.
Johnsson, William, ed. "Ordination of Women to the Gospel Ministry." *Adventist Review,* July 3, 1990.
Kant, Immanuel. *Critique of Pure Reason.* Translated by Max Müller. Garden City: Doubleday, 1966.
Kantrowitz, Barbara. "The Messiah of Waco." *Newsweek,* March 15, 1993.
Käsemann, Ernst. "The Beginnings of Christian Theology." *Journal for Theology and the Church* 6 (1969) 17–46.
Kee, H. C. "Testaments of the Twelve Patriarchs." In Charlesworth, *Old Testament Pseudepigrapha,* 1:775–828.
Kelsey, David H. *The Uses of Scripture in Recent Theology.* Philadelphia: Fortress, 1975.
Klijn, A. F. J. "2 (Syriac Apocalypse of) Baruch." In Charlesworth, *Old Testament Pseudepigrapha,* 1:615–52.
Koch, Klaus. *The Rediscovery of Apocalyptic.* Translated by Margaret Kohl. Studies in Biblical Theology 22. London: SCM, 1972.
Ladin, Jay. "Fleshing Out the Chronotope." In *Critical Essays on Mikhail Bakhtin,* edited by Caryl Emerson, 212–36. New York: Hall, 1999.
Laeuchli, Samuel. "Christianity and the Death of Myth." In *Parable, Myth and Language,* edited by Tony Stoneburner, 7–18. Newton Center, MA: National Institute for Campus Ministries, 1968.
Lakoff, George, and Mark Johnson. *Metaphors We Live By.* Chicago: University of Chicago Press, 1980.
Lorde, Audre. *Sister Outsider: Essays and Speeches.* Freedom, CA: Crossing, 1984.
MacIntyre, Alasdair. *After Virtue: A Study in Moral Theory.* Notre Dame: University of Notre Dame Press, 1981.
Mack, Burton L. *The Lost Gospel: The Book of Q and Christian Origins.* San Francisco: HarperCollins, 1993.
Malina, Bruce J. *On the Genre and Message of Revelation: Star Visions and Sky Journeys.* Peabody, MA: Hendrickson, 1995.
Marshall, Jay W. *The Ten Commandments and Church Community.* Harrisonburg, VA: Herald, 1996.
Martin, Ralph P. *Worship in the Early Church.* London: Marshall, Morgan & Schott, 1964.
Maxwell, C. Mervyn. *God Cares.* Vol. 2. Boise, ID: Pacific, 1985.
May, William F. *The Physician's Covenant: Images of the Healer in Medical Ethics.* Philadelphia: Westminster, 1983.
McFague, Sallie. *Literature and the Christian Life.* New Haven: Yale University Press, 1966.
———. *Speaking in Parables.* Philadelphia: Fortress, 1975.
Miller, Donald E. "Worship and Moral Reflection: A Phenomenological Analysis." *Anglican Theological Review* 62 (1980) 307–20.
Moltmann, Jürgen. *The Coming of God: Christian Eschatology.* Translated by Margaret Kohl. Minneapolis: Fortress, 1996.
———. *Theology of Hope: On the Ground and the Implications of a Christian Eschatology.* Translated by James W. Leitch. New York: Harper & Row, 1967.
Morgan, Douglas. *Adventism and the American Republic: The Public Involvement of a Major Apocalyptic Movement.* Knoxville: University of Tennessee Press, 2001.

Morson, Gary Saul. "Bakhtin, Genres, and Temporality." In *Critical Essays on Mikhail Bakhtin*, edited by Caryl Emerson, 171–89. New York: Hall, 1999.

———. "Introduction to Extracts from 'The Problem of Speech Genres.'" In *Bakhtin: Essays and Dialogues on His Work*, edited by Gary Saul Morson, 89–90. Chicago: University of Chicago, 1981.

Morson, Gary Saul, and Caryl Emerson. *Mikhail Bakhtin: Creation of a Prosaics.* Stanford: Stanford University Press, 1990.

Moule, C. F. D. *The Birth of the New Testament.* New York: Harper & Row, 1962.

Mowry, L. "Revelation 4–5 and Early Christian Liturgical Usage." *Journal of Biblical Literature* 71 (1952) 75–84.

Murdoch, Iris. *The Sovereignty of the Good.* New York: Routledge & Kegan Paul, 1970.

Murphy, Nancey, et al., eds. *Virtues and Practices in the Christian Tradition: Christian Ethics after MacIntyre.* Harrisburg, PA: Trinity, 1997.

Nestle, Eberhard, et al. *Novum Testamentum Graece.* 27th ed. Stuttgart: Deutsche, Bibelgesellschaft, 1993.

Newport, Kenneth G. C. *Apocalypse and Millennium: Studies in Biblical Eisegesis.* Cambridge: Cambridge University Press, 2000.

Newsom, Carol A. "Bakhtin, the Bible, and Dialogic Truth." *Journal of Religion* 76 (1996) 290–306.

Niebuhr, Gustav. "Adventists Break Ranks, Ordain Women." *New York Times*, September 23, 1995.

Niebuhr, H. Richard. *Christ and Culture.* New York: Harper & Row, 1951.

———. *The Meaning of Revelation.* New York: Macmillan, 1941.

Nussbaum, Martha C. *Poetic Justice: The Literary Imagination and Public Life.* Boston: Beacon, 1995.

Perrin, Norman. "Apocalyptic Christianity." In *Visionaries and Their Apocalypses*, edited by Paul D. Hanson, 121–45. Philadelphia: Fortress, 1983.

———. *Jesus and the Language of the Kingdom: Symbol and Metaphor in New Testament Interpretation.* Philadelphia: Fortress, 1976.

———. *The Kingdom of God in the Teaching of Jesus.* London: SCM, 1963.

Peterson, Eugene H. *Reversed Thunder: The Revelation of John and the Praying Imagination.* San Francisco: HarperCollins, 1988.

Piper, Otto A. "The Apocalypse of John and the Liturgy of the Ancient Church." *Church History* 20 (1951) 10–22.

Pittman, Barbara L. "Cross-Cultural Reading and Generic Transformation: The Chronotope of the Road in Erdich's *Love Medicine*." *American Literature* 67 (1995) 777–92.

Prigent, P. *L'Apocalypse de Saint Jean.* Paris: Delachaux et Niestlé, 1981.

Reddish, Mitchell G. *Apocalyptic Literature: A Reader.* Peabody, MA: Hendrickson, 1995.

Ricoeur, Paul. *Interpretation Theory: Discourse and the Surplus of Meaning.* Fort Worth: Texas Christian University Press, 1976.

Rogers, Corish R., and Joseph R. Jeter Jr., eds. *Preaching through the Apocalypse: Sermons from Revelation.* St. Louis: Chalice, 1992.

Rowley, H. H. *The Relevance of Apocalyptic: A Study of Jewish and Christian Apocalypses from Daniel to the Revelation.* Rev. ed. Greenwood, SC: Attic, 1980.

Rubinkiewicz, R. "Apocalypse of Abraham." In Charlesworth, *Old Testament Pseudepigrapha*, 1:681–705.

Russell, D. S. *Apocalyptic: Ancient and Modern*. Philadelphia: Fortress, 1978.

———. *The Method and Message of Jewish Apocalyptic*. Old Testament Library. Philadelphia: Westminster, 1964.

Saliers, Don E. *The Soul in Paraphrase: Prayer and the Religious Affections*. Cleveland: OSL, 1991.

———. *Worship as Theology: Foretaste of Glory Divine*. Nashville: Abingdon, 1994.

Samples, Kenneth, et al. *Prophets of the Apocalypse: David Koresh & Other American Messiahs*. Grand Rapids: Baker, 1994.

Sanders, E. P. "Testament of Abraham." In Charlesworth, *Old Testament Pseudepigrapha*, 1:871–902.

Scholz, Bernhard F. "Bakhtin's Concept of 'Chronotope': The Kantian Connection." In *The Contexts of Bakhtin*, edited by David Shepherd, 141–72. Amsterdam: Harwood Academic, 1998.

Schüssler Fiorenza, Elisabeth. *The Book of Revelation: Justice and Judgment*. 2nd ed. Minneapolis: Fortress, 1998.

———. *Revelation: Vision of a Just World*. Proclamation Commentaries. Minneapolis: Fortress, 1991.

Schweitzer, Albert. *The Quest of the Historical Jesus: A Critical Study of Its Progress from Reimarus to Wrede*. Baltimore: Johns Hopkins University Press, 1998.

Scriven, Charles. "Fundamentalism Is a Disease, a Demonic Perversion." *Spectrum* 23 (1993) 45–46.

Shea, William H. "How should SDAs Respond?" *Spectrum* 23 (1993) 43–45.

Shell, Penny. "The Women Pastors Respond." *Spectrum* 25 (1995) 59.

Shepherd, Massey H., Jr. *The Paschal Liturgy and the Apocalypse*. Ecumenical Studies in Worship 6. London: Lutterworth, 1960.

Spohn, William C. *Go and Do Likewise: Jesus and Ethics*. New York: Continuum, 1999.

———. *What Are They Saying about Scripture and Ethics?* Rev. ed. New York: Paulist, 1995.

Steinglass, Matt. "International Man of Mystery: The Battle Over Mikhail Bakhtin." *Lingua franca* (1998) 33–41.

Stone, M. E. "Greek Apocalypse of Ezra." In Charlesworth, *Old Testament Pseudepigrapha*, 1:561–79.

Stortz, Martha Ellen. "Vision and Choice: Insights from Weil and Murdoch." Paper presented to the Society of Christian Ethics, January 6, 1996.

Tabor, James D., and Eugene V. Gallagher. *Why Waco? Cults and the Battle for Religious Freedom in America*. Berkeley: University of California Press, 1995.

TEAM (Time for Equality in Adventist Ministry). *Ordination to the Gospel Ministry*. Video. Langley Park, MD: TEAM, 1995.

Teel, Charles. "Kissing Cousins or Kindred Spirits?" *Spectrum* 23 (1993) 48–49.

Thompson, Leonard. *The Book of Revelation: Apocalypse and Empire*. New York: Oxford University Press, 1990.

———. "Cult and Eschatology in the Apocalypse of John." *Journal of Religion* 49 (1969) 330–50.

———. "Hymns in Early Christian Worship." *Anglican Theological Review* 55 (1973) 458–72.

———. *Revelation*. Abingdon New Testament Commentaries. Nashville: Abingdon, 1998.

Torres, Arthur R. "The Future Is Now." *Spectrum* 25 (1995) 56–58.

Tracy, David. *The Analogical Imagination: Christian Theology and the Culture of Pluralism.* New York: Crossroad, 1991.
von Rad, Gerhard. *Old Testament Theology.* 2 vols. Translated by D. M. G. Stalker. San Francisco: HarperCollins, 1965.
Warren, Ron. "Our Brothers and Our Sisters . . ." *Spectrum* 23 (1993) 50.
Weber, Eugen. *Apocalypses: Prophecies, Cults, and Millennial Beliefs through the Ages.* Cambridge: Harvard University Press, 1999.
Westermann, Claus. *The Praise of God in the Psalms.* Translated by Keith R. Crim. Richmond, VA: John Knox, 1965.
Wheeler, Gerald. *Wisdom: Timeless Treasures From Proverbs.* Hagerstown, MD: Review and Herald, 2000.
Wilder, Amos N. *Early Christian Rhetoric: The Language of the Gospel.* Peabody, MA: Hendrickson, 1999.
———. *Eschatology and Ethics in the Teaching of Jesus.* Rev. ed. New York: Harper, 1950.
———. "Scenarios of Life and Destiny." In *Jesus' Parables and the War of Myths: Essays on Imagination in the Scriptures,* edited by James Breech, 71–87. Philadelphia: Fortress, 1982.
———. *Theopoetic: Theology and the Religious Imagination.* Philadelphia: Fortress, 1976.
Wilgoren, Debbi. "Three Women's Act of Devotion and Defiance." *Washington Post,* November 4, 1995.
Witham, Larry. "Sligo Rebels, Goes against Vote." *Washington Times,* September 24, 1995.
Witherington, Ben, III. *The Jesus Quest: The Third Search for the Jew of Nazareth.* Downers Grove: InterVarsity, 1995.
Working Woman. "350 Women Who Changed the World 1976–1996." November–December 1996.
Yarbro Collins, Adela. *Crisis and Catharsis: The Power of the Apocalypse.* Philadelphia: Westminster, 1984.
———. "The Early Christian Apocalypses." *Semeia* 14 (1979) 61–121.
Yoder, John Howard. *The Politics of Jesus.* Grand Rapids: Eerdmans, 1972.
———. "To Serve Our God and to Rule the World." In *The Royal Priesthood: Essays Ecclesiological and Ecumenical,* edited by Michael G. Cartwright, 127–40. Scottdale, PA: Herald, 1994.

www.ingramcontent.com/pod-product-compliance
Lightning Source LLC
Chambersburg PA
CBHW062039220426
43662CB00010B/1561